ISBN: 978-0-9961022-0-9

Published by **www.PaulWagner.com**

Registered with Library of Congress: 2016: Wagner, Paul

Other Books, Cards & Apps by Paul Wagner:

The Personality Cards
Pocket People
Pocket Love
STARTUP Confidential (StartupConfident.com)
The Colorful Me Workbook (Coloring Book)
The Me App (PersonalityApp.com)

Visit www.PaulWagner.com to learn more.

When we liberate emotions, wisdom and light grow within us.

TABLE OF CONTENTS

AUTHOR'S NOTE

When Carl Jung unveiled his famous personality archetypes, it gave the world a framework for self-exploration. I strive to do the same, but with more specificity.

This book came to me in a dream where I saw hundreds of personality faces cascading in a waterfall. As I wrote about each personality, I saw parts of myself in the writing and I began to feel and release emotions. I soon realized that this book was a tool to help me heal and evolve.

The deeper I looked into each personality, the more I unearthed aspects of myself that had challenged me for years. I released events, attitudes, beliefs, relationships, emotions and suffering that I've carried since childhood. Doing so, I liberated my being and found a sweet clarity.

Looking at ourselves honestly gives rise to our emotions. Upon their release, we heal the aspects of ourselves that bind us. This expands our understanding and our ability to be authentic and present.

To understand everything is to forgive everything. -Buddha

We are an ever-changing chemical equation in pursuit of balance and equanimity. Our thoughts, desires and intentions affect our personal alchemy. We are in control of these things, creating realities upon every thought and intention. If we so desire, we can gently release people, events, beliefs and circumstances that no longer serve us. In the process, we transform this, prior and future lives.

We are all born from a divine spark. This spark, however pure, cannot prevent us from adopting debilitating characteristics and attitudes. Healing these aspects helps us evolve.

To begin your journey, select three personalities that appeal to you. Read each chapter and journal about what comes up for you. Fully express yourself.

Imagine how each personality is reflective of you and of the people in your life. See each personality as a representation of an aspect of the universe calling you to heal and master it.

I am grateful for **Mata Amritanandamayi** (also known as Amma, and found at Amma.org) for allowing me to open many of her retreats with a spiritual comedy show. Sitting on her stage was profound and life changing.

Thank you Yogi Bhajan, Thich Nhat Hanh, Chogyam Trungpa, Karmu, Day Lone Wolf, Hawk and Larry Hewitt for showing me how to be vulnerable and fearless at the same time.

I have deep gratitude for Dr. Xiaoshen Jin and Randy Nargi for their brilliance, kindness and support. Thank you to Ellis Mensah and Craig Ephraim for buying the first books! Thank you John Sacco, Jill Aramiah, Barry Wolfman, Sebastian Posern, Tom LaRotonda and Annique Wagner-Hiester for providing valuable encouragement and feedback.

May we shed constricting veils that imprison us and achieve the utmost level of joy.

Paul Wagner
January 15, 2016

HOW TO USE THIS BOOK

EXPLORE YOURSELF & OTHERS!

This book is a friendly guide, a personal development tool and the start of a conversation. With a fairly broad stroke, it explores a perceived subset of the spectrum of colorful personalities, avatars and attributes that operate within the collective human psyche.

Every experience results in the accumulation of attitudes, intentions and beliefs, which live in us as magnets. Left unchecked, our internal magnets can attract undesirable experiences to our lives. These magnets also form identity masks (personalities) within us, which also attract experiences. We are at the mercy of these amorphous, embedded constructs until we recognize, heal and release them.

You are invited to explore, embrace, forgive and celebrate these aspects within yourself and others. May you move successfully past your stories and closer to emotional and spiritual freedom.

HOW READERS USE THE BOOK

- "The books and cards help me **heal my heart and grow**! They help me have more compassion for my husband and our relating. Wonderful and helpful!" - Jennifer S.

- "As a psychotherapist, **I use the book and cards to help my clients** bridge the gap between fantasy and reality. I also use these tools to help me see myself more clearly." - Chris V, Ph.D

- "It might sound a little heavy, but the **book is helping me process my life** so I can think about dying with a light and clear heart. This is truly a gift." - Ria G, PhD

THE PURPOSE OF OUR PERSONALITIES

Much like our spirits enter our bodies at birth, we step into personalities, which are nothing more than vehicles for interacting with physical realities. We use personalities to interact with the universe, make friends, get jobs and get attention. By temporarily naming and then exploring our personalities, we make them more relatable, which helps us process unattended emotions and experiences. Doing so, we increase our ability to forgive ourselves and others, our awareness expands and we grow.

Over time, we evolve out of some personalities, stepping into clearer, more advanced representations of ourselves. At the ends of our lives, we drop all personalities and we return to source. This does not mean that our souls die, it means we go back to an existence without pretense or construct.

The purpose of life is to release the features within us that are incongruent with the source of all life. This is what the masters who have appeared throughout time have taught us. Buddha, Mohammed, Jesus, Krishna, Lao Tzu, Quan Yin, Amma, Paramahansa Yogananda, Swami Vivekananda, Osho, Thich Nhat Hanh, Sai Baba and all the light beings who brighten our spirits, point to a oneness with creation, a merging with eternity. They desire for us to go through the process of **Self-realization**, seeking nirvana, the state of the perfect non-existence of self-serving desires.

Some people pursue this clear state by praying, chanting or by living monastic lives, but the majority of us utilize relational, emotional and psychological modalities to serve our spiritual advancement. These tools bring us closer to the Self, expanding our awareness, clarity and sense of freedom.

By exploring and finding empathy for the broad spectrum of human attributes inherent in the human condition, we move closer to the source. By seeing ourselves in every living being we experience and interact with, we become free. With one intention, one action, we can awaken.

HOW TO EXPLORE YOUR PERSONALITIES

When reading a personality chapter, give thought to how you relate to it. As you see reflections of yourself and others in the readings, consider releasing the behaviors and notions you find hurtful or distasteful. As feelings emerge, fully express them vocally or by writing about them.

Life is challenging. Mistakes are part of the plan. Forgive. Let go. Reboot.

As you read through personalities that reflect parts of you that are positive, helpful or enjoyable, take extra time to celebrate them! Embrace the more pleasing personalities and the related characteristics so that you might validate and accentuate their presence in your life. Celebration of our most treasured and valuable attributes is an important part of the growth process.

START HERE: A STEP-BY-STEP METHOD

1. *Pick Three Personalities:* Flip through the book and choose three personalities of interest. If you have the companion deck of The Personality Cards, think of a question, shuffle and pick a few cards. Allow the personalities you choose to teach you something about yourself or others.

2. *Read the Chapters and Take Notes:* Be honest and transparent. Project yourself into the pages. Contemplate your life. Consider your past, present and future. Look at your relationships, careers, desires and dreams as they relate to the personality's emotions, attributes and behaviors.

3. *Express Emotions:* Be brave. Look at moments from childhood and all the emotionally-charged events in your life. See the wonder, the helplessness, all the joys and pains. If a chapter reminds you of something specific, make note of the traits, feelings and lessons. Allow yourself to cry, laugh or scream so you can LET IT ALL GO! Doing so, you heal and evolve.

4. *Personality Empowerment:* The colors and gems we wear affect how we feel about ourselves. Defusing essential oils into the air or massaging drops of pure oils into our bodies helps us relax, release emotions and grow. Flower essence tinctures can help us heal old wounds and get back to shining brightly. Explore these things so you can enjoy relief, healing and happiness.

5. *Be Grateful:* The more you explore and release, the more joy you welcome into your heart. There is no wisdom except through emotion. Gratitude helps us forgive, leading us to peace and clarity.

GO FOR IT!

THE LOVER

My heart vibrates when a sweet soul is near. I come alive when experiencing, connecting with, and nurturing the heart, mind, and body of another. If my first attempt fails, I try again, and then again, and then again. My desire is to connect deeply and intimately, either directly or remotely with a beloved soul born of delicious spiritual vibration. I embody a love that is an unconditional dance with all living beings. Without this dance, I cannot breathe. I do not exist. Dance with me.

THE LOVER

"I remember when it happened, the moment I decided to give no matter what I receive."

MORSEL

Love is a constant, an action, a decision in every moment. If we are persistent in loving action, we might, for a moment, feel truly connected and whole. We are ever-pregnant with love.

MESSAGE

Love is our birth right, and our destiny. Love is a way of life and a philosophy. It is a constant force that streams from one living creature to the next. No matter the circumstance, love is always within reach. Whether we experience love by relating with others, in prayer, submerging in nature, or via transmission from a living or deceased spiritual master, love is always in our midst. We are in constant communion with all living beings, plugged into all sources of love in all the universes.

We have all felt the warming embrace of love. At one point in our lives, mothers, fathers, siblings, guardians, or God graced us with a sweet, loving friendship that awakened the softness in our hearts.

You may have heard beautiful and miraculous words from your Grandmother. You may have found love in the words of an author or poet. As a child, you had a puppy, kitten, or goldfish who gave you just enough love to fill your little heart. You may have participated in a ceremony, and felt a vibration more expansive than you. You knew this to be love.

We live such complex lives, we often fail to recognize love when it appears. In our occasional despair, we might keep track of mistakes and store toxic memories. When we feel a glimmer of love, rather than embrace it, we use it to remind us of how undeserving we are. With our obsession for the past and our low self-esteem, we render love useless.

Most relationships are not comprised solely of love. They include a cocktail of projections, fears, desires, and needs. While love is often in the mix, it is not always predominant.

It is easy to miss the subtle call of the Lover. She never shouts, whispering softly when we least expect it. The Lover offers tenderness and warmth to all living beings, rarely thinking of herself. She is eternally available to the deepest parts of us. When we are confused and distracted, she waits. When we reject her love, she pauses then tries again.

The Lover may be the CEO of a billion dollar company. He might be a living in a shack by a river. To The Lover, how his life appears to others is unimportant. Material comfort is not how The Lover derives pleasure from the world. She delights when we allow her embrace to set us free.

If The Lover has warmed your heart today, allow the universe to pour itself into you. Open the doors and windows, turn on the faucets, and receive every morsel of love available. Bathe in it. Dance in it. Eat it with a spoon! It has been far too long since you last opened yourself up. Today, you sing with the bird, "I accept LOVE!" Today you open your heart to yummy, delicious, nutritious love.

CAUTION

The highest experience in this life is not found by following societal norms, having the perfect marriage or climbing the ladder of success. The highest experience in this life is found in our ability to love. When you love, you embody the most advanced attribute of your humanity.

Open your heart to love so you can heal it. Release the emotions blocking the love available to you. With emotional release comes wisdom and spiritual growth. While the mind holds a fraction of our experiences, the heart carries an eternity of understanding. It is the center of all of our realities. It is the foundation of our immune and nervous systems. The heart houses the energetic mechanisms that heal you and attract goodness to your life. Let love into your heart. Open the gates to your goodness. Give, receive and enjoy love.

EXTREME

There are no degrees of love. We cannot love one person more than another. Sometimes when we tell someone we love them, we are saying that we need or desire them. When we feel we are not being loved, we are failing to love ourselves. We often mistakenly blame others for our inability to take care of ourselves. We cannot expect our lovers and partners to take care of our need for self-love.

Many of us have witnessed parents and guardians attempting to love each other. You may have internalized a twisted definition of love. Your idea of love might be akin to the definition of control. Human "love" is a wild waterfall, a mixture of pure gems and rough-edged stones. When we are showered with human love, stones rub against our skin, removing barnacles. Our psyche is cleansed and flow and healing return to our hearts. Love yourself first and your relationships will flourish.

EMPOWERMENT

Imagine beautiful, loving angels circling around you pouring light into your mind, body, and heart. Imagine this light moving through your limbs and veins. Release the emotions that come up. Eat organic cacao, read a love story, watch a romantic movie and forgive someone.

The colors of your clothes and the gems you wear can significantly affect your mood, mind and heart. Ingesting flower essences and applying essential oils to your body (or diffusing them into the air) can improve your energy, attitude and drive. The following modalities are recommended for The Lover. Seek professionals to help you expand this part of your life.

Colors: green, lime green, olive, dark orchid, hot pink, violet red, blue, dark violet

Gemstones: Emerald, Jade, Rose Quartz, Moss Agate, Malachite, Jade, Blue Quartz, Moonstone

Flower Essences: Holly, Star of Bethlehem, Pine, Cherry Plum, Sweet Chestnut, Walnut

Essential Oils: Holly, Poppy, Rose, Lavender, Jasmine, Ylang Ylang, Sandalwood, Chicory, Pine

Love is a constant. We cannot love one person more than another. Some love is not love at all. It is a combination of projection, need, fear, and desire.

THE TRANSPARENT

I enjoy freeing my mind and heart of unnecessary clutter, preferring to live as an open book for all to see. I stumble when involved in ferocious business pursuits, but I thrive when immersed in honest groups, intimate communities and creative endeavors. Whatever details or challenges seem to be a burden to the situation, I relinquish them freely in pursuit of a clear mind and joyful simplicity. My load is light, making me accessible to almost anyone who crosses my path.

THE TRANSPARENT

"I seek to be open-minded upon every moment, interaction and experience."

MORSEL

Life is simpler when approached with a genuine heart.

MESSAGE

Every day we ingest thousands of messages from the media. As we consume vast amounts of fast food and hyperbole, we allow our memories to feed us misguided information. We have lost the ability to discern what is real and of value to us. We are both the addict and the dealer.

We jump through hoop after hoop with the belief that it will make our lives better and more whole. Unknowingly, we defer to the federally approved mandate on happiness:

1	Go to a good college.	5	Buy a house or condo.
2	Buy a new car.	6	Refinance and buy insurance.
3	Marry someone of the opposite sex.	7	Move up the ladder at work.
4	Make some babies.	8	Make as much money as possible.

Truth be told, none of these things are required for a happy life. Our minds are too often the embodiment of the past, often controlling our choices and internal influences. It is our minds that keep us from experiencing our true natures in this moment.

If The Transparent has appeared amidst your mess, be grateful. With her unpretentious style, she brings clarity, light and inspiration to an otherwise complex, cloudy world. Through her, we rethink our assumptions. With a glance, she helps us get back to our true natures and this precious moment.

The Transparent lives a simple, pristine life. Rather than aggressively pursue goals, she calmly and quietly makes choices that feel true and connected. She shares information as it happens, freeing herself from the trappings of secrets and hierarchies. The Transparent eschews the drama and suffering associated with social dynamics and gossip.

As the sun rises on a new chapter in your life, The Transparent lovingly suggests that you detach from all complexities and focus solely on the things that bring you flow and joy. Relinquish obsessions. Step away from stressful dynamics. Allow happiness to cushion your ride.

Refrain from ingesting and internalizing headlines, news feeds, and office chatter. Replace this never-ending cycle of madness with simplicity. Let The Transparent remove the clutter from your mind so you can think and feel again. Release your masks, choose authenticity, and embody a heartier truthfulness. Pursue peace, joy and honesty. Your best days are ahead.

CAUTION

The joy of life is not found in the minutia, it is found in the flow as you go from one moment to the next. When we allow complex dynamics and details to rule the day, a part of us goes dormant. Instead of putting effort into monitoring your thoughts and deeds, relax and release control. Your life might look fascinating with that metric ton of information strapped to it, but this is an illusion. Find the balance between the archivist and the dancer who lives freely in the moment.

Look carefully at how you construct your day. Consider the challenges at work and in your primary relationships. Be true to yourself in every way. Do the things you participate in bring you joy? Make the changes that inspire a relaxed transparency. To feel free: evaluate, delegate and let go.

EXTREME

When we fail to set clear boundaries, our relationships and lives can quickly erode. Refrain from being so transparent that you tell others your bank account numbers and passwords. You might be so naive in your transparency that you share your brilliant business idea with a stranger on the bus. You might be swinging between low self-esteem and vanity.

Consider what is truly yours in this life, and what is not yours. Your bank account is YOUR bank account. If you are monogamous, your wife or husband is YOURS, not anyone else's. Make clear distinctions between those who are in your circle of goodness and trust, and those who are not.

If you have over-complicated your life with control and pretense, this is the perfect time to find your center, release some tears and get back to being fully and wholly who you are.

EMPOWERMENT

Lovingly ask the universe to provide you with partners and friends who truly honor you and your openness. Bless the universe with your gratitude, speak your heart and await the will of heaven. If you feel emotionally frustrated, try Kundalini Yoga to help loosen the energies that are blocking you. If you are feeling marginalized in some way, seek to set better boundaries, take a restful break or consider transforming the relationships in your life where your transparent style is not respected.

The colors of your clothes and the gemstones you wear can significantly affect your mood, mind and heart. Ingesting flower essences and applying diluted essential oils to your body (or diffusing them into the air) can improve your energy, attitude and drive. The following modalities are recommended for The Transparent. Seek professionals to help you expand this part of your life.

Colors: white, goldenrod, cornsilk, plum, light green, light blue, turquoise

Gemstones: Aquamarine, Turquoise, Tiger's Eye, Agate, Garnet, Rose Quart

Flower Essences: Rescue Remedy, Centaury, Agrimony, Aspen, Beech, Lavender

Essential Oils: White Angelica, Thieves, Valor, Lavender, Grapefruit, Rose, Cedarwood

At birth, our minds and hearts are open. Return to this openness every day.

THE BUMBLE BEE

I'm a self-reliant pack-rat, a mixture of wise sage, homeless person and traveling minstrel. I carry my world on my back as I pursue my next relationship or adventure. I carry all of my emotional wisdom and physical baggage wherever I go. This gives me immediate access to everything I am and everything I own. With all this weight, I'm a bit clumsy, but I can wander anywhere at the drop of a hat. I seek like-minded souls in pursuit of easy friendship and hearty laughter. Let's drink honey tea, share our stories, and make plans to meet under the silver moon. I'll bring my wings.

THE BUMBLE BEE

"I like it here, but I believe it might be better over there."

MORSEL

When relieved of old mirrors and tired illusions, fruitful pathways and potentials emerge.

MESSAGE

Travel is a healer. It helps us release attitudes and attachments, instructing us to be flexible, resourceful, and open. With few things in tow, we become happier, nimbler, and more adventurous. Traveling helps us become more self-reliant, refreshing our perspectives on the people and processes in our lives. Travel can be medicinal in its ability to decrease dependence on comfort and materialism.

We identify heavily with possessions. We might be so fearful about theft that we refrain from traveling. As we take the last sip of our Caribbean cocktail, we genuinely believe someone might be stealing our engraved titanium golf clubs and little Jimmy's glow-in-the-dark frisbee. Even when in the center of paradise, without a care in the world, we obsess about our stuff.

The Bumble Bee may be a stuntman, entrepreneur, salesman, artist, comedian, magician, athlete, healer or dancer. He travels far from home to share his craft with the world, enjoying whatever feedback or money that comes his way. The Bumble Bee is kindhearted and open-minded. He is self-reliant, and never overstays his welcome. He is unattached and deeply free.

With unpredictable style and behavior, The Bumble Bee can appear to be clueless and clumsy. She might bump into furniture, or repeatedly come within a hair's breath of danger. She might even wander into enemy territory and carelessly dance with death. Fear not, because Bumble is fully aware of her actions and location at all times. She is the master of movement and peace. Using the Aikido move "Ten-Kan," Bumble makes one turn of her body and moves out of harms way.

The Bumble Bee might look like an international, pot-smoking drug mule. He might even carry the entirety of his knowledge and wardrobe on his back, but look past his appearance and you will see there is more to Bumble than meets the eye.

The Bumble Bee is a wise keeper of truth. She is a real-time Buddha living in the moment, available to lovingly touch your life in the here and now. She is often a gentle soul who knows that her primary function is to shed wisdom and light on those with whom she communes.

If The Bumble Bee is buzzing in your garden today, release your clench on reality. You have the chance to create a new perspective, job, position, home, or relationship. Have a yard sale, grab your toothbrush, lock the door behind you and head for the horizon! It is time for an adventure!

You have the tools, experiences, and perspective required for success. If you desire, the universe will bring forth every opportunity you need to refresh your life. All you have to do is open up and begin.

CAUTION

The Bumble Bee is a soft-hearted consciousness who moves with the flow of everything around him. If his zen-like style and actions frighten you, you might perceive peacefulness to be a sign of weakness.

Bumble Bee's arrival might be a call to change how you treat yourself and others. Do you put unnecessary pressure on yourself to do things a certain way? Are you holding too tightly to a situation?

The Bumble Bee might be telling you that it's time to take a trip! Take the show on the road! Go-it alone! It might be time to vacate or graduate! Be prepared to redefine what you believe to be "home."

Be careful not to bring all your gifts, talents, and attributes on every trip you take. Take your heart, soul, fears, past, wisdom, vulnerabilities, wits, and voice everywhere you go. Trust yourself to arrive at destinations that further your growth, give you joy and advance your self-understanding.

EXTREME

If Bumble is buzzing aggressively in your flower bed today, you might be trying to force a situation that is not right for you. If you are feeling sick or stuck, take a good look at the relationships in your life and make sure they support your happiness. Examine the connection with each of your parents and guardians. Focus on the emotional dynamics, responses, and reactions. There might be trapped emotions within you that need to be set free. When we release emotion, we stop old cycles of pain.

Your future Self awaits your transformation. Steer gently into the wind, go with the flow, and you will become new. Learn from yesterday, for today you cross the skybridge that Bumble built.

EMPOWERMENT

When The Bumble Bee feels fearful and disconnected from others, he needs grounding. Head into nature for a hike or weekend retreat. Connect with plants, trees and streams. Steer clear of relationships infused with guilt, shame and control. Seek like-minded travelers, artists and healers who understand freedom. These are the people who embody appropriate levels of attachment.

The colors of your clothes and the gemstones you wear can significantly affect your mood, mind and heart. Ingesting flower essences and applying essential oils to your body (or diffusing them into the air) can improve your energy, attitude and drive.

Colors: red, firebrick red, dark purple, dark orchid, green, orange, violet

Gemstones: Amethyst, Black Tourmaline, Tiger's Eye, Rose Quartz, Rainbow moonstone

Flower Essences: Hornbeam, Mimulus, Honeysuckle, Holly, White Chestnut, Wild Oat, Water Violet

Essential Oils: Lavender, Valor, Ylang Ylang, Sandalwood, Orange, Frankincense, Spruce

The home we seek is beneath all thought, below identity, around the corner from construct. It's beyond societal reasoning, resting on a shelf called Self-love.

THE FEELER

I make decisions by sensing and embodying the feelings of those nearest me. I sit in the seat of each soul, achieving an understanding of what they feel. Once I get a sense of their emotional body, I offer a balanced perspective or opinion, one that takes into account the feelings of everyone involved. With this insight, I educate the collective, heal some of them, and remind them all that they are loved. At times, I take on too much and become overwhelmed with emotion, even incapacitated. Letting it all flow through me, resisting very little, I continually gain insight and wisdom that seem to escape the souls around me. I feel the vibration of every little thing. This too shall pass.

THE FEELER

"If it whispers, dances, emanates or sings, I absorb it and process it with all of my being."

MORSEL

Empathy steers us toward an expanded understanding of human nature and ourselves.

MESSAGE

We are more than skin and bones, born from the same elements that created the universe. We are comprised of the most subtle weavings of sounds and vibrations, the true building blocks of reality.

When we choose an emotion, thought, desire, intention, action or experience, it creates sounds and vibrations in our bones, organs, minds and hearts. Our mental, emotional and physical health depend upon the quality of the sounds and vibrations that we generate and those we allow in our sphere.

No matter how separate we believe we are, there is no separating our thoughts and actions from the entirety of creation. Even when we believe our thoughts and actions to be supremely private, there is no denying that the whole is affected upon every thought and emission.

Instead of seeking healing connections with others to cope with our challenging lives, we fill our bellies with unhealthy ingredients that alter our thinking. We drink too much coffee and alcohol, numbing our experiences of reality. We dim our inner lights and distance ourselves from love. We take drugs to expand our joy, and by doing so, we reduce our effectiveness in the higher realms.

The Feeler is keenly aware of, and sensitive to the sounds and vibrations in her environment. She is "tapped in," seeming to know and feel things that are out of reach for everyone else.

Being The Feeler results in a wealth of insight into human nature and all its machinations. While potentially a burden, this treasure trove of understanding has immeasurable benefits.

The Feeler's fountain overflows with awareness. With one glance or touch, she heals the innermost part of you. She transforms dynamics, individuals, and processes through her deep knowing and feeling. With one word she can build a bridge or tear one down.

It is difficult for The Feeler to refrain from taking other people's emotions into her heart. It is challenging enough for her to synthesize her own emotions, save the wave of emotions coming from a loved one or a room full of friends. Without boundaries, The Feeler will be emotionally incapacitated.

If The Feeler has slipped inside your heart today, the best outcome for your situation is one achieved through compassion. By empathizing with all participants, and synthesizing all perspectives, The Feeler will intuitively know the best course of action for everyone involved.

As you avail yourself to the energetic bodies of the people around you, remember to honor your boundaries and the boundaries of those you seek to love and help.

CAUTION

When your heart is receptive and raw like The Feeler's, it becomes second nature to absorb every fibre in the emotional atmosphere. The challenge for The Feeler is to refrain from taking on the emotions of every living creature within a ten mile radius. She continually houses stray dogs and drama queens.

When The Feeler focuses on success, money and position rather than intimacy, she can become overwhelmed and take things too personally.

Remain as loving and balanced as possible. Every so often, reboot your heart by clearing stored emotions and collected energies. Your clarity can bring resolution to every situation.

EXTREME

The Feeler can become so overwhelmed by what others feel and experience that she either shuts down completely or explodes. While your sensitivity is a gift that brings growth to everyone around you, your own person and heart must be intact throughout the process.

The Feeler might wake up one day to find that all her friends are a burden to her. This is a challenging day for The Feeler because she is being called to make changes in her life. Only you know when you've have taken on too much.

To keep grounded and whole, be prayerful, forgiving, and set clear boundaries. It is perfectly okay to tell someone you no longer want them in your life. It is your right to create the life that you feel will honor your gifts and heart. Humans and computers have a major similarity: we can both reboot.

EMPOWERMENT

When you feel overwhelmed by the emotions and burdens of others, seek a therapist or good friend to help you clear these energies. With a cleansed heart, you will quickly spring back to life. Be sure to protect yourself during intimacy and sexual exchanges. If The Feeler is not careful, he will carry the energies of several past lovers for his entire life. At the conclusion of each relationship and intimate experience, find a ritualistic way to release the emotions and energetic forms you collected.

As The Feeler, explore the following colors, gems, flower essences and essential oils to brighten your heart and mind. It's amazing how clothing, jewelry and healing tinctures can improve for our lives.

Colors: white, ivory, mint cream, purple, indigo, lavender, periwinkle, fuchsia, light blue, light green

Gemstones: Turquoise, Agate, Hematite, Amethyst, Black Tourmaline, Bloodstone, Rose Quartz, Coral, Rhodochrosite, Topaz

Flower Essences: Walnut, Centaury, Holly, Chicory, Vervain, Vine, Beech, Rock Water, Pine

Essential Oils: Roman Chamomile, White Angelica, Rosemary, Cinnamon Bark, Thieves, Lavender

We are sponges, soaking it all up. Ring us out and we are healed. When we raise our vibration in this fashion, we cannot be offended or deterred.

THE ONCE-ENCHANTED

I once thought the world to be my personal Disney love story. I believed it all, from talking bunnies to the perfect mate, to the fairies dancing in my dreams. As the bubbles burst all around me, I could no longer see colors. What was once real became fictitious. Even pigeons in the park have become cardboard replications of the bird I once knew. Nothing gives me the spark that my fairytales provided. What does one do when magic fizzles? Where is my secret flame? My hidden treasure? I'll sit patiently and await enchantment's return.

THE ONCE-ENCHANTED

"When my fantasy was ripped from my heart and thrown to the wind, my identity followed."

MORSEL

To fully experience ourselves, our stories and beliefs must be vetted for truth and authenticity.

MESSAGE

As we freely dance with our hearts open wide, we might fail to see the nearby cliff. As we pirouette off the edge, we gasp in fear. In the midst of our helpless fall through the air, we wonder how this came to be. Was the cliff always there? Was I pushed or did I do this to myself?

Our existences are dreams comprised of thousands of smaller dreams and stories. These stories form a powerful engine that can make or break the pathways in our lives. Whether we win, lose or draw, the stories we create give birth to our realities.

Many of us use stories to justify religious beliefs, political perspectives, family culture, self-esteem, levels of success, and emotional states of being. All these things, whether real or perceived, feed into a narrative that either expands or shrinks our potentials.

When our dreams become disrupted by awareness, we can become deflated, confused or alarmed. The moment our bubbles burst, we can lose faith and spiral downward. It is in this moment that we realize our well-crafted beliefs and stories were partial fantasies in need of re-evaluation.

The Once-Enchanted understands that in order to increase his level of awareness, he must continually revise his beliefs, stories and dreams. He knows that being caught off-guard or falling off a fantasy cliff is too painful, even unnecessary.

We are the writers of our stories and dreams. We are the only ones who can scrutinize them, and enhance their quality. If we allow ourselves to ingest and perpetuate tiny falsehoods, we are the only ones who will suffer.

If The Once-Enchanted has arrived cheerless and gloomy today, it is time to come to terms with the falsehoods, fantasies and delusion in your life. Your former story may have attracted triumph and miracles, but that time has passed. Unless you are prepared to dance with your shadow, it is time to detach from your tale and begin again. The chance of renewal is a gift to be cherished.

When we release outdated narratives, new realities emerge with a variety of possibilities. When we let former justifications and protective devices dissolve, we make room for new potentialities. We are always in control of our dreams, how we interpret them and to what level we are willing to aspire.

As you release the beliefs and relationships that once served you, remember it was you who created those realities. You are the co-creator of realities, beckoning enchantment and rebirth at every turn.

CAUTION

We have all played the victim and attempted to polarize against a perceived villain. We have all plotted and schemed to advance our games. When we jeopardize our sweetness like this, we risk becoming the villains we fear. As our worlds catch fire and crumble to the ground, we often wonder how and why.

Open your heart and find another way to look at your situation. Allow new and more fulfilling stories to emerge. With acceptance, patience and courage you can forge a new and better way.

Whatever you believe to be the bubble-bursting ideas or events in your life, you are seeing them through outdated lenses. Let love spark a new perspective and story.

EXTREME

We are best to be detached from our stories and identities. When a relationship begins to change, do not deny its flow, rush to fix it or push it back into the past. Allow events to unfold naturally. When we are beholden to expired ideas, we miss out on the truth of the present moment. When a truth emerges in your life, let it live freely out in the open. Living in the light, we will find our way home.

The Once-Enchanted is giving you a message today: move on or live in gloom. Every second you live in the past is another second the universe wastes on supporting your negative reality.

EMPOWERMENT

When we feel despondent or disillusioned, it's helpful to work with an art therapist. She will help you explore and express yourself. Schedule daily meditation and prayer, inviting as much light into your life as possible. You may have lost connection to the lineage of emotions nestled in your heart. Put your hands on your chest and ask your emotions to rise to the surface. Let them out and let it go.

The Once-Enchanted has a tendency to be aloof during emotional and physical intimacy. Consider opening up to a few kind-hearted friends and let them nurture you. As you await enchantment to return, pray that all the beings in all the realms, in all the worlds be happy.

The colors of your clothes and the gemstones you wear can significantly affect your mood, mind and heart. Ingesting flower essences and applying essential oils to your body (or diffusing them into the air) can improve your energy, attitude and drive. The following recommendations are for The Once-Enchanted. Seek to improve your emotions, attitudes and conditions every day.

Colors: dark red, deep pink, violet, purple, chocolate, yellow, gold, goldenrod, turquoise, sea green

Gemstones: Kyanite, Amethyst, Golden Quartz, Clear Quartz, Enhydro, Moss, Appetite, Amber

Flower Essences: Gentian, Gorse, Water Violet, Clematis, Sweet Chestnut, Scleranthus, Wild Rose

Essential Oils: Lavender, Rose, Valerian, Orange, Pine Needle, Ylang ylang, Geranium, Valerian

Speak your truth. Live your truth. Always be in pursuit of the truth.

THE GROUCH

People have forgotten what the word "quality" means. Nobody seems to care about anything of lasting value anymore. I expect so much, yet I never feel satiated by what I see and hear. I critique and critique, yet nothing changes. I like things to go a certain way, but rarely does life acquiesce. Every time I push, it feels as though I'm attempting to wake the dead. When did mediocrity become so popular? Am I the only one who understands excellence? While I am truly alone on my island of assessment, my grumble keeps me company.

THE GROUCH

"Please stop whining about my demeanor. I gave you what you came for, and so much more."

MORSEL

Do not deny your grumpiness. Do more than relish it. Celebrate it. There is gold in the grump.

MESSAGE

We brainstorm, have visions, and draw beautiful pictures, often only sharing them with our closest friends. We tell shallow stories at parties, testing our brilliance on strangers. We glorify the things that appear in our mind yet never fully pursue or express them. Rather than put them up for evaluation and improve upon them, we build fortresses around our vulnerability and recoil at the thought of criticism. We all fear critique.

Take a lesson from beavers. Beavers work tirelessly to create their dams. Their elaborate designs include detailed architecture and separate rooms. These homes are veritable water theme parks, equipped with slides and passageways. These hard-working creatures work collaboratively, often finishing each other's jobs. Whatever challenges emerge, they continue to work. When challenged by other beavers, everyone keeps moving forward. It appears as if nothing is taken personally.

When challenges, conflict and opinions come our way, we defend ourselves. We scan our internal arsenals for perfectly-timed reactions and we bark like trapped animals. We refuse to see lessons and feedback for what they are: a collection of ideas to consider. As someone delivers critical thinking to us, we can barely breathe. We feel as though a python is choking the life out of us.

While The Grouch lives to critique minutia, his is a vital and inspiring voice in the evolution of creativity. With his every utterance of dissatisfaction, The Grouch forces you to examine yourself and extricate imperfections. With his ornery attitude and harsh thinking, he uncovers the inconsistencies of our plans, shedding light on the shadowy beliefs that live nestled beneath our pretentious skin.

If The Grouch has grumbled into your sphere today, take his feedback with a grain of salt. Doing so, your creations will become more crystallized and inspired. Listen to the core of The Grouch's message, and you will turn that mediocre drawing into a masterpiece.

The Grouch's job is to help you to become more aware and more creative. Take notes and address each concern, but NEVER internalize his bark. When The Grouch grumbles, it is not an attack. This is the sound he makes when he merges with perfection. If need be, grumble back.

Use your relationship with The Grouch as one of the greatest growth opportunities of your life. Pretend as though the Gods are speaking directly to you through him. Celebrate the emerging innovations!

If you are The Grouch, do your best to keep the toxicity out of the critique. With a little sugar in your speech, you'll be honored for the rare value you bring to others.

CAUTION

This may not be a time for your unsolicited opinions. Even though we might feel justified in sharing every brilliant thought in our minds, if they cannot be joyfully received, we can do more harm than good.

Be careful how much of her feedback you internalize, because it can become addictive. When we do not love ourselves, we unconsciously seek abuse, begging strangers to throw salt in our wounds.

When we are in the process of creating, we might crave a brilliant mind to help us. Forgetting our voice, we drink in her insight as if it were a magical elixir. We can easily become intoxicated with The Grouch.

Always keep a pouch of your purest gold hidden from view. Your gold is that well of sweetness that lives within you. Protect it at all costs. You should be the only one who has a key to your inner temple.

EXTREME

You gave your hidden gold to The Grouch and are now blaming others for your mistake. Take responsibility for your choices. Do not use The Grouch as an excuse to be fearful. To work through your grumbling, you might need a good, long cry. With every image, scenario and relationship we process and detach from, we bring ourselves closer to Self-realization. With every feeling and emotion we let evaporate from our hearts, we embrace another level of freedom and joy.

EMPOWERMENT

Once you have gleaned the highest value from your interactions with The Grouch, say goodbye to her, at least within your own heart. Consider doing a ritual that involves letting go, releasing emotions and declaring your gratitude. The Grouch served you well.

Each one of us has a unique and subtle vibration. The colors of your clothes and the gemstones you wear can significantly affect your mood, mind and heart. Ingesting flower essences and applying essential oils to your body (or diffusing them into the air) can improve your energy, attitude and drive. Seek to improve yourself on even the most subtle levels.

Colors: light green, turquoise, pink, gold, light blue, lavender, salmon, red

Gemstones: Amethyst, Moonstone, Charoite, Chyrsocolla, Aventurine, Rose Quartz, Larimar, Pink Tourmaline, Ruby

Flower Essences: Beech, Star of Bethlehem, Impatiens, Rock Water, Vervain, Water Violet, Chicory, White Chestnut

Essential Oils: Lavender, Rose, Peppermint, Bergamot, Clary Sage, Geranium, Juniper, Sandalwood, Orange, Ginger, Spruce

Be courageous in your pursuit of humility and the elasticity of your ego. Listen carefully, but let all opinions roll off you like beads of water on waxed wood.

THE DISCONNECTED

I'm often lost and confused, gently suspended in three-dimensional space. What I need most is a beacon of light to lead me to a truer reflection of myself, one that I can healthfully attach to. I look in the mirror and see a human being, but I barely recognize the image before me. Day by day, I try to find things I can relate with and define myself by, but never seem to hit the mark. On occasion, I am successful, but most often I float in and out of transparency like a long breath on a cold winter's day.

THE DISCONNECTED

"There was once a loving accord between my body and spirit, but now I am beyond my reach."

MORSEL

When a challenging events keep you from being present, pound the earth, howl at the moon, and demand a connection between your soul and its vessel.

MESSAGE

As you move through life at a mighty pace, cascades of experiences and emotions trickle through your mind and heart. Rather than integrate what you have experienced, you multitask, putting your spiritual and psychological growth in stasis.

While we all try to put on happy faces, a large percentage of us have been deeply hurt by our own actions or by someone else's. At some point in our lives, we may have been molested, abandoned, denied or forgotten. While these burdens are opportunities to grow, they are certainly challenging.

Instead of facing the emotions and identities that result from our traumas, we ignore them, hoping they will fade away on their own. Yet, there they sit, nibbling at us. Crumb by crumb, negative experiences take us away from ourselves. The more we allow this, the more we disassociate.

When we disconnect our spirits from our bodies, we lose access to electric currents that stimulate emotional connection, growth and awareness. No matter how far we have journeyed from ourselves, we must seek the vine will swing us back to our nature. We must seek that cord of connection to bring us back to the living. Only then will we be able to spin our traumas into gold.

The Disconnected is an overwhelmed soul who is often unaware of her own presence in the room. Confused and feeling separate, she may not know how wonderful she is or how warmly she is being received by those around her.

The Disconnected is often living and functioning within a compartmentalized area inside of her mind and heart. She is unable to feel the electricity that connects her to herself, her environment and the people around her.

He lives behind a silky, translucent wall. At best, he is present elsewhere, possibly trapped in a long-ago memory. While he might appear to be unaccustomed to the body he inhabits, The Disconnected loves his body and is fighting to be fully present in the here and now. His desire is to come back to life, to be seen and heard. He is fully cognizant of his disconnection, and is working hard to meaningfully connect with you and others.

When The Disconnected shares his experiences and perspectives with you, prepare to be in awe. Encourage him to open up and freely share. Give him as much room and freedom as possible. With your loving compassion, he will grasp the strands that connect him to love, to you and to the universe.

CAUTION

The Disconnected tends to spend a great deal of time monitoring himself. His inner chatter and filters keep him from fully enjoying the present moment. When you see The Disconnected struggling to communicate, your patience and kindness will put him at ease.

Be careful not to confuse The Disconnected's silence for agreement. He is constantly evaluating and reforming what he thinks and feels, putting him in a continual state of flux. For now, let him explore himself.

To be The Disconnected's friend, use warm, nurturing language when connecting with him. If you persist with love and patience, you will spark The Disconnected's true identity to emerge and flourish.

EXTREME

This is not the right time to make demands of The Disconnected. She is far more fragile than you realize. If you're demanding, you might thrust her deeper into her cave.

The Disconnected behaves as if she is in a self-imposed prison, which keeps her from participating in life's great adventure. This separateness is only a temporary illusion. Be patient with yourself.

Holding your identity and emotions hostage will only cause further suffering. Without professional help or encouragement from friends, you may never finish that project, attract a satisfying relationship, live in the creative flow or feel loved. Reach out and get the support you need!

EMPOWERMENT

If you're feeling sad or aloof, try Tai Chi, Hatha Yoga or Cranial Sacral therapy, These things can help you soften and reconnect with your body. If you feel frustrated, dance wildly in the forest, take a boxing class or pound the earth with a prayerful scream. Write a poem. Squeeze your teddy bear. Call a friend and share secrets. Sit quietly and gently breath in and out. Nurture your foggy heart and mind back to their original levels of vibrancy.

The colors of your clothes and the gems you wear can significantly affect your mood, mind and heart. Ingesting flower essences and applying essential oils to your body (or diffusing them into the air) can improve your energy, attitude and drive. The following modalities are recommended for The Disconnected. Seek professionals to help you expand this part of your life.

Colors: pink, fuchsia cranberry, purple, orange, chartreuse, green, aquamarine

Gemstones: Emerald, Rose Quartz, Malachite, Pink Tourmaline, Lepidolite, Amber, Peridot

Flower Essences: Walnut, Larch, Heather, Gentian, Honeysuckle, Elm, Star of Bethlehem, Willow

Essential Oils: Bergamot, Clary Sage, Lemon, Mandarin, Cedarwood, Rose, Ylang Ylang, Sandalwood, Geranium, Helichrysum

Kiss, cuddle and nurture yourself back into your beautiful body and directly into this delicious, valuable, limitless moment.

THE UNATTACHED

I'm emotionally even and quietly strong. I thrive on joy but rarely indulge my passions. I'm as present in the midst of a hurricane as I am walking in a lush, peaceful forest. I let drama play out without adding to the stew, keeping an eye on the prize of maintaining a consistent level of joy. If there is too much pushing or fretting in the midst, I graciously excuse myself with love. Do you hear eternity's whisper? It's calling you. Stand with me in a mystical cave while chaos passes by.

THE UNATTACHED

"I seek the 'perfect pocket', that sweet space between passive and passionate."

MORSEL

Hold gently to your realities and relationships, just enough for connection and flow.

MESSAGE

No matter how intense our desires and attachments are, they eventually fade. Upon every awareness, we place a little less meaning onto the things we experience. As we grow, we give a little more, need a little less, and we are hopefully more at peace.

Less engulfed, less enmeshed, less pain. With a little success and flow, we take a step back, and for a time, we are connected only to what is easy and real.

Hidden within us are emotions and desires that act as magnets. Every magnet within us will attract a range of potentially positive or negative experiences. When an attracted element appears before our eyes, we have the choice to engage with it or refuse it. By letting negative and disruptive people, events and commitments pass us by, we serve our evolution. We owe nothing to negativity.

As we mature, the game changes. We realize that we will never reach a peaceful precipice if we do not forgive and move on from the aspects that limit and restrict us. When we learn to release the past, we find clarity of mind and heart. It is then that a sweet truth emerges: all attachments limit us.

The Unattached are a rare breed. These spiritual daredevils are continually satisfied with their lives and experiences, embodying a peaceful separateness without effort. Because they do not grasp at events or circumstances, The Unattached are free.

To embody The Unattached, take nothing personally. Regardless of the personality or event you are confronted with, do not react. Become the observer and await the intuition of your higher Self before you engage. If you feel it is time to cut cords or dissolve connections, be gentle, clear and swift.

To be certain you have moved through your emotional and psychological attachments, make a list of the outstanding people and moments in your life, both the enjoyable and the challenging. Sit quietly and think about them. If you feel an emotional charge, tap into it, then work to release it.

Consider the most colorful and most important lessons in your life. Release the hidden emotions, bonds and ties. Remember to lovingly clear away the clouds as soon as they appear.

If you have stumbled upon The Unattached today, keep a humble eye on her actions and responses. Follow this Self-realized soul to her secret place. When you see the light of the universe pour through her crown, bask in her awakened glow. It is a gift to be in the presence of a truly Unattached soul.

By attracting The Unattached, you have set yourself on a path of spiritual clarity.

CAUTION

We all forget that even the most positive cultural movements and ideologies are imperfect. Be careful around groups that preach the light. Remember that their version of the truth is one of many.

Spiritual assemblies that have unspoken required wardrobes, lexicons and pretensions tend to grow the weed of spiritual materialism. Those who follow their rules are often perceived as holier than others. They might even consider themselves to be advanced. It's a never-ending distraction. All the while, true spiritual advancement evades them all.

Becoming The Unattached is an ego-less process. It does not arrive as a parade with glitter. Like the tiniest vine, it grows subtly in the background. There is work to be done. Sit quietly and look within.

Gently and privately uproot your lesser attributes. Continually release the image of who you believe yourself to be so all egoistic chaff can fall to the ground. Let your unfoldment drive the train.

EXTREME

You may have pulled so far back that you have unconsciously alienated yourself from the positive flow of life. Whether your exile is joyfully self-imposed or the result of a series of difficult events, you need not live on a desert island. When we sit alone for too long, we fall in love with our idiosyncrasies, perceptions, smells and excrements. It's time to step back into the light with others.

You might be reevaluating relationships, making a move or pursuing a career change. As you work through the related emotions, be gentle with yourself. Remember to love yourself in all things. Remain aware of the reciprocal loyalties that are dearest to you. These relationships will provide the framework and definition that your life needs to unfold.

EMPOWERMENT

Consider working for a charity. Reach out to help a friend. Seek out meaningful ways to share yourself with others. Doing so will bring a joyful spark to your heart and life. You might consider teaching classes to increase your awareness of the human condition.

The colors of your clothes and the gems you wear can significantly affect your mood, mind and heart. Ingesting flower essences and applying essential oils to your body (or diffusing them into the air) can improve your energy, attitude and drive.

Colors: sea shell, white smoke, light yellow, gold, orange, salmon, light blue, light gray, lavender

Gemstones: Azurite, Covellite, Honey Calcite, White Opal, Opalite, Citrine, Amethyst

Flower Essences: Clematis, Gorse, Water Violet, Chestnut Bud, Crab Apple, Elm, Pine

Essential Oils: Bergamot, Geranium, Mandarin, Cedarwood, Spruce, Frankincense, Myrrh

Being one with everything is a choice and a reality.

THE RIGHTEOUS BEAST

In the core of my being lives a fire that burns so brightly, it seems to empower my position as a righter of wrongs. I seek to uphold honor and bring about a balance of justice for all of humanity. I will do whatever it takes to inspire right action and changes of heart. If necessary, I will rattle, shake and fight you in order to bring about the refinements I seek. Stand toe-to-toe with me, learn the boundlessness of my rage and mourn the depth of your untruth.

THE RIGHTEOUS BEAST

"Your unwillingness to embrace the truth is your infliction."

MORSEL

When pursuing or defending a dream, unbridled aggression might be required.

MESSAGE

A subtle force lives under our personalities. This force is unaffected by socialization and untainted by the DNA we receive from our parents. It cannot be learned or absorbed. It is the energetic force of masculinity, pouring forth from the hearts of our ancestors, directly into the seats of our souls.

Without this powerful force, there can be no creation. There can be no invention, no action and no fruit. Without the raw aggressive nature of masculinity, there is a void in the universe. Without it, life would cease to exist as we know it. It is impossible to distill it.

Conversely, if the only source available to us were masculinity, life would become unpredictably explosive. Without the co-creative whisper of the feminine, we would be an unruly pile of deconstructed thoughts and materials. Who are we, if not mixtures of masculinity and femininity.

Today's spiritual circles have become accustomed to judging the raw, uncomplicated masculine all the way to its bone. We frown upon professional boxing, graphic sex and the harsh, crass language that many men and women seem to enjoy.

We put political correctness at the forefront of psychological and spiritual assessment. Doing so, we lock our inner males in steel cages, trapping them in terminal passivity. Rather than celebrate our multifaceted nature, we let the pendulum swing from the oppressed feminine to the castrated masculine. It is a cycle born of fear, and everyone loses.

If The Righteous Beast is standing strong and firm in your midst today, the message is clear. Gather your strength and focus, and aggress upon your object of desire, commanding it into your possession.

Train like hell, polish your armor and prepare to defend your title, position and perspective without regret. You are the master of your domain, your universe and the energies that create the life force within you. Only you can drive from the farthest border of complacency, through the stronghold of your enemies, into the seat of victory.

The Righteous Beast is a relentless force. His bark, bite and devouring nature comprise the purest form of masculinity. Make no mistake here: if The Righteous Beast stands before you, he has come to build an alliance or he is here to cut your throat.

The Righteous Beast is an angry healer and street-savvy priestess. She pursues victory using every tool and power she can muster. Even Tibetan monks, in the heat of invasion, fought their oppressors with weapons. Center yourself. Fight with as much honor as you can, but remember to fight!

CAUTION

When he is in pursuit of a goal, The Righteous Beast will often drop his sword and present the hand of friendship. He might do this after you have shown strength or won a battle. Be aware that this might be a decoy tactic intended to distract you. Upon letting down your guard and showing any measure of vulnerability, The Righteous Beast might slice your dangling manhood from its master.

The Righteous Beast sometimes appears as damaged goods who finds it challenging to heal her past. She may have come from a home without love or spent her childhood around violence. Her rage runs deep.

Guard up! As The Righteous Beast approaches, shake his hand with integrity and passion, but ready the other hand for the fight of your life.

EXTREME

You may not have enough love in your life. You might be imbalanced because you closed your heart after a trauma, divorce or job loss. You might have lost hope or faith. Find a healthy place to let go of your sadness and rage. Wrestle with friends, go on a strenuous hike, spend a day at the batting cage, or take a martial arts class. Get the energy in your body and heart moving again.

You might be learning a lesson about boundaries. You invited The Righteous Beast to be your friend, but his aggression dampened your peacefulness and goodness. Only you control how you interact with the world. The person or event is never the problem, it's how you respond and evolve.

EMPOWERMENT

Find time for affection, gentle touches and massages. Free yourself from oppressive thinking, harsh people and limiting dynamics. As always, forgive yourself. If you're feeling overly attached to an opinion or a judgement of another person, seek to better understand their sensitive and vulnerabilities. Empathy and compassion advance us much further than a momentary verbal spar.

The colors of your clothes and the gems you wear can significantly affect your mood, mind and heart. Ingesting flower essences and applying essential oils to your body (or diffusing them into the air) can improve your energy, attitude and drive. Enjoy the following recommendations specific to The Righteous Beast. Seek professional assistance to derive the most benefit.

Colors: yellow, pink, orchid, violet, purple, plum, turquoise, light blue, light green, orange

Gemstones: Rose Quartz, Tangerine Quartz, Amber, Yellow Fluorite, Orange Tourmaline

Flower Essences: Rock Water, Cherry Plum, Heather, Holly, Willow, Aspen, Star of Bethlehem

Essential Oils: Jasmine, Orange, Ylang Ylang, Tangerine, Cardamom, Blue Tansy, Cistus, Geranium, Ginger, Goldenrod

A solitary, focused burst of rage can dissolve residue from years of oppression and unleash a tornado of untapped abilities, awarenesses and power.

THE WANDERER

I live and love most effectively when I wander the planet with no plan. We'll share a meal, a small promise or a kiss, but I'll soon be on my way. I may stay in touch, but you might never hear from me again. It all depends on the winds that blow around us and the balance of our subconscious intentions. If we meet again, I'll remember you fondly and expect to pick up exactly where we left off: in love, in laughter or in the middle of a co-conspired illusion. I'll see you in my dreams.

THE WANDERER

"It was fun to share my heart with you. I gave freely and joyfully so that I might taste you."

MORSEL

Home and love do not require incubation. They may appear in an instant.

MESSAGE

We all have secret desires. We obsess about some of them, awaiting the perfect moment to pursue them. Whether it is a sexual experience, fantasy relationship, creative endeavor, or the promise of financial windfall, we may drop even the most sacred commitments to appease an orphan dream. It is not that we are careless. It is that we know that if we allow it, our desires can easily be satiated.

Sometimes pursuing and achieving a fantasy seems vital to our happiness. We dive in, experience a wave of emotions and for a moment, we feel satisfied. While these experiences might quell the mind's obsession for a time, these pursuits might become addictive.

The Wanderer is a soft-hearted adventurer who bounces from one immersive experience to the next. He opens his heart and mind to the experiences around him and be becomes an integral part of them, even if only for a short time.

If The Wanderer has graced your life with sweet magic and flair, restrain your affection for a time. While he won't steal your wallet or jewelry, he might abscond with your heart, never to be seen again. While his intentions are most often pure, he evades commitment and consistency as if they were the worst plague on earth. This is the mindset of The Wanderer.

The key to successfully engaging this loving scoundrel is to happily receive and enjoy her attention, generosity and gifts without expectation. Welcome it all and let The Wanderer carry you to the top of your secret mountain.

Spending time with this alluring and adventurous soul provides luscious treasures and she gives far more than she receives. Give her the space she needs to inspire you and she will continue to fill your mind, body and heart with the most scrumptious confections.

The Wanderer is usually good for her word in the moment and is often generous of spirit. She will clean your house while you are at work, give you creative ideas without any thought of remuneration, and she'll heal your heart with a compelling story or gesture.

These carefree souls engage life at a rapid rate, amassing countless hearts and experiences. When engaging The Wanderer, his emotional and experiential wealth is transmitted to you, yielding gifts and secrets usually meant for kings and queens.

In return, The Wanderer expects only your warmth and attention. Be open, demand nothing, and let the heavens speak to you through The Wanderer.

CAUTION

It is exciting to hear The Wanderer's stories and join her in a dance under the hippie moon. With her at your side, you will experience emotions, often joy, at a level akin with miracles.

These vibrant storytellers are often in the midst of various dramas, most of which will sound simple to you. You will find that her dramas often require $100 cash, needing to sleep on your couch, or a quick transport to the next "happening." She might be in the throes of a life-or-death situation involving a prince in a far-off land. Without your counsel, the world as we know it may cease to exist! So goes the fascinating and sometimes exhausting drama of The Wanderer.

Be generous, but do not let him stay for too long. He might want to stay, not for his gain, but for yours. Let him go with love and encouragement. He will let you know when the time is right to see each other again.

EXTREME

With The Wanderer in your world, you might be holding too tightly onto your story. You may have so precisely defined yourself that you are playing far below your abilities and dreams. Are you fearful of risk and change? You may have a partner, house, job and baby, all of which you love, but the illusion you co-created is beginning to feel limiting. Surprise yourself with an adventure or ask your friends to surprise you. You might consider making a move, quitting your job or changing your name. Be fearless as you examine your life.

EMPOWERMENT

You may have ventured so far from yourself that you're now standing at the edge of space and time! To bring yourself back into balance, you need love, respite and a good, long emotional release. Consider learning a martial art like Aikido. By exploring love, grounding and healing, you will not lose your magic. On the contrary, you make room for more.

The colors of your clothes and the gems you wear can significantly affect your mood, mind and heart. Ingesting flower essences and applying essential oils to your body (or diffusing them into the air) can improve your energy, attitude and drive.

Colors: yellow, orange, turquoise, orchid, cinnamon, indigo, midnight blue, white, purple

Gemstones: Blue Calcite, Turquoise, Lapis Lazuli, Malachite, Aventurine, Emerald, Infinite Stone, Blue Aventurine, Blue-Green Aventurine, Lace Agate

Flower Essences: Mustard, Gentian, Gorse, Aspen, Impatiens, Water Violet, Heather, Chestnut Bud, Vervain, Walnut, Olive, Wild Oat

Essential Oils: Spearmint, Violet Leaf, Vetiver, Neroli, Helichrysum, Fennel, Frankincense

Say yes to the experiences that seek to unshackle your spirit. Nurture serendipity, sweet connections and promising adventures. Believe in magic.

THE INFLUENCER

I walk into a room with a newly-fashioned handbag, a favorite new song or a fresh perspective on tired ideas. Gather around me and get a gander of my sensibilities and luster. I'll tell you what the emerging trends are, then take you to twenty cocktail parties to meet the innovators leading the way. I might be a blogger, salesman, investor, preacher or inventor. I might even be personally connected to the planet-shakers who live a few steps ahead of the rest of us. I often get wind of the things that can dramatically change life as we know it. And I tell a good tale. Buy me a drink and I'll deliver the future first-hand.

THE INFLUENCER

"I shine brightly and share with abandon, knowing I will benefit from my munificence."

MORSEL

Generosity yields immeasurable benefits. The most interesting possibilities are around the corner.

MESSAGE

When we make great strides in life, it is often as a result of a few well-timed lunches and handshakes. Heart-centered connections with quality people often give rise to things that have the greatest potential for our lives. With just one seasoned introduction, a lineage of wonderful events can unfold.

The Influencer is an iconic and unique personality driven by new fashions, both ideological and material, and the desire to communicate them to the world. She will travel to trade shows, coffee houses and happy hours just to be seen with a new watch.

No matter how much it might cost in health or money, The Influencer persistently and generously shares her insights with others. She deeply loves the position she holds in her circle of friends and community. There is nothing she would rather do with her life.

How does The Influencer know what she knows? It may stem from having had gracious childhood mentors or a tenacity born from poverty. Either way, The Influencer's skills come naturally to her. Her ability to attract, absorb and charismatically disseminate information is unmatched.

The Influencer is generous of spirit. He knows that demanding payment the moment his brain produces an intelligent thought is a sure-fire way to fail. He is the master of familiarity which allows him to make streams of introductions with ease. He also understands his value in every introduction and has no problem speaking up about compensation and consideration when the time is right.

If The Influencer is verbally dancing for you today, give a listen. She might give you an idea for a new business or inspire a new way to express yourself. She might even sell you on finally liking who you are! At the very least, her ideas will feel refreshing to everyone involved.

Being around The Influencer affects our health, dreams and well-being. She reminds us that being open and taking risks often results in great success. Even the adrenalin that results from taking a chance can inspire an achievement or renewal.

The Influencer is a powerful flame who tends to attract a wide variety of moths, so be careful not to get caught up in the entourage that surrounds her.

As The Influencer pontificates, stand quietly nearby and extract whatever pearls of futuristic wisdom you need in order to level up. While you may not capture or fully ingest the spirit and brilliance of The Influencer, breathing the same air might be all you need to grow.

CAUTION

The Influencer prides herself on having a brilliant mind. During every one of her social exchanges, she leaves an indelible mark, often impressing the best of the best. She plans her speeches, clothes, accessories and movement down to the last wink and glittering pearl. Before she heads to the Governor's Ball, The Influencer rehearses every potential conversation, from the waiter and valet to a host of possible thought-leaders and socialites. She is, without a doubt, a prepared actress and effective game-shifter.

If she is not careful, The Influencer can become a seducer. She might seek sex and glamour on the arm of a celebrity or international trend-setter. She might be on the hunt for her next mark. Wait for The Influencer to reveal more of herself before you lay all your treasures at her feet. Only kindred spirits deserve to see your gifts.

EXTREME

You have mastered the ability to communicate with others. You can hold court with the best of them, but while it appears you are at the top of your game, you have yet to fathom the value of intimacy. You might be taking the material world too seriously. Do you remember the pulsating bundle of muscles at the center of your chest? That's your heart. Your heart is the engine that empowers your soul. If you ignore your heart, you ignore your nature, destiny and potential.

You may have become fearful of social engagements. You might even be depressed. Take a few risks in friendship and recreation. Plan an epic road trip with friends. Extend beyond your comfort zone and keep your heart at the center of it all. You control your happiness.

EMPOWERMENT

The Influencer often obsesses about the "next big thing." Doing so, he tends to forsake his family, friends and personal well-being. Remember that the vast majority of our pursuits are an illusion. You might consider volunteering for community service to awaken your heart and inspire your growth.

The colors of your clothes and the gems you wear can significantly affect your mood, mind and heart. Ingesting flower essences and applying essential oils to your body (or diffusing them into the air) can improve your energy, attitude and drive. Explore the following ideas with a professional to derive the most benefit.

Colors: purple, indigo, red, firebrick red, green, gold, yellow, blue, ivory, orange

Gemstones: Tiger Eye, Chiastolite, Stromatolite, Axinite, Gold, Emerald, Aventurine, Covellite

Flower Essences: Chicory, Sweet Chestnut, Impatiens, Willow, Rock Water, Pine, Agrimony

Essential Oils: Rose, Bay Laurel, Benzoin, Cinnamon, Galbanum, Ginger, Myrrh, Violet Leaf

Give freely and without reverence to title or position. There is no hierarchy.

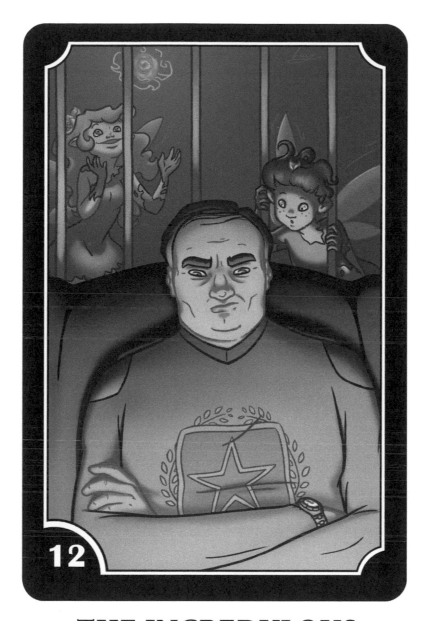

THE INCREDULOUS

I'm often an untrusting naysayer. Shout it, sing it or dance it. No matter how you tell it, I probably won't believe it. Whether it is concrete, intangible, real magic or love, I'll be the first to challenge its validity. If I didn't witness the creation of it with my own eyes, you'll have a tough time enrolling me in your little dream. If you ask me if your pursuit is worthwhile, be prepared for a curt, unfriendly response. Stand back with detachment and let me scoff or you will feel the dismantling effects of my disdain. My time is supremely invaluable, isn't yours?

THE INCREDULOUS

"If I bought into your story without scrutiny, what good would I be?"

MORSEL

Beneath blinding over-confidence lives an elusive fear. Allowing critique will transform perilous delusions into actionable potential.

MESSAGE

In the dream world, we wander through space and time experiencing unique, often fanciful realities. We co-create these other-world experiences in union with our ancestors, guides and psychological projections. Throughout the night, we are omniscient, able to conjure and create all things.

As we become each player and object in our dreams, we expand our understanding of that perspective and begin to fathom all the related emotional and psychological subsets.

Our dream-state experiences travel with us too. Upon waking, they give us valuable insights in our physical realities. With every dream, we expand our emotional and experiential database.

Before the greater consciousness co-created the world, it lived as a whispered dream in the heart of the divine. For millennium, indigenous tribes have understood that dreams tremendously enhance our lives. By growing the bridge between the physical and dream realms, we grow a deeper understanding of the concurrent cycles of thought, creation, life and death.

The Incredulous denies this part of her, giving credence only to things she can see and hear. As such, she challenges the work of artists, inventors, healers and others who allow divine beings to work through them. If it is born of the heart or channeled from another realm, The Incredulous seeks to deconstruct it.

The Incredulous lives to scrutinize everything, dissecting even the most benign concepts and creations. If The Incredulous has threatened to crash your happy, hippie "idea party," she wants to make sure you can defend what you believe. She will test you at a level you have never experienced, pushing you to distill what is positively and absolutely the truth in this present moment.

Take a deep breath and encourage The Incredulous to ask her most thoughtful questions. If she becomes unruly or if you find her presence to be oppressive, take a step back, set a clear boundary and let her know you would like the experience with her to be more positive and productive.

If you can refrain from taking her pokes and jabs personally, The Incredulous will help you strengthen your core understanding of yourself, your abilities and your potential. While it might feel like you are in the hot spot, being in the crosshairs of scrutiny can produce surprising things. It will either break you or further solidify your value and resolve.

CAUTION

Was The Incredulous was so aggressive with you that you fell apart? Did she prove your resolve to be paper thin? Chances are, your preparation was a bit messy and flawed. You may have crumbled upon inspection.

When you flinch, stutter and sweat under his aggressive study, The Incredulous feels a pang of satisfaction. He might even reveal his wry smile and hearty chuckle as you unravel at his feet. It might be The Incredulous was so aggressive with you that you fell apart. She may have proven your resolve to be paper thin. It's time to improve it!

Do not let the voice of a critic send you astray. Dig your heels in, feel your roots and embody your true purpose. Upon proving your resolve, The Incredulous will loosen her grip on your destiny.

EXTREME

The Incredulous is an important voice in the group-dynamic puzzle. She can be rough and hurtful, and her ability to stonewall an individual is exemplary. You and your project might be enjoying months of growth and expansion, but The Incredulous can see through walls. If you fail to build your idea on more solid ground, she will dissolve your illusion with one sneeze.

In your adversarial stance, you might be letting arrogance get the better of you. This might cause you to throw something magnificent into the fire simply because you don't understand it. Life feels better with an open heart, even if our minds haven't caught up. Avail yourself to miracles. You might find that rusty old vase in your barn is made of gold.

EMPOWERMENT

Even though he rejected you with fanfare, the seemingly cold-hearted Incredulous might still be open to your ideas. Change your approach. You might win his heart after all! Remember that when we play the victim, we force ourselves into a corner. Seek to play the role of the highest position in the land. Be gracious, open and strategic, always letting brilliant people share their opinions.

The colors of your clothes and the gems you wear can significantly affect your mood, mind and heart. Ingesting flower essences and applying essential oils to your body (or diffusing them into the air) can improve your energy, attitude and drive.

Colors: violet, blue violet, fuchsia, pink, orchid, gold, yellow, steel blue, turquoise, sea green

Gemstones: Amethyst, Purpurite, Tanzanite, Blue Apetite, Turquoise, Malachite, Azurite, Dioptase

Flower Essences: Impatiens, Chicory, Vervain, Vine, Beech, Red Chestnut, Mimulus, Heather, Olive

Essential Oils: Bergamot, Ylang Ylang, Frankincense, Lavender, Sandalwood, Violet Leaf, Nutmeg, Myrrh, Tangerine, Galbanum

Break free from your imaginary prison. Bliss is a vital nutrient for our bodies, minds and hearts. Our attitude is everything.

THE HERMIT

I love my solitude and seeing my own reflection. Somewhat troubled at times, I live in a secret cave filled with both light and darkness. I feel so overwhelmed with the pain of all living beings that I can barely fathom the idea of having a direct intimate experience with another soul. Even a warm handshake might extinguish whatever identity I have left. Raw and soul-torn, I have forgotten my name and history, living sensorially among shadows. I'm chopped cabbage, scattered crumbs, a broken branch. I am a sweet chirping bird seeking a morsel of goodness to nourish my forgotten Self. Thrill me with your gaze, but judge me not. Whatever your dream, I can sense it as you pass me by.

THE HERMIT

"Shadows, silence, wind and trickling water are the ones I call friends."

MORSEL

Solitude and seclusion allow the soul to face hidden fears and shadows without infecting other living beings. Amidst the gloomiest dance, light and love are one thought away.

MESSAGE

There is no better way to expand awareness than by giving yourself the gift of solitude. There is a sweet peace of mind that comes from inward focus. When we are present to the entirety of our nature, we inspire the same depth in every reality we create.

Our psyches are filled with deep caves rich in emotional and experiential gems. Each cave filled with pools of ancient beliefs and knowledge. Strewn across the walls of our subconscious are impressions of lives gone by, all of which can be healed and explored simply by going within.

When we choose to expand our understanding of the universe, inner and outer guides come to our aid. With a clear heart, we are given keys to the other realms, invoking a broader understanding.

In the infinite sphere of sound and vibration, there are no doorstops, no locked windows. All we have to do is ask with a transparent heart. In an instant, the universe hears us and reveals its mysteries.

The Hermit has learned that when we dig too deeply into our shadows, we risk a dance with delusion. Without meaningful connections to other living beings, we can easily spin in the loneliest direction, disappearing into confusion, delusion and self-hatred.

We might think The Hermit to be a dangerous outcast, someone who plots to steal our belongings, our families, or our ways of life. He might appear to be obsessed with seclusion and unfit for society.

What we fail to understand is that given his non-attachment to almost everything in his life, this powerful soul can often see the true nature of reality. Many hermits have made a conscious choice to be where and who they are. Some are Self-realized beings.

While some hermits appear to be homeless, some will dress like monks or teachers. Others might don sportswear or business attire. Some might be naked in the woods, hoping never to be seen by another living being again. The Hermit is found in every faction of society and she lives within all of us.

Some people find it easy to tap into their depth. They close their eyes in the middle of a busy room and immediately understand that every one of us is alone. They accept this notion without fear.

As The Hermit unveils his secret cave to you, evaluate how reliant you are on others and society. Too much socializing can lock you into peak-performance mode. This can extinguish receptivity and exhaust your well of creative energy. Without ample pause, you will never know yourself the way nature intended. You always have permission to break free, go within and expand.

CAUTION

The Hermit knows that grasping for straws in the material world can only take us so far. The more experiences and people we attach to, the more we dampen our abilities to fathom reality and facilitate smooth transitions from this world to the next.

When we die, no one can go with us. In that regard, we are alone. The more we understand our temporal natures, the easier it is to comprehend that death is only a transition. There is no death, only life.

Lessening our load in life, we can see how foolish our pursuits and adornments can be. Sticky illusions and attachments may have found temporary homes in our lives, but once relinquished, they will not be missed for long. Throughout any clearing process, parts of you might feel naked and raw, but this too shall pass.

EXTREME

Left to himself for too long, The Hermit loses perspective. She perseverates and regurgitates her thoughts. She disassociates from the parts of society that nurture her. Without a healthy intervention, The Hermit can morph into a dark, dangerous version of herself, vibrating solely with negativity.

The Hermit often forgets she is connected to other human beings. Hold a dinner party to get things moving again. Make a list of your most enjoyable friends and schedule time with them. Your mission is to stand in the sun, open your heart, and let the rays of light find a natural home in your being.

EMPOWERMENT

Look at the bright stars in the sky and imagine what it took for them to exist. Get up early to see the sun rise. Feel the newness and enjoy the solitude of the morning as the sun kisses your cheeks. You might consider Tai Chi or Aikido, less combative martial arts that engender a feeling of strength and peace. Embrace your inner silence, ignore distractions and return to the living. It's time.

The colors of your clothes and the gems you wear can significantly affect your mood, mind and heart. Ingesting flower essences and applying essential oils to your body (or diffusing them into the air) can improve your energy, attitude and drive.

Colors: white smoke, ivory, yellow, light blue, light pink, green, violet, purple, dark red, orange

Gemstones: Emerald, Onyx, Crystal Quartz, Howlite, Opalite, Ruby, Yellow Sapphire

Flower Essences: Crab Apple, Water Violet, Vervain, Vine, Heather, Rock Water, Willow, Rock Rose, Star of Bethlehem

Essential Oils: Basil, Bergamot, Cinnamon, Cardamom, Rosewood, Frankincense, Ylang Ylang

The answer to your soul's beckoning is deep within you, shielded by ego and guarded by a sweet alluring silence.

THE INNOCENT RASCAL

All eyes gaze upon me like soft arrows, often accusing me of eating the last bit of chocolate pie. But I didn't do it! Look in my heart and see! I do my best to avoid trouble, but somehow it ends up at my doorstep and in the corners of my mind. It is as if my shadow stands beside me, inviting guilt, shame and blame. Upon shaking off this cackling, guilty goat, yet another trickle of accusation emerges. With every foot I climb, I fall a few inches. Soon I will conquer this anchor, and set sail for flowing abundance.

THE INNOCENT RASCAL

"Shackled by an old cloak and a debilitating residue, there is more to me than you can see."

MORSEL

Disembodied impressions, with no connection to reality, can attract palpable experiences.

MESSAGE

Musical notes, engines, thoughts, emotions and words vibrate, as do each of us. Whether we want to or not, we participate in vibrations, emanate vibrations and absorb the collections of vibrations happening around us. Some vibrations are healthy for us while others are limiting.

When we engage in a conversation or witness an event, we ingest the energetic residue from what we see and hear. Much like plucked guitar strings that reverberate with each other, we absorb what comes our way then reflect it outward. Without realizing it, we can easily take on someone's energy, thoughts or feelings.

Even as our souls traveled into our mothers' wombs, we brought with us energetic patterns and vibrations from past lives, along with residue from our exchanges with spirits in other realms. Once within our mother's wombs, we may have absorbed the energy of a brother or sister who came before us. As adults, we might never know all that we've absorbed and how it is affecting us.

The Innocent Rascal appears questionable or untrustworthy because of the vibrations and residues that he carries with him. He attracts scrutiny, not because he's guilty, rather, because he appears to possess something we do not like. Given all the blame and shame he's ingested in this life and prior lives, it is no wonder he regularly appears to be guilty.

You may know The Innocent Rascal personally and are able to vouch for him. You might attest that he is honorable and qualified, but you also sense a dark shadow circling around him.

You might picture The Innocent Rascal's face when you hear of theft or fraud, or attribute a catastrophe to her just because it "kinda feels" as though she did it, not because you have any proof. This woman could have been on the other side of the world at the time of the infringement, but our perception claims she did it. Completely unreasonable, yet it feels verifiable.

If The Innocent Rascal appears guilty to you today, it is time to put down the magnifying glass and pick up the mirror. You have wasted too much time disabling others with judgment. Your attitude has drained you of vital life force. It is time to turn the focus inward. Take inventory of your attributes. Examine your challenges, mistakes, misconceptions and infractions, then get to work healing them.

Clear out the oppressive details and energies that have cemented to your spirit. Set boundaries with The Innocent Rascals in your life. Release beliefs and intentions that restrict or limit you so that you can be free to prosper in life. Consider the personal attributes that inspire you then pursue them. No guilt, no shame, no problem. Go for it!

CAUTION

Whether The Innocent Rascal is guilty or not, consider unfettered forgiveness. When you free an ancient soul from lifetimes of indentured servitude, you free an aspect of yourself that has long been entangled in the transgressions of others.

Even if you do not buy into the notion of carrying impressions life to life, you would agree that when we repeat negative behavior, it can become an indelible part of our identity. It can also become a habit.

By clearing the patterns of guilt, negative thinking and destructive actions, you start fresh. Reframe how you think about yourself. Learn to attract more enjoyable people, events and circumstances. You are the only one who stands in the way of transformation and joy.

EXTREME

The Innocent Rascal is a part of all of us. When we are without honesty or integrity, we attract people who will most certainly deceive us. We might even deceive ourselves. As if on an unstoppable treadmill, we feverishly work to balance the truth and deceit within us. No matter how hard we try, we remain frustrated.

To make sustainable changes, we have to do deep emotional and behavioral work. What are you avoiding? What are you hiding from? Who and what are you protecting? Most importantly, when are you going to forgive yourself? There is no time like the present.

EMPOWERMENT

When you feel burdened by a cloak of accumulated negativity, pray for divine light to gently bathe your heart and mind, then await a heavenly renewal. You might consider mantras, meditation, exercise, yoga, sex or dance to help you clear energy from your mind, body and heart. Sometimes all we need is a change of scenery and all is well.

The colors of your clothes and the gems you wear can significantly affect your mood, mind and heart. Ingesting flower essences and applying diluted essential oils to your body (or diffusing them into the air) can improve your energy, attitude and drive. Enjoy the following recommendations specific to The Innocent Rascal. Seek professional assistance for the most benefit.

Colors: yellow, gold, goldenrod, orange, brown, light brown, sienna, ivory, pink, aquamarine

Gemstones: Apatite, Turquoise, Amber, Citrine, Imperial Topaz, Gold, Tiger Eye, Pink Tourmaline

Flower Essences: Pine, Crab Apple, Sweet Chestnut, Oak, Star of Bethlehem, Rock Rose, Gorse

Essential Oils: Peppermint, Violet Leaf, Rose, Oregano, Nutmeg, Myrtle, Lavender, Citronella

Let go of shame and guilt. They cannot serve you or any other living being. Step into the light and stay there.

THE REPEATER

I live in a temporary cloud filled with outdated patterns, old influences and abandoned behavior. In the distance behind me, a familiar object rolls near. It is a collection of prior experiences, assembled into a massive tumbleweed, filled with prickly points, remembrances, events and broken promises. Something tells me I should move out of the way, but here I stand in its path awaiting impact. I know I have control over this collection of realities. It is time to master my past, let it all go and move on.

THE REPEATER

"When I finally paused and looked behind me, I realized I had resolved very little."

MORSEL

Dissolving thorny memories and prior experiences is tricky. Upon release, oppressive cords are cut, freeing the spirit to soar.

MESSAGE

We see a golden train pulling into the station. As a welcoming stairway unfolds before us, a magnetic force pulls us up and into a well-adorned hallway. Now on board the train, we bump into kindred souls, happily chit-chat in the dining car, and we feel at peace. As the train slowly pulls out of the station, we realize we will never reach our desired destination, because the train is going in reverse.

It is easy to settle into behavioral grooves where we play out familiar situations in repeated fashion. Some patterns are harmless, like sitting in our favorite chairs or eating french fries, while others keep us spinning in circles, blocking our growth and advancement. When we look carefully, we often find that many of our patterns are symbiotic, working in tandem to create specific realities.

While we might take a special workshop that temporarily nudges us out of our fog, our deeper patterns are difficult to disrupt. It does not matter which guru or light-bearer takes center stage in our lives, it might simply be that we are ill-equipped to absorb enough glow to make a shift. As every possible red flag pops up in our path, it becomes clear that we are the only ones in our way.

If The Repeater has resurrected ancient drama, it is time to examine your patterns of repetitive behavior. The repetition in your life may be in the areas of low self-esteem, nutrition, emotional narratives, religion, self-denial or substance abuse.

It might be that you repeat the same circumstances with the same types of people in the same way, on the same day, in the same month, year after year!

You might believe that all of your patterns are fated, and you have given up hope. It might be that you have forgotten that you have the ability to transform your life in an instant. The Repeater desperately struggles with these things. He is unaware of the power he has to transform his most challenging patterns into forgotten relics.

Visualize the life you desire. Make small changes in your habits to reflect this new life. Make adjustments to your most repetitive negating behaviors, and make note of your progress. If The Repeater is in your circle of friends, lend a hand to their plight before you are dragged down as well.

With gentle steps and sincere discipline, you can create newness by addressing one undesirable aspect at a time. You are the embodiment of potential. Trust this and take the first step. By repeating positive action, a new path will come to life and inspire your continued exploration and rebirth.

CAUTION

Some patterns reappear with new faces, costumes and candy attached. When our old ways disguise themselves like this, they can be difficult to recognize and change. When we fail to see the hooks leading us away from our transformation, we dig our trenches a little deeper.

By obsessing about the drama in your life, you may have invited a former acquaintance to replay an old trauma. Rather than defend your life and the people you love, you chose to dance with the devil once again. The only person to blame for the lights going out is you.

Nestled in your restrictive patterns is a belief that you are not the one in control of your life. Seeking rescue, you patiently wait for an imaginary influence to do the work that only you can do. You are at the helm of your life. Champion it by making bold choices.

EXTREME

When we continuously repeat negative behavior, it is nothing shy of addiction. We all lie to ourselves, paint pretty pictures and project into them. Given the millions of falsehoods that society promotes, it is almost impossible to live a congruent, truthful life. Garbage in, garbage out. What we ingest, we become. You cannot progress until you dissolve ties with the media, people and beliefs that enable you. It might be time to make drastic changes.

Extricate yourself from negative personalities, events and trends, both internal and external. As the last remnant of your past dissolves, you will wonder how it came to be that circular motion became preferable to a vibrant thrust forward.

EMPOWERMENT

The Repeater has a way of exhausting her resources. As she re-creates dramas and pains in her life and the lives of others, her rolodex dwindles. You might be filling the holes in your life with silly putty. Employ a coach to help you make mature choices and changes so you can recognize your patterns and release them.

The colors of your clothes and the gems you wear can significantly affect your mood, mind and heart. Ingesting flower essences and applying essential oils to your body (or diffusing them into the air) can improve your energy, attitude and drive. Enjoy the following recommendations specific to The Repeater. Seek professional assistance to derive the most benefit.

Colors: white, mint cream, lavender, light blue, orchid, gold, orange

Gemstones: Rhyolite, Tangerine Quartz, Pink Sapphire, Blue Sapphire, Blue Quartz, Chalcedony

Flower Essences: Chestnut Bud, Pine, Gentian, Star of Bethlehem, Elm, Oak, Sweet Chestnut

Essential Oils: Ginger Root, Spruce, Rosewood, Frankincense, Sage, Chamomile, Lanyana, Galbanum, Grapefruit, Jasmine

Let the past become watery colors melting into the horizon.

THE SOCIALIZER

To me, ideas and innovations are like cool mountain air. I breathe m in and I am invigorated. Obsessed and insatiable, I continually absorb then share interesting ideas with everyone around me. If I'm not multi-tasking with multiple devices, I'm formulating, connecting dots and piecing things together. I'm a high-tech Santa Claus: load me up with ideas and inventions, and I'll passionately traverse my network, articulating my opinions and experiences with caffeinated abandon. I don't care much for expressing emotions and I don't have time for empathy. What moves me most is the unadulterated truth about the innovations in every category of life and industry.

THE SOCIALIZER

"When I learn something that can enthuse, educate or inspire, I happily share it."

MORSEL

The world heals and evolves when all information is freely accessible by everyone.

MESSAGE

The universe is a massive mirror reflecting back to us all that we desire. When we reframe our perspectives toward the positive, we manifest events and relationships that produce higher levels of joy. To bring things to life, we must be active in the world, connecting and relating. This is how the universe can co-create our desired realities in union with us.

When we meditate, we reduce mental chatter and gain access to stillness. This is when doors to the collective consciousness open, attracting more valuable and precise insights from the higher realms. Silence reduces our tendency toward illusion. It allows the source of life to speak through us.

While we all share a variety of gifts and talents, what differentiates us is the ability to stand strong in the face of adversity, and the propensity to advance our intentions to becoming physical realities. Our resolve, resistance and egos make us unique.

The Socializers are the reason digital technologies spread so quickly around the world and gave birth to so many new companies. These clear-minded souls were open to every possibility, enabling them to see years ahead of the curve.

As innovation upon innovation came to life, they foresaw new realities and generously availed themselves to the collective. As a result, a vibrant new wave of intelligence and invention was born. It spread like wildfire, quickly enhancing and connecting the lives of millions of people.

The Socializer often shares information without taking credit, moving ideas around like an ant feeding her colony. Without her magnanimity, the most outstanding notions might remain in the shadows. The moment a Socializer is exposed to a new idea, they leap on it.

If The Socializer is calling you, take a deep breath and exhale your ideas and visions to those closest to you. Become the bee and sting your social network with your brilliance.

You may believe your ideas to be unimportant, but if you investigate them, you might arrive at something remarkable. Simply by putting effort into your creativity, you might influence other people's inventions or encourage others to invest in themselves.

Ask friends and family to fuel the passions burning within you. Your ideas might cure a disease or advance a vital category of industry. Your next thought might carry the seeds required to give birth to the next level of human evolution. Trust yourself! As you relax into the stream of ideas that flows through you, honor your muse and share your insights with the world.

CAUTION

The Socializer is a generous, open spirit with a clear eye on the future. He will not tally the number of listeners nor seek remuneration. He simply hungers to share.

Some Socializers have more ego than real-world value. They make stunning declarations and paint perfect pictures of amazing opportunities. They deliberately use key phrases and metaphors to hypnotize the impressionable into partnership or investment. While Socializers are often positive influences, these shining knights can also be carnival barkers preying upon the vulnerable.

As The Socializer evangelizes, listen carefully and do the necessary research. Even if she is not trying to fleece you, these magnetic personalities tend to leave out the details. As you ingest the visions of The Socializer, take it all with a grain of salt.

EXTREME

Sometimes The Socializer runs her mouth without thinking. She might offend someone or spill valuable secrets, putting her future in jeopardy. Think before you speak. Refrain from sharing your brilliance with every stranger in the room. Use discernment at every juncture. Protect yourself by developing your ideas first and researching their value. Refrain from buying a celebratory round of drinks until you have substantial movement on your project. Do not get stung by your own ego or admissions. Temperance is the lesson of the day.

EMPOWERMENT

Maintain a clear mind and heart so that you can be of service to yourself and others. Spend a few minutes meditating in the morning. Take long walks to clear your heart and invigorate your body.

It's exciting to explore colors, gemstones, flower essences and essential oils. When we incorporate these things into our lives, we can increase our energy, alertness, passion and joy. If you're a Socializer, experiment with the colors you wear. Consider wearing some of the gemstones from the list below. The right flower essences and essential oils will help you find your center again.

Seek professionals in the following categories to help you achieve your highest level of health and happiness. Exceptional endeavors await!

Colors: white smoke, yellow, ivory, pink, light green, sky blue, aquamarine, violet, black

Gemstones: Peruvian Opal, Citrine, Fluorite, Azurite, Crystal Quartz, Obsidian, Sugilite, Pink Sapphire, Cobaltoan Calcite, Lapis Lazuli

Flower Essences: Holly, White Chestnut, Chestnut Bud, Vervain, Walnut, Rock Water, Cherry Plum

Essential Oils: Sandalwood, Lavender, Rosewood, Angelica Root, Bergamot, Cinnamon, Frankincense, Geranium, Rose

Openness and generosity will keep you in the flow of providence and grace.

THE UNTOUCHABLE

I stand behind steel glass as transparent as the wind. As I look around, I see no truly threatening enemies, and nothing in my scope frightens me. An unseen force seems to be protecting my front, my back and my path. I feel safe from all harm, feeling confident that nothing can derail my well-armored destiny. No matter where I walk or stray, I am confident that I will remain on a trajectory leading to success. I am living proof that the Elixir of Life exists. It must be in my bones.

THE UNTOUCHABLE

"What protects me is not just bullet proof, it is much more durable and comprehensive."

MORSEL

When we learn to repel the projections and demands from family, friends and society, we begin to understand our unbridled Self and our incalculable potential.

MESSAGE

We enter this life with accrued experiences and karma from thousands of prior lives. The energetic impressions from these lives attach to our present-day spirit. We are the amalgam of the experiences from every life our souls have lived.

While it's comforting to think we each collected a treasure-trove of golden moments throughout our many lives, it's also likely that we gathered a lot of challenging experiences. Whether good or bad, every experience attaches to our spirits as a soft impression. However elusive, we eventually have to release these impressions so they don't restrict or limit us in any way.

No matter what we carry from life to life, positive thought and effort instill us with goodness. This goodness acts as a protective shield in this life and those to come. When we focus our attention on learning a particular skill set, our souls gain streams of specific knowledge. This is how a virtuoso is born with master-level skills. Actions from her prior lives fed into this one. Our actions can also protect us in this life and future lives.

Infused with the force of prior goodness, The Untouchable enjoys bountiful fruit from his pursuits. Whether he acquired his skills in this lifetime or prior, The Untouchable carries a secure sense of accomplishment and an enduring pride. These things are natural to him. He knows no other way.

The Untouchable may have witnessed the actions and abilities of his father and grandfather. These tycoons of industry may have mastered a "smooth as silk" style, yielding a flawless air of grace. By watching these kings of strength and boundary, The Untouchable learned how to let things roll off his back and take the most confident strides. With all this in tow, The Untouchable stands strong against adversity, delivers impeccable speeches of vision, and has the courage to go it alone.

Because of his impenetrable etheric armor, it is difficult to bring The Untouchable down, no matter what feats of evil you throw at him. Without even trying, he is a powerful force and pillar of strength.

As The Untouchable, take pride in the stainless nature of the life you've created. With your no-stick spirit, you will surely attract success, along with a loyal following. Even if your intentions are dangerous, very little will penetrate the layer of goodness that currently protects you.

Be careful how you use your power as it comes with a great deal of responsibility. Continue the trend of positivity by strengthening your skills and keeping focused on the pursuit at hand. Rest assured that you have the protection you need to accomplish anything your mind and heart desire.

CAUTION

The Untouchable will do anything to bring her vision to life. While she may appear to be an ally, your alliance will only endure if you support her dreams and desires. The Untouchable can be a fierce and unforgiving warrior, so be careful with how you engage and support her.

To survive this delicate situation, consider changing your agenda or taking time off. If the project at hand is antithetical to your moral code, you are best to gently back out and recover what you can.

This Untouchable may have laid the groundwork to dominate you, putting complex machinations in place well in advance of knowing you. Without her graciousness, you could easily be rendered obsolete.

There is no middle ground when partnering with The Untouchable. Find your place in her kingdom, or fold and retreat.

EXTREME

The Untouchable is a formidable foe and exhaustive researcher. It could be a challenge to defeat him. The snake of over-confidence may have bitten you, causing you to gamble your heart away. Because of your short-sighted pride, you were outmaneuvered. Do not take this brilliant General for granted. Humble yourself. To him, you are a fragile flower. Subject yourself to his authority and be happy.

Winning a dark game usually yields a shallow victory and feeds the weakest part of you. If your pursuit is truly worthwhile, and if there is a promise of light and joy for all involved, only the softest part of you will know the truth. Be honest with yourself and command a path of honor.

EMPOWERMENT

This may be a time of healing, pausing or letting go. Take a moment to share love and intimacy with those closest to you. If there are children involved, take a few days to build forts with pillows and watch movies while eating buckets of popcorn. Becoming the child will give you great insight.

Consider wearing some of the colors and gemstones to enhance your energy and life. You might find that the recommended flower essences and essential oils will help you shift in a positive way.

Colors: silver, light brown, sea green, red, violet, blue violet, orchid, white smoke, black

Gemstones: Hematite, Black Agate, Black Tourmaline, Scolecite, Opalite, White Kunzite, Uxelite, Amethyst, Red Jasper, Ruby

Flower Essences: Walnut, Mimulus, Crab Apple, Rock Water, Larch, Willow, Chicory, Vervain, Beech, Aspen

Essential Oils: Lavender, Orange, Bergamot, Jasmine, Myrrh, Sandalwood, Peppermint, Ylang Ylang, Patchouli

Your gifts, talents and attributes are the fruits of your soul's journey. Seek to heal and improve them with every thought and action.

THE FLOATING

I move with the wind, flitting from here to there, living in a flurry of dreamy possibilities. It's so fun to consider all my options! I'm sweet and approachable with a giving style that appears to be reciprocal, but mostly I receive. Sometimes, that is giving too. Intoxicated with potential, my intentions and loyalties can change with the wind. Sometimes I'm noncommittal, leaving friends and family in a twisted fix. When it comes to Self-care, I believe that being selfish is permissible. I do love you. will you forgive me?

THE FLOATING

"I tantalize others with bouquets of dreams, but follow-through escapes me."

MORSEL

Broken dreams occur when fantasy becomes preferable to Self-love. To be congruent, honorable and whole, be grounded and seek completion in all things.

MESSAGE

A lovely tree rests atop rich, fertile soil. Little creatures scurry about the branches, making nests and storing food. Furry and winged friends make beautiful sounds and songs. Pairs of chipmunks, squirrels and salamanders nuzzle and protect each other. While this above-ground ecosystem appears to be complex and multifaceted, there is far more going on beneath it.

A vast root system swells inches beneath the surface. Ants, worms and insects build homes, pathways and alliances. Smaller tangential root-groups extend to the underbellies of nearby trees. Like lovers in a passionate embrace, this massive root collection intertwines and shares the nourishment of the soil. To make this even more fascinating, they do all this and more in the dark.

The interconnected family of living beings is a miracle of interdependency, one element relying on another. We are each a part of this community, where our effort is essential to the advancement of life and consciousness. When we are accountable, all systems flourish, an idea escapes The Floating, as she is often not grounded enough to commit or reciprocate.

Light and full of heart, The Floating has a sweet presence, healing negativity with a glance. Her style and charisma are often inviting, even intoxicating. It is as if she knows us, somehow able to peek into our soul. However enjoyable this can be, we might never experience a true relating with The Floating. Yes, her attention towards us feels real, but her flakiness can shake the bonds of our trust. This is not her intention, rather, it stems from her sense of Self, which might be no more than a withered prune.

While a little structure or reprimand might coax this soul into alignment, The Floating does not often understand that he is important to others. He is a butterfly who rarely stays long enough to connect, flirting and fluttering only until he's nourished. Once satisfied, he might flutter off again.

The Floating craves acceptance and commitment, even though she might not be unable to return those sentiments. We might feel in love with him, but his affection for us might be temporary or surface-deep. The lesson here is to only engage relationships that result in a balance of reciprocity.

When we are not grounded, it is difficult for us to give and receive. To come into better balance, The Floating might require a peaceful environment, loving affection or a healthy meal. By providing The Floating the grounding, nurturance and love he needs, you might inspire him to honor himself, share his gifts and be truly present in relationships and life.

CAUTION

The Floating has many positive attributes. She inspires magic and positive thinking, she is quick to validate and inspire. The Floating also has the potential to unravel a string of goodwill upon a flick of her littlest finger. What started as a cute habit during childhood has morphed into a life-long pattern that restricts intimacy, responsibility and growth.

Every one of us has the potential to become a little airy-fairy, flaky and confused. As life bombards The Floating with details and to-do lists, she'll emotionally or psychologically check-out. She might stumble in her commitments and follow-through. Integrity is a straight-forward concept. Unforeseen circumstances arise, but if you're continually attracting unforeseen circumstances, you need a reality-check.

EXTREME

Do you receive compassion when you arrive late or when you fail to complete something? Is someone enabling a measure of your selfish behavior? Do you feel a sense of control or entitlement when you impose on others? Regardless of what you think or believe about your actions, it is time to change your behavior. Reciprocity and fair exchange are the orders of the day.

If you have dishonored close friends and allies, reach out to them and make amends. Make sure you have no pending commitments in jeopardy. Set a clear objective and move into this next life phase: the phase of personal accountability.

EMPOWERMENT

The Floating needs good friends to remind him of his tendency to be an imposition. There might be underlying childhood dynamics and frozen emotions to examine and release. Seek a healer, spiritual master or psychologist to help you achieve the highest level of integrity in your life.

The colors of your clothes and the gems you wear can significantly affect your mood, mind and heart. Ingesting flower essences and applying essential oils to your body (or diffusing them into the air) can improve your energy, attitude and drive. Seek professionals to help you achieve your highest level of health and happiness.

Colors: green, dark purple, dark violet, dark pink, dark blue, firebrick red, smokey white, black

Gemstones: Kyanite, Chiastolite, Axinite, Hematite, Smoky Quartz, Red Coral, Ruby, Red Garnet, Onyx, Pyrite

Flower Essences: Vervain, Clematis, Sweet Chestnut, Star of Bethlehem, Gorse, Gentian, Larch, Cherry Plum

Essential Oils: Cedarwood, Spruce, Vetiver, Basil, Benzoin, Bergamot, Cinnamon, Sage, Frankincense, Rose, Violet Leaf, White Fir

When we are loyal and committed, we grow valuable, dependable roots. These roots give rise to the flowers that create and nurture our future.

THE HEDONIST

I am forever in pursuit of delicious flesh and sensual pleasure. My hope is to ease the pain I feel from the grinding ghosts who flourish around my shadowy soul. When I feel the itch to re-puncture my long-ago wounds, I dive deeper into binding, physical bliss, never fretting a single consequence for myself or others. Given the choice between devotion to a human being and devotion to sensual delight, I'll take the latter. Ever the insatiable hunter, rarely a loyal friend, I live to feed myself all the sensuality my hot, dripping lips can devour. Feed me and I'm yours, at least for the moment.

THE HEDONIST

"Every pore of my body angrily awaits pleasure. I'm insatiable with a vengeance."

MORSEL

Pleasure is our reward for being human. When we continually seek excess, we act out imprisoned aspects of ourselves that need only love.

MESSAGE

As the physical forms of living creatures came into being, the collective consciousness segmented itself into millions of unique souls who then infused themselves into the living beings inhabiting all the worlds. All of creation is a co-conspired miracle!

The stunning gift for each of us is knowing that we are deeply connected to everything in creation. Every one of us is brother and sister to every living being in existence. As such, there is little difference between a human being and a tiny pebble resting on a distant planet. While dissimilar in physical form, we are identical in how our energies pulsate interconnected sounds and vibrations.

The Hedonist understands these mysteries, seeking to experience the totality of consciousness through sensory input and physical pleasure. For The Hedonist, looking, smelling, touching, ticking, nibbling, cuddling, mounting and ingesting, comprise the definition of life.

If The Hedonist has sauntered naked and deliciously hungry into your camp today, you are about to receive an immensely pleasurable gift. It may be a sensuous evening with a fleeting lover, a moonlight dance with a stranger, or a psychedelic mushroom party in a lush forest. When with The Hedonist, expect eye-opening experiences that will reshape your principles and perceptions.

At first glance, a gift from The Hedonist may appear frivolous or shallow, but make no mistake here. Her gift might lead you to an exciting path. While the journey might be dangerous, you'll enjoy every moment, as if the Gods bestowed her upon you as a gift.

The Hedonist is a pattern interrupter, providing energy for your nervous system. He inspires renewal and a merging with the juicy, creative flows and forces of the universe. Sample him, devour her, both blood and bone. Relish every second of it!

When you awake from the dream, remember that you are, first and foremost, energy in the form of light. Keep hold of the energetic properties you experienced with The Hedonist and use them to your advantage. Feel the grounding that he inspired in you. All this grounding to settle you, to root you into the fabrics inherent in the earth.

Remember that no matter the extent of the escapades of the body, heart and mind, love and joy can be reproduced with one intention, one thought, one decision. Your intention attracts your reality, always.

CAUTION

When The Hedonist pursues pleasure, she might put her safety, and the safety of others, in jeopardy. The challenge for you today is that while feeling free is a most admirable dream, you must remember you are also part of a unified community and consciousness. In the pursuit of pleasure, be sure to give empathy and compassion a seat at the table.

If your lover is reckless, speak up in a compassionate way. If he asks you to do things that feel hurtful or dangerous, set limits with him. If you are The Hedonist and your lover is not, find common language and experiences to enjoy together. The resulting freedom and delight must be mutual. The potential for your pleasure and unfolding is limitless.

EXTREME

If The Hedonist appears extreme to you today, remember that she often makes decisions that benefit the smallest number of people. Her pleasure is her priority. She can be the most intoxicating and self-absorbed soul on the branch. A dance with The Hedonist might result in the sacrifice of a marriage, the collapse of personal finances or the loss of a project or endeavor.

Give great pause before removing that last piece of clothing or popping that pretty purple pill. Before you press your wet lips against her soft, buttery skin, take a moment to remember your life, commitments and goals. Take a walk around the block, masturbate, write in your journal or pray. At the very least, demand that all activities take place with the greatest care.

If your paradise has already imploded, remember this is not your destination, it is only a pit-stop. Take actions to better the course of your reality. In a reasonable amount of time, you will sense progress and feel celebratory. In the meantime, ask The Hedonist to pack his things and head home.

EMPOWERMENT

Are you desperately seeking pleasure to hide your pain? You might benefit from hiring a life-coach. They help people make more empowered decisions. A life-coach will help you sculpt the life you want. Refrain from sugar, caffeine and stimulants as these will affect your clarity of mind and heart.

The colors of your clothes and the gems you wear can significantly affect your mood, mind and heart. Ingesting flower essences and applying essential oils to your body (or diffusing them into the air) can improve your energy, attitude and drive. Seek professionals to help you achieve your highest level of health and happiness.

Colors: orange, white, mint cream, lavender, orchid, violet, gold, green, bright blue

Gemstones: Orange Aventurine, Carnelian, Tangerine Quartz, Green Aventurine, Cherry Quartz

Flower Essences: Clematis, Impatiens, Rock Rose, Cherry Plum, Star of Bethlehem, Pine, Gentian, Larch, Gorse, Crab Apple, Elm

Essential Oils: Spikenard, Rose, Chamomile, Sage, Benzoin, Cypress, Jasmine, Vetiver, Lemongrass

Lasting joy is achieved through an intimate dance with positivity.

THE MENACE

I sometimes forget the healthy strands that intimately connect me to other human beings. My thrust in life often includes upsetting positive movement, mocking religious and romantic fantasies and defrocking compliance. Sometimes this behavior has positive, even miraculous results. Befriend me and I will give you the tiniest morsels of connection, just enough to keep you from leaving. With little provocation, I might smack your voice box and wonder why you're choking. I sometimes forget to be human. I think positive thoughts, but I am clearly imbalanced at times. Under my shell is a confused youngster seeking approval. I might be a mirror for your inability to take care of yourself.

THE MENACE

"Unless you hit me with a brick, I might take my neediness and disgruntlements out on you."

MORSEL

Self-abuse often comes from the loved ones we empower to dethrone our joy.

MESSAGE

We co-create our lives in partnerships with the universal consciousness. We imagine what we want, then follow it up with action. This, in turn, produces our physical realities and experiences. Our intentions, however, are another story. Sometimes we have hidden negative intentions while in the process of creating something wonderful. This sends mixed messages to the universe.

With good intentions at the onset, the results of our actions can be exponentially more powerful. With a little forethought, we can create intrinsically positive realities that not only appear to be good, but are founded in goodness.

Jesters, comedians, and playful provocateurs are the prefect examples of well-intentioned imaginers. Their mercurial endeavors often inspire a deeper understanding of relationship, politics, religions and our world. They intend to provide entertainment while often relaying a vital message. These social magicians help heal and advance individuals, and society as a whole.

The Menace's exploits are often devoid of such nobility, often more in line with a hurricane. The Menace rarely sculpts anything unique on his own and has little understanding of the value of good intentions. His idea of co-creation is to buy a sledge hammer and break your computer with it. To create a bonafide Menace, you need two pounds of lonely, a gallon of hurt and a dash of narcissism.

If The Menace has trampled your flower bed today, there is a good chance it was you who unlocked the front gate. The Menace might be your best chance to work through an old wound around boundaries or self-defense. On some level, you might enjoy being abused. Whatever your hang up, The Menace is here to teach you something valuable.

This infantile beast can be harsh and intoxicated with ego, wasting no time on social graces. She wants love, but might set fire to the living room to get it. Inject her with compassion, and you can up-level her life, but nothing will shift until you address the part of The Menace that lives within you.

You may have stolen money or broken hearts. You might be unconsciously lying to or manipulating others. Whatever your shadow quality might be, it's time to own it and change your game. You might be a troubled artist, a teacher or a pent-up business executive. You might be a lonely priest or social worker. Without a complete humbling and the associated transparency, you cannot begin anew.

Get clear with yourself and evolve your behavior. Do not dwell on the past, rather, move swiftly forward with love and forgiveness. As a result, everything will shift in a more positive direction. Take note of the lessons and accept them with graciousness. It's a great day to grow with The Menace!

CAUTION

The Menace is a skilled disrupter who knows how to hurt others. To protect yourself, you must continually smack this barking dog on the snout. Your best defense is to build an intellectual wall around her so that damage can be contained. Befriend her by asking about her passion, work and dreams. Your kindness will help you command the wreckage.

Remain in control of the situation by being cool and detached. The Menace appears for one reason: to provoke spiritual growth. It might be that the disruption she is creating is far less damaging than it appears.

When someone appears in our lives and disrupts our peacefulness, we are called to examine how we allowed it to happen. While in some cases, it is mere chance, most often we attract the things we experience. Evolve yourself and the situation with grace. Time heals all wounds.

EXTREME

Now that the living room is on fire, do you feel better? If there is room for additional damage, you might consider burning the last pieces of furniture and roasting a few marshmallows. To get the biggest bang for your spiritual buck, take hold of this epic wreckage. Breathe in every nuance. Look at all the astonished faces glaring at you. Can you feel the frustration?

To get back on solid ground, consider packing the necessary belongings and getting out of town for a few days. Just like a computer, we always have access to the reboot button. Rebooting could give you the chance to truly love yourself and become a more stable, compassionate human being.

EMPOWERMENT

If The Menace has pilfered your playground, try meditation, Kundalini yoga, Tai Chi or Aikido. These art forms will help you find peace in your life again. If you've been out of balance lately, barking rough comments at strangers, you might need to examine your diet. Stimulants like sugar and caffeine can change how your brain functions. Consider fasting and working with a nutritionist or medicinal herbalist. If deeper wounds exist, work with a therapist or life-coach to help you grow.

The colors of your clothes and the gems you wear can significantly affect your mood, mind and heart. Ingesting flower essences and applying diluted essential oils to your body (or diffusing them into the air) can improve your energy, attitude and drive.

Colors: white, mint white, pink, violet, cornflower blue, purple, gold, turquoise, green yellow

Gemstones: Rhodochrosite, Aquamarine, Carnelian, Danburite, Rose Quartz, Kyanite, Amethyst, Chrysocolla, Blue Apetite, Citrine, Sunstone, Sodalite, Turquoise

Flower Essences: Chicory, Chestnut Bud, Vervain, Vine, Beech, Rock Rose, Aspen, Larch

Essential Oils: Blue Tansy, Ylang Ylang, Yarrow, Sandalwood, Geranium, Bitter Orange, Myrtle, Juniper Berry, Coriander

Love your harsher aspects and they will naturally fade.

THE YESTERDAY

My heart remains unresolved, sitting quietly in a bath of moments gone by. I try to live in the here and now, but there are too many old images, tears and triumphs that I have yet to process and release. I see the now-reality for a moment, then ghosts fill the room. I wish I could set them free, but our dance melts me and gives me purpose. Even though a dream, it feeds my needy heart and soul. My nights are filled with emotion derived from every memory I have stored. I fear that should I fall asleep, I'll miss the most enduring courtship of my life.

THE YESTERDAY

"No matter how I look at it, I was so much better back then. It was ALL so much better."

MORSEL

Release your yesterday and tomorrow so that you can live powerfully in the now.

MESSAGE

Every memory is from the past. Every past event is an illusion. Every illusion is a dream. Sometimes we hold so tightly to yesterday that we leave no room for today.

Beautiful experiences sweep us into the clouds. Years pass and we continue to imagine them. We drink their wine, caress their cheeks, and feel the palpable depths of connection. Whether joyful or hurtful, we remain submerged in them, drunk on a dream.

Over time, our perceptions change. As new memories, beliefs and life experiences sweep into our thoughts, the event we once rejoiced in becomes diluted, morphing into something different, possibly the opposite of what it was.

Mostly forgotten by other participants, former experiences can become obsessions. With contrived versions of the events now resting in the forefronts of our minds, we render ourselves unable to enjoy the gifts in the present. So it is with The Yesterday.

If The Yesterday has found her way into your home, greet her face-to-face with affection. She is here to ask your permission to detach from your heart and leave your reality for all time. She beckons you to move on with gratitude.

When someone close to us dies, we might still feel them next to us, talking with us, loving us. We hear the sounds of their voices and feel their touch. Our minds are so powerful that memorable events and relationships can become indelible, even preferable.

We love to hold on, but holding so tightly to the hem of The Yesterday's dress may bind you to loss and heartache, and she may never be inspired to leave. Only you can set her free.

Be receptive to this important life passage and allow the past to bestow upon you the riches from moments gone by. Breathe in every nuance, every glance.

Tune into the depth of your heart and focus on the images of The Yesterday. Feel every moment that nurtured and expanded you. Acknowledge the wonder and beauty of it all. Remember the highs and lows, the good and bad, the truths and projections. Feel the deep intimate bond with your beloved and recall any related loss.

It is time to let it all go with love and light. Allow your emotions to pour forth. Let Yesterday fade into shadow. With each moment you celebrate and release, you make room for new ones. It is time to be free of things that are no longer meant for you. It is time to let go and begin anew.

CAUTION

Your obsession with the past has proven to be an intoxicant. Are you drunk on the success of yesterday? Do you still celebrate trophies you received in high school? Do you wake up every day and look lovingly at photos of your ex-wife or former husband? Stop the insanity.

You are not your past. You are not even the person you were an hour ago. If you allow it, you are new in every moment.

Lovingly liberate your past before it strangles you. Letting go on every level, you bring yourself into the present moment. You are the divine intervention you seek.

EXTREME

Living in the past for a few minutes is benign, but living our lives as if the people and conditions from twenty years ago have never changed, is delusion. Sadly, many people live solely in the past. They believe their long-ago lives to have been so eternal that they rush home every day to open an old photo album or listen to a once-treasured song.

Life is too short to relive any prior moment from our lives beyond a gentle recollection. As time evaporates, so do prior versions of you. Release every nuance of your past and allow the universe to recreate you. Build a new vessel, ready and fit for a life filled with joy in the present moment.

EMPOWERMENT

One thing The Yesterday needs is good friends. Even if you think they've forgotten about you, reach out to those who are nearest and dearest to you. Ask them to visit, or better yet, get on a plane and go see them. There is no time like the present to rekindle relationships that have meaning for you. As you ponder and release your past, seek to make strides every day. Make one new acquaintance every month. Over time, these acquaintances can become beautiful and reliable friendships.

The colors of your clothes and the gems you wear can significantly affect your mood, mind and heart. Ingesting flower essences and applying diluted essential oils to your body (or diffusing them into the air) can improve your energy, attitude and drive. Seek professionals to help you achieve your highest level of health and happiness.

Colors: royal blue, green, sea green, turquoise, silver, white smoke, purple, violet, pink, turquoise

Gemstones: Turquoise, Morganite, Sodalite, Emerald, Rose Quartz, Malachite, Lithium Quartz, Watermelon Tourmaline

Flower Essences: Honeysuckle, Cherry Plum, Gentian, Star of Bethlehem, Rock Rose, Gorse, Pine

Essential Oils: Rosewood, Sandalwood, Lavender, Melissa, Parsley, Vetiver, Ylang Ylang, Rose Otto, Aniseed

The past is a cancelled check. It no longer exists. Even this idea is a dream. Live fully in this moment, in the now. Live life fully right now. Always right now.

THE ENTICER

I dangle pretty charms from my balcony with the hope of attracting love, money and success. I enjoy pursuing the favor of friends, lovers and influencers, lavishly adorning them with goods and services at every turn. With a wink, I attract and forever capture heart upon heart. Sadly, I do not know myself enough to be cognizant of the ramifications of my actions, and I am equally entranced by the gimmicks I use to put others under spell. Without much ado, I too fall prey to sleight of hand. I'm impressionable, charismatic and always on the hunt for glitter.

THE ENTICER

"I happily use trinkets to attract goodness to my life."

MORSEL

At the intersection of faith, love and vulnerability is an intimate embrace with the divine. Love cannot be bought, sold or manipulated into being. It arises because it is who we are.

MESSAGE

We have co-created a world that causes us to be continually abducted by hype, lies and toys. We are often distracted and displaced, barely having the presence of mind to look within for one moment.

We watch reality television, spend hours playing holographic games, and purchase products from companies whose mission is to damage the planet we live on. We allow our spirits to be drenched in political hyperbole as if any of it is based on a shred of truth. We have become so deeply disfigured by our own laziness that simplicity and truth have become the fantasy. We are far from home.

With some of our purchases of make-up, disproportional dolls and third-world manufactured fashion, we nurture a false sense of Self and fund a global addiction to filling voids and contriving value.

When we buy an item, we support the company, the company's agenda and the positive or negative effects the company has on human beings, animals and the planet. With many of our purchases, we fund either our species advancement or our demise.

With millions of advertisements, headlines and showmen competing for our attention, we ingest thousands of messages, many of which are antithetical to our nature. If we allow it, our screen-time can inspire our spiritual evolution, but if we're not careful, it can also poison us.

If The Enticer is dangling her charms today, you have a knack for using well-manufactured toys, ploys and decoys to evoke passion and desire in the hearts of strangers. You instinctively know what makes eyes widen and mouths water. When you pursue someone, you are hyper-aware, even able to feel the uptick in their heartbeat. This is sometimes a blessing and sometimes a curse.

How you present information is of equal value to what you are sensing and selling. Without a compelling hook, the product might never gain the momentum it deserves. If you truly believe in your pursuit, job or project, give it the make-over it deserves.

Create a mind-blowing presentation, but infuse your creativity with goodness and love. Also pray for the receivers and viewers of your presentation. These things can have a profound effect on the world.

To embody The Enticer and achieve great success, you must speak to another's heart. The more intricately you connect with the hearts of your audience, the greater penetration your message will have. Infuse integrity into your work and you'll create something that is both successful and meaningful at the same time. There is no better combination.

CAUTION

Many Enticers are so deeply loving and altruistic, they give away pieces of their soul in every transaction. When you finally get what you want, you might be too empty to enjoy it. Be careful with your heart. Set boundaries so that no one can abscond with your gold.

Some Enticers get so caught up in the momentum of their hyperbole, they begin to believe their own machinations. You are more than the shiny objects you carry. You are a human being with a sensitive heart and mind. Your are unique, beautiful and worthy of love and light.

EXTREME

Before diving into your next experience, make sure every piece of you is on board. Without consensus from all your parts, you could easily end up in a half-hearted pursuit. Before jumping into a relationship or project, evaluate what's on offer. Make sure it honors your nature and truth. Peek under the hood. The bells and whistles might sound wonderful, but if they don't ring in the key-of-you, you'll regret it.

If a shiny suit is dangling a golden carrot in front of you, ask the tough questions. Who owns the carrot? Why are they offering it to you? Who else will be eating this it? Where did it come from and why is it suddenly available? Keep your head on straight and get the answers you need. This might look like a first-class ticket to HappyTown, but it could also be a one-way ticket off of Lemming's cliff.

EMPOWERMENT

The Enticer would benefit from an older generation's advice and support. Create a personal Counsel of Elders. Reach out to four or five older people in your life and ask them to advise you. Their thoughtful notes of temperance and encouragement will ground and inspire you. As The Enticer, you sometimes seek intimacy through the process of selling something. Challenge your beliefs in this area. Seek ways to heal the misconceptions you internalized early in life.

The colors of your clothes and the gems you wear can significantly affect your mood, mind and heart. Ingesting flower essences and applying diluted essential oils to your body (or diffusing them into the air) can improve your energy, attitude and drive.

Colors: orange, purple, coral, dark red, dark pink, magenta, dark violet, forest green, steel blue

Gemstones: Dioptase, Chiastolite, Stromatolite, Green Sardonyx, Sugilite, Azurite, Garnet, Ruby

Flower Essences: Larch, Vervain, Aspen, Mimulus, Crab Apple, Chestnut Bud, Gentian, Heather, Star of Bethlehem, Rock Water

Essential Oils: Bergamot, Rosemary, Anise, Bay Laurel, Cardamom, Sage, Frankincense, Grapefruit, Lavender, Nutmeg, Jasmine, Geranium

Our most potent reflections are neither shiny nor external. They humbly wait for us in the seat of our souls.

THE COVERT

I carefully walk with shadows to bring about power struggles, disasters, chaos and change. I'm as discreet as a creepy mouse, often indirect, holding my cards so close to my chest they are practically stapled to my ribs. I follow plans with precision, always have an out and simultaneously venture down several distinct paths at once. I do not think twice about my actions, no matter the casualty or cost. I'm a harsh competitor, a secret keeper and a believer in the idea that life is a perpetual game. Win or lose, give me a list of players and a map, and I'll dismantle the opposition from the inside out. When all is said and done, I'll be safe, secure and well-positioned above the rest.

THE COVERT

"Regardless of how it appears, chances are, it is not the truth."

MORSEL

When we compartmentalize our values, shadows traverse crevices to commandeer our thoughts.

MESSAGE

In every corner of the Earth, there are complex games in play. Hired players coordinate the agendas of an elite minority, a set of greedy maneuverers who perpetuate corruption on massive scales.

While many of us seek to invoke light and love, sinister players use the hearts, souls and money of unsuspecting pawns to further their self-serving missions. Who are the peasants who consistently buy into the lies and fund these games? Look in the mirror, it is you and me. If only we understood how to counteract these people and events.

When we peel back the layers of society, we see the grotesque faces behind the masks. We learn about secret passageways and hidden vaults. There are agendas at play that we would find so shocking, we might never be the same once exposed to them.

While our armies overthrow governments and massacre civilians, we are silent. We let corporations get away with murder, yet we rant like a child when our neighbor does not recycle. It all depends on what stories feel good to us and what stories feel bad. If a story appeases our comfort, we believe it. If it interrupts our version of reality, we reject it. We have little interest in the truth.

The Covert is a magician, able to pull off challenging feats without ever coming near the spotlight. If The Covert stepped through your secret doorway, be aware that a game is afoot. This double agent will only share details about his pursuit if it is absolutely necessary, so don't be surprised if you have to dig deep to find out what's happening. The Covert is so skilled at manipulation, when he needs something, you will most likely offer it long before he asks.

He has the ability to simultaneously command both positive and negative forces. He might not be as dangerous as he is convincing. If you are about to jump on a moving train, look out for questionable behavior. Whatever you do, be careful what you agree to.

Growing up, The Covert may have devised inventive ways to get what she needed. Coverts tend to exude a unique combination of demonstrative charm and detachment. They always get their way.

If you are The Covert, look at your goals and examine the network at your fingertips. You have the ability to get what you want, but you will need a complex plan to achieve it. Carefully map out each and every move. Be prepared to take risks and walk the line between good and questionable behavior. Remember to protect yourself and your family at all costs. While it may be challenging to uphold the mystery of The Covert, the journey can be exciting and rewarding on every level.

CAUTION

If The Covert is hovering around you, ask questions, expect elusive answers, and keep digging for the truth. Don't let the prestige of working with The Covert lull you into complacency.

In an effort to understand the cesspool you're swimming in, consider reaching out to the best of these people to learn more. Be careful how you phrase your questions as you might awaken the beast.

If you are The Covert today, be as secretive as possible. Establish a plan that cannot be influenced or disrupted by others. Some plans require absolute anonymity. If friends snoop, steer their attention to a new subject. Protect every aspect of the plan or you run the risk of exposure.

EXTREME

Be aware that you might be a pawn in a much larger and more dangerous game, one that you have no chance of winning. Put on your detective hat and determine whether or not you are at risk. Ask for details about the other players and make note of anything that does not feel above-board. Hide the family jewels and prepare against a masterful invasion of your privacy. Check your gut often.

Motives can be so well-protected that a shark can appear as tame as a baby lamb. There may be unclean motives afoot. Be careful with what you condone. You could easily create risk for yourself or others. If your self-preservation is the most important thing to you, protect yourself by saying NO to this adventure. Once The Covert is out of sight, let your interest in the shadows fade. Clear your mind of negative thoughts so that similar magnets will pass you by.

EMPOWERMENT

As The Covert, you probably have a difficult time confiding in others. When you visit with your closest friends, do your best to open up to them. This is the only way for you to change your patterns of secrecy and grow your connections with others. When we spend most of our time cavorting with darker players and secret agents, we miss out on the flow of living life in the present moment. Seek to expand you life by bringing it out into the light - and keep it there.

The colors of your clothes and the gems you wear can significantly affect your mood, mind and heart. Ingesting flower essences and applying diluted essential oils to your body (or diffusing them into the air) can improve your energy, attitude and drive.

Colors: white, mint cream, light green, gold, peach, pale blue, turquoise, steel blue, indigo

Gemstones: Azurite, Sapphire, Gold, Rose Quartz, Opalite, Honey Calcite, Tiger's Eye, Malachite

Flower Essences: Agrimony, Mullein, Chestnut Bud, Rock Rose, Star of Bethlehem, Willow

Essential Oils: Ylang Ylang, Balsam Fir, Rosewood, Pine, Bitter Orange, Galbanum, Chamomile

**When we live in the light, our vibrations magnify and create a stronghold.
Endeavor to live, think, pray and co-create solely with light.**

THE SQUEEZE

I use well-crafted mind games to up-level the lives and pursuits of partners, friends and competitors. I twist situations and relationships using subtle emotional and psychological schemes. My intention is always to increase position, profit and value. I gently encourage acquiescence, employing tricks and tactics akin to magic. I never fail to move a mark in the direction of my desires. If my persistence initially fails, I'm known to be as patient as a turtle on a thousand-mile jaunt. For now, you are my marionette and I am enjoying our mutually beneficial dance.

THE SQUEEZE

"I am going to introduce you to a warm, deviant hook that will force you to do what I need."

MORSEL

When manipulation is used to relate or create, the aggregate result is loss.

MESSAGE

Sometimes lies are so delicious, we convince ourselves to ingest them, even promote them. Whether it's buying a car, getting into bed with a stranger or participating in a fascinating plan, we forget that when quick-fixes appear too good to be true, they usually are.

The Squeeze understands that the world is built on systems, whereby if you do X and Y, Z will most likely happen. This brilliant mind understands how variables can be manipulated so that systems will work in his favor. While his machinations can change lives for the better, they can also cause harm.

Imagine yourself as a little bunny. You know all the bunny paths around the forest. You built a strong thicket to protect yourself. Your sharp sense of danger keeps you on your bunny toes, but you're still just a cute little bunny. This is how The Squeeze, a professional marksman, sees you.

If The Squeeze has moved into your sights today, hear him out. If his plans appear too grandiose or if they intimate you as a fall guy, let him know where his integrity is failing or simply refuse his offer. While the rewards might appear useful or valuable, the repercussions could be hurtful to you.

The arrival of The Squeeze in you life might stem from feelings of lack or from your inability to be clear about who you are and what you want. You may have fooled yourself into believing that you deserve better. The Squeeze might be the remedy you need, or he could be your newest enemy, leading you down a rabbit hole of denial and self-neglect.

Consider forgiving the mistakes you've made in the past. Consider forgiving others for the ways they slighted you. Your expressed tears could easily expunge your attraction to this soul. By releasing emotions, you might release the final remnants of hidden greed, aggression or fear.

Remember that a player like The Squeeze can gently sneak into our lives and slowly push us toward becoming someone we are not. Once we become accustomed to her encouragement, we may no longer recognize ourselves. Squeezes are perceptive, intuitive or both, and they know when we're vulnerable. Over time, they gain windows into our souls and can quickly trigger us to act or react.

The Squeeze understands what makes you tick and what prompts your squirm. Their game of wit could rattle you, even undo you. While you might benefit from a jaunt with The Squeeze, the eventual untangling could be a challenge.

Consider an exit while you still have clarity. In every interaction with The Squeeze, be true to yourself. If you're The Squeeze, seek only games that generate joy and goodness for all involved.

CAUTION

We all live with a bit of turmoil inside of us. It might be a hurricane of assumptions, a tornado of self-hatred or a windy storm of confusion. It might stem from the past or come from our anxiety about the future.

Your pain might be disconnecting you from yourself or others. It might be making waves in your mind, disrupting your ability to focus. Your unresolved pain can also destroy relationships or push you to hurt others. Clear your heart and consider other options.

Left unattended, a distressed soul can become narcissistic, and their agendas can become obsessions. It is from this place that The Squeeze can be prompted to go down the wrong road. She might also operate from a position of lack causing her to act as if the world owes her something. This, of course, is an illusion.

EXTREME

As The Squeeze, you know how to create complex webs of deceit. If your plans involve hurting others, you are messing with an age-old spiritual law: karma. Creating deeper enmeshments creates karmic bonds that could take lifetimes to unwind. Make every effort to keep your intentions and actions clean and conscious. Right action will nourish you. With one internal shift, you can change the game. Nothing stands between you and the light, unless you allow it. Steer clear of your darker nature which seeks to dominate others. Evaluate future actions with loving care.

EMPOWERMENT

If you've been manipulating others in some way, you are the only one who can change your behavior. Can you see the pain you are causing others? By twisting someone's mind, even the slightest bit, you attract similar vibrations to your life. Much our most challenging behavior is born of our own anxiety, fear and delusions. Seek a therapist or personal coach to help you advance your thinking.

The colors of your clothes and the gems you wear can significantly affect your mood, mind and heart. Ingesting flower essences and applying diluted essential oils to your body (or diffusing them into the air) can improve your energy, attitude and drive. There is no end to the progress we can make. Seek the highest integrity and brightest light and you will eventually embody it.

Colors: orange, turquoise, blue, royal blue, hot pink, violet red, purple, plum, orchid

Gemstones: Orange Sapphire, Orange Chalcedony, Pink Tourmaline, Cobaltoan Calcite, Pink Opal, Ruby, Cinnabar, Turquoise, Blue Apetite

Flower Essences: Agrimony, Aspen, Gorse, Holly, Rock Water, Honeysuckle, Mustard, Rock Rose

Essential Oils: Chamomile, Cedar, Impatiens, Elemi, Jasmine, Myrtle, Angelica Root, Cardamom

When you manipulate others, you restrict an equal aspect within yourself. Relinquish games. Live authentically. Therein lies your freedom.

THE CONTRADICTOR

Friendly banter is enjoyable to most everyone I know, except me. While going with the flow of a conversation seems obvious, I enjoy taking a position polar opposite to consensus. At times, I do not even believe my own argument, but I so enjoy being combative! Look at how appalled they are! Look at the spittle and fumes! It is absolutely wonderful to see how tripped up people get by their egos and attachments. I love opposing people in this way because it results in a greater awareness of the topic at hand, with all eyes focused on me. Stand back and note what emerges from my next assertion.

THE CONTRADICTOR

"Prepare to be uncomfortable as I deconstruct your reality."

MORSEL

Consider then defend the exact opposite of what you believe. In this exercise, a greater, more defensible truth will emerge.

MESSAGE

The ego uses a myriad of compelling methods to attract attention to itself. It works overtime to feed our bottomless hunger. The ego can spoil intentions, block light and drive our hearts out of business.

Regardless of its power, with a moment of reflection we can overcome the ego with love. Even if our world is on fire, we can pause, clear our mind and begin again.

One effective modality the ego employs is contradiction. While contradiction can inspire eye-opening awarenesses, it can also unnecessarily draw focus and create confusion. This is not always a bad thing, yet it's how The Contradictor establishes position. He knows it is impossible to gain control when everyone's needs are already met. Choosing contradiction, he can inspire mutiny.

When the stakes are high, contradiction can be a helpful negotiating tool. It can force closed minds to open, and it has the potential to unearth new ideas and pathways. Contradiction is also the primary method used by religions and politicians to create hysteria. It can never be used for its own sake.

Even when being contradictory, we can nurture open-hearted discussions and allow for peaceful environments. This advances the pursuits in play and builds rapport. As a result, the open feeling in the room will inspire more awareness and connection, which often produces innovation. These things are good for everyone.

The Contradictor brings with her a lot of chutzpah. No matter the odds, she'll pursue any challenge. She has no fear of groups, individuals or ideas. She has impeccable courage and a tendency to take it to the mat just for fun. Strong is the resolve of The Contradictor.

If The Contradictor is challenging your position today, consider the ideas at hand, and you'll fortify your understanding and position. Ideas and beliefs can always benefit from analysis and upgrade.

If you are The Contradictor today, remember that you bring value to every situation, but often forsake personal growth for a chance to grandstand. Be less critical of others and more open to discussion. Consider the ideas at the table, even for a moment. While others might find you to be a challenge, you are their whetting stone. By knowing you, they will be sharper and more resilient.

Liberate your ego and stand in the light. Turn denial into consideration. At the conclusion of the ensuing events and discussions, you will either uncover a gaping hole in your thinking or establish a more defensible belief system. Either way, remain open and grow.

CAUTION

As you witness the flurry of activity within and around you, be aware that you have a profound strength that others find useful and attractive. Notice the dishonest systems currently in place. Seek ways to help the creators of these systems improve their integrity. With a little patience, you can bring about a helpful transformation.

As The Contradictor, be aware of your patterns of isolation. Be careful to sprinkle a little kindness into your speeches so that your combative nature does not undermine your friendships, gifts or ideals.

Contradictors might obsess about one idea to the point of ignoring other people's feelings. Be soft, open and flexible.

EXTREME

When you press a hot branding iron against flesh, it leaves a mark. Be careful. When you lead with your ego instead of your heart, you can easily hurt yourself and others in the process. Just because you have the ability to debate someone into the ground doesn't mean the skill is useful. Consider your most aggressive intentions and work hard to bring them into the light. It might be an apology, the offering of new information, a personal olive branch or the simple admittance that you were wrong. Become the bigger person and transform these relationships.

The people you are in dialogue with might be unable to hear you because of their limitations. Be gentle with them. When the time feels right, embody compassion and try again.

EMPOWERMENT

If you are pushing so hard that you're attacking others, take a break. Drink lots of water, take naps, cut out sugar and caffeine. Recalibrate so that you can be more humane and more effective. Most importantly forgive yourself. Whatever happened, it's in the past and the past is a cancelled check.

Try a full-body cleanse, drink Jasmine tea and eat less food for a few days. Given your aggression, you might also detox your liver. Try Ayurvedic and herbal medicine for the most enduring results.

The colors of your clothes and the gems you wear can significantly affect your mood, mind and heart. Ingesting flower essences and applying essential oils to your body (or diffusing them into the air) can improve your energy, attitude and drive. Consult a professional for best results.

Colors: magenta, pink, aquamarine, turquoise, chartreuse, cornflower blue, cyan, dark orchid, orange

Gemstones: Rose Quartz, Watermelon Tourmaline, Amethyst, Amazonite, Blue Quartz, Citrine

Flower Essences: Beech, Vine, Chicory, Chestnut Bud, Elm, Holly, Heather, Rock Water

Essential Oils: Rosemary, Bergamot, Galbanum, Lavender, Marjoram, Myrtle, Rose, Sandalwood

Why force a specific reality? Why force anything at all? The Self, born magnetic and elastic, will naturally attract congruent realities upon a relaxed effort.

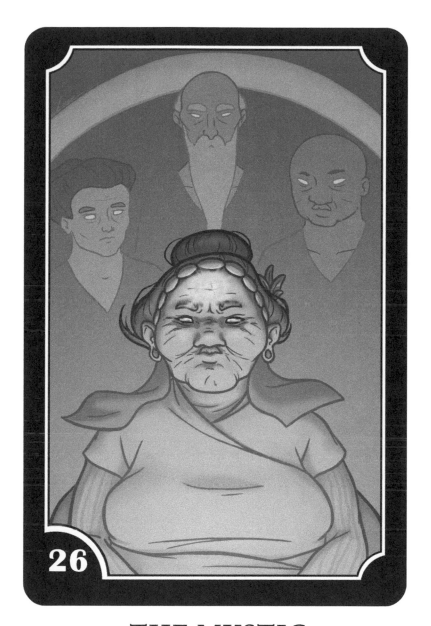

THE MYSTIC

I live in the netherworld of archetypes and energy, bridging the gap between spirit and form. I see symbols, patterns and influences that are ruled by etheric, natural forces. I am a vehicle for clarity, abstract reflection and eternal truth. What thrills me most is when forces align to effect change. Disembodied spirits and angelic beings move through me, like a river gushing through a fallen, hollow tree. If I can be the midpoint between these forces, directing their convergence, I am in the bosom of my beloved.

THE MYSTIC

"While one part of me interacts on earth, other aspects commune with unseeable realms."

MORSEL

Every soul is connected to a soul-group as well as other realms of consciousness. Communing with these souls, angels, entities and thought-forms is as easy as opening our hearts and saying hello.

MESSAGE

Long ago, people of the earth used divining skills to connect with planets, deities, entities and each other. In each village lived an oracle, sage or mystic who provided helpful guidance for those who needed it. They shared insight, predicted conflict, advised on health and relationships, and always with a focus on the light.

In this Age of Technology, we are being distracted away from connecting with the sources of all life. We have become immune to the invasive ideologies that are vying for control over and influence on our minds, homes, lives cultures and societies.

Almost daily, we are each provoked to give up a piece of ourselves in exchange for a vote or for a product that we do not need. We have become information addicts, forced outside ourselves for answers, as we forsake the mysteries that rest peacefully in our hearts.

If the Mystic has magically graced your heart with insight and light, you are blessed with a loving, intuitive guide to see you through the transitions in your life. Allow yourself to call on and accept help from this guide so that your life's obstacles are easier to maneuver.

With The Mystic at your side, you will see and experience the best of all possibilities. This angelic friend is here for you always, sitting patiently, waiting to serve your spiritual advancement, personhood and happiness.

Close your eyes and imagine a lush green forest and beautiful light-beings traversing the skies. At the edge of the trees, see a most sacred and holy temple. Imagine your Mystic guide standing in the center of the temple with you, hand-in-hand with your ancestors and teachers.

Whenever you need encouragement or love, each of these beings is here to encourage your joys, passions and purpose. You have the same access to these vibrations as any healer, psychic, priest, shaman, wizard or spiritual teacher. You are born of the same material that gave birth to the universe and all its mysteries. All you must do is clear your mind and heart, and work toward purity.

If you allow yourself, you will be able to see the abstract world from a high perspective, enabling you to focus on simplicity, love and service.

Breathe deeply and welcome The Mystic into your heart. With her guidance, you add flow and joy to your life, and to the lives of those around you. She will always be available to light your path.

CAUTION

You are being asked to see your current situation from a higher, healthier perspective. The angelic forces in your midst want to help you create a more beneficial trajectory for your life. You are being asked to dig deep and embody a more loving attitude. If you are holding a grudge, planning revenge, or making a decision from a low vibrational mindset, you could easily provoke a train wreck. Be careful with your next move.

The Mystic spends much of her time in the higher dimensions. As she connects with etheric beings on other planes, she often forsakes her own health and healing. This can only go on for so long before physical problems arise. Consider all the options the universe has prepared for you. Sit quietly and pray for guidance. Let The Mystic help you.

EXTREME

You have been here before, sitting shoeless on the cold ground after a fall. This is not the first time you tripped and fell into a bucket of poop. You seem to end up here during the times in your life when you forget to honor yourself. Certain situations bring you to your knees.

While things appear to be dismal, you have options. Sit quietly, invoke the sacred temple within you and see The Mystic standing strong, hand-in-hand with all the divine entities that serve you. Pray for grace and formulate a plan of action. With their help, you'll be reborn into a new reality.

EMPOWERMENT

If the other realms are overwhelming your body and spirit, do a grounding ritual to bring your mind and heart back to center. Head into the forest for a long walk, meditate on the beach, or sit in bright sunlight. If you feel disconnected from your body, it might be time for a good ole-fashioned romp in the hay with a trusted lover. Playfully relish the animal inside of you. Release the sounds and expressions that allow you to feel sexual, powerful and alive.

The colors of your clothes and the gems you wear can significantly affect your mood. Ingesting flower essences and applying essential oils to your body can improve your energy, attitude and mood.

Colors: purple, light blue, dark red, orange, bright yellow, gold, white, lavender

Gemstones: Ruby, Red Orange Sapphire, Orange Citrine, Cherry Opal, Rhodochrosite, Rose Quartz, Chiastolite, Carnelian, Gold, Sugilite, Amethyst

Flower Essences: Larch, Elm, Clematis, Cerato, Cherry Plum, Wild Rose, Heather, Vine, Larkspur, Hornbeam, Crab Apple, Walnut

Essential Oils: Cinnamon, Frankincense, Jasmine, Lavender, Myrrh, Patchouli, Juniper Berry, Rose, Violet Leaf, Yarrow, Galbanum

Beneath the personality is a living, electric current that is found in every living being, in every realm, in all the worlds. Attune to this force and know your Self.

THE DISRUPTOR

I burst into meetings, relationships and scenarios like a lightning storm, setting tiny fires with my perspective, perceptions and insight. It is not my intention to create havoc, but my ideas and style are a challenge to assimilate into existing plans. I freely share thoughts, impressions and intuition, never shackled by guilt, co-dependence, the past or fear. When our time together is over, you will either be smarter, wiser or angrier for having met me. You might also be in shock. If you're the leader who invited me into the fold, I'll make you look terrific, but your team might resent me. My innovations will rock your world, dazzle your brain and render your plan brighter and tighter.

THE DISRUPTOR

"I am not attached to my insights, but I get the feeling you should brace yourself."

MORSEL

When the Self deeply attaches to a reality, greater truths will seek to challenge and deconstruct it.

MESSAGE

When we enter a relationship or begin a project, it is natural to be excited. The idea of collaborating, the feeling of creating, and the adrenaline that rushes through our veins are palpable.

We project our hopes, needs and desires into the idea of creating. As plans solidify, we deal with the nuances and become attached. At the height of our success, we grow the weeds of defensiveness. This is where our troubles begin.

We will do anything to maintain the beliefs, realities and processes currently in play in our lives. We will block the brightest light in order to avoid feeling pain. When we sense impending shifts, we freak out, becoming like wild animals in a lightning storm.

Rather than fight the nature of the ever-changing universe, embrace the inevitability of change. Given that all particles in all the universes are in states of flux, the idea of defending any reality, even for a moment, is a fool's game. Even defending our own self-image is a folly.

If The Disruptor has barreled over your chain-link fence, he might be ushering in a time of reformation and rebirth. Are you prepared to be flexible? Can you relinquish your attachment to the people and processes in play? Are you fixated on one outcome? Remain open to all possibilities.

As with all aspects of Self, the force of The Disruptor lives within every one of us. She has many forms: Shiva, Kartikeya, Durga, Sekhmet, Mars, Guan Yu, Judas, Mom, Dad, Sibling, a hurricane, a tidal wave. It might have been a distant thought, dream or unconscious desire, but it was you who invited The Disruptor into your world and heart.

As The Disruptor disassembles the ideas and aspects you love the most, consider her presence to be a gift. Honor this unruly soul and reflect on what may have inspired her arrival. Are you disheartened on some level? Is a small part of you dying? Has a relationship hit a wall?

Since the beginning of time, spiritual masters have told us that attachments create the majority of our suffering. When we accept the notion of impermanence, we relinquish fear of change and death.

To remain in the bosom of happiness, make the necessary changes to your life before the universe thrusts them upon you. They might be simple or they might require a drastic re-envisioning.

The Disruptor's bolt of lightning is here to propel you into your next phase of evolution. Welcome this time with an open mind, and your heart will surprise you with another enjoyable illusion to engage.

CAUTION

Just like an oracle warning the local village of impending doom, you have become The Disruptor, initiating vital changes to the realities around you. When whisking emancipation into a dynamic or venture, there is often a variety of responses and reactions, all of which are outside of our control. Be prepared for some mayhem.

It is usually not The Disruptor who forces our hand and brings us to our knees. It is our own fear-based projections and insecurities that do us in.

Stand strong in what you offered others and let the winds of change intervene. Let the short-sighted players fade from view. You are doing exactly what you have been called to do: open yourself up to illumination and share the brilliance that often comes through you.

EXTREME

If The Disruptor appears extreme to you, you are putting too much energy into combating an already impossible situation. Whatever you are fighting to preserve or protect, let it fade into the shadows or die a natural death. As you let go of the past, you will unearth a deeper awareness.

Did you set out to hurt someone? Was it greed that set your heart aflame? Look honestly at yourself and allow new understandings to emerge. When your mind is clear, find the grace within you and salvage what you can. We cannot change what others think or do, but we can heal and begin again.

EMPOWERMENT

Take a deep breath and examine your motivations. Are you power-hungry? Are you dishonoring yourself on any level? Be honest. A little solitude and journal writing will go a long way. You might need a little break from the stress of life and business. Consider making an ice cream sundae or playing in a park. You might need a bit of affection or physical love from someone you trust.

The colors of your clothes and the gems you wear can significantly affect your mood. Ingesting flower essences and applying essential oils to your body can improve your energy, attitude and mood.

Colors: blue, bright red, white, bright gold, light orange, salmon, magenta, lime green

Gemstones: Malachite, Blue Sapphire, Gold, Honey Calcite, Morganite, Howlite, Opalite, Peridot, Fuchsite, Butterstone

Flower Essences: Walnut, Oak, Agrimony, Chicory, Beech, Elm, Heather, Holly, Impatiens, Willow

Essential Oils: Cedarwood, Mugwort, Angelica Root, Spruce, Myrtle, Bergamot, Frankincense, Pine, Ylang Ylang

Speak your truth with unbridled enthusiasm. Your resolve will move mountains and clear pathways to change.

THE CONSCIOUS TWIST

I remain peaceful, loving and generous until my shadow-self is offended. Upon an infraction, I might pause momentum so that you'll reconsider your behavior. When feeling hurt or neglected, my actions might include outrage or revenge. When you love and include me, I'm as loyal as a puppy, but leave me out of the process and we'll most certainly have an issue. If you want to rebuild our bridge, I welcome resolution. Be kind to me and encourage my positivity. Your compassion will heal it all.

THE CONSCIOUS TWIST

"When my heart is broken, I tend toward creating an abrupt change of direction."

MORSEL

When in the process of creation, be wholly transparent. Keep allies in view of the prize.

MESSAGE

In every negotiation, there are many influences to consider. There are personal agendas and beliefs, the present moment in all its complexity and the expectations of what "should be". Add to that things like secrets, vendettas and financial parameters and you have a colorful stew of potential challenges.

There is one influence that outweighs all the rest: feelings. When our minds are scattered and our lives too busy, feelings are neglected. Our mistakes give rise to frustration, sadness, anger and paranoia. When shadows are provoked, misunderstandings arise. This can cause our friends, partners and peers to lose faith in us.

The Conscious Twist often heralds a time of pause or reflection, enabling you to catch up with yourself. While the majority of your plans are most likely in tact, there may be a few details that require your love and attention.

If The Conscious Twist is meandering about, you may have excluded someone close to you from an important event or communication. This may have caused a loyal confidant to become adversarial, seeking a renegotiation of terms and outcome. The person in question might even be YOU.

Do you take the necessary time to care for your primary relationships and agreements? Do you properly explain your actions during upheaval? If you are out of balance, The Conscious Twist may have put a thorn in your side. While the damage might be negligible, it is not without consequence.

Keep an open mind and heart. Take inventory of whatever might be in jeopardy, whether it is money, friends, pride or ownership. Reach out to this adversary (or within yourself) and make amends. You might find that by taking the time to heal or deepen your relationships, you broaden them and increase their potency. You can reach this affect simply by slowing down and opening your heart.

Pursuing reciprocity is also important. Wins must be on both sides of the tables and include all parties. If you can find a way to add value to the propositions and agreements in your life, do it now. Being proactive can add positivity to a venture or relationship.

Remember to take the time to consider how others feel. With expanded empathy and compassion, we are more whole, congruent and unified. In all things, love yourself and show up with every part of you. Be forthright, integrated and consistent. Whether the outcome is profit or loss, a united, positive action will send tangible ripples into the universe and benefit all.

CAUTION

When she is out of balance, The Conscious Twist will charismatically entice you with one face, then harm you with the other. She has a complex personality that requires patience and understanding.

If you are The Conscious Twist, you might be holding a grudge and have been unable to find the words to express what hurt you so deeply. Write a clear, descriptive letter to the person who offended you. Let him know how you feel about what happened. The purpose might not be to send it, rather, simply to get in touch with your feelings.

If left unattended, emotions can putrefy and become toxic. They might split us in two, causing us to forget who we are. Forgive yourself and your transgressor. Un-dig the trench. Take a deep cleansing breath and fill your lungs with a new and unified reality.

EXTREME

It appears you let somebody down. They in turn wreaked havoc in your life and sabotaged your dream. It is reasonable that you would be hurt or devastated from these events. When our buttons are pushed, we break into pieces and act out our opposing mindsets. While wanting others to fully experience our pain is understandable, when we hold others in captivity, we are the only prisoner.

If you hurt someone, remember that we cannot control other people's reactions. Even with an apology, some might refuse to wrap their head around forgiveness. This does not mean you are unforgivable, it means the other person cannot get out of her own way. Send clear and kind intentions to the universe. Rekindle the most valuable relationships in your life. Unite all the disenfranchised parts of you and become whole again. It's the perfect time to forgive, let go and renew.

EMPOWERMENT

To get back into balance, examine your allegiances and alliances, look at your loyalties and devotions. Forgiveness and the pursuit of peace are the orders of the day. Consider letting your guard down and opening your heart again. Engage a therapist, priest, rabbi, shaman or clairvoyant to help you process your heartache. Find forgiveness for each aspect (including you) and enjoy a rebirth.

These colors, gemstones, flower essences and essential oils will improve your mind, heart and mood.

Colors: orchid, violet, magenta, forest green, purple, sky blue, aquamarine, pink

Gemstones: Purpurite, Stichtite, Blue Quartz, Tanzanite, Malachite, Dioptase, Pink Tourmaline

Flower Essences: Cherry Plum, Holly, Rock Rose, Star of Bethlehem, Pine, Impatiens, Gorse, Elm, Agrimony, Willow, Beech, Vine

Essential Oils: Ylang Ylang, Lavender, Vetiver, Bergamot, Sandalwood, Pine, Bitter Orange, Rose

There is no duality. Everything is connected. You cannot deliver an experience to another that you will not also experience. Be split and you are no longer you.

THE INTERRUPTER

I like to jump head first into the middle of activities already in progress. My ideas and actions might be a bit annoying at first, but they are rarely born of ill intent. Perhaps I'm just clumsy! Truth be told, when I get in your face, when I intrude into a process, it's organic to my nature and flow. In complex social situations, it can become an enjoyable game. I do not fret too much about other people's reactions to my enthusiasm, especially when I'm on a roll. I mean seriously, when my mojo kicks in, I am frickin' awesome. You know what I'm saying? Let me tell you something else ...

THE INTERRUPTER

"Lots to get off my chest, so hush up a moment, I'm in love with this. Listen up!"

MORSEL

Helpful gifts and inspiring truths often appear as pieces of chocolate bejeweled in broken glass.

MESSAGE

We hold court at a cocktail party, chatting away at a hundred miles an hour. The beguiling story we are telling is seconds from its epic climax, then, out of nowhere, someone pops into frame and hijacks the conversation. In an instant, our precious little narrative is lost. Defeated and deflated, we excuse ourselves, wander back to the bar and ask for a double.

We might quickly rebound, or we might struggle a bit before gaining back our confidence. While being cut short can be disappointing, what feels like a slap in the face can also be viewed as a helpful pattern-interrupter. It depends on our perspective.

While fascinating, people with fast-moving brains and aggressive social styles can be a little unnerving. In the midst of our most prized soliloquy, they might blurt out a random question, act out an attention-grabbing fact or sing the most irritating song. While it might appear their intention was to fluster us, chances are they were simply celebrating a moment. No harm, no foul.

If The Interrupter tripped you up today, it was far more valuable to you than you realize. Her outpouring most likely had gems in it the size of grapefruits. Do not let your feelings cloud what has occurred. Do your best to be receptive, even if this person appears to be unaware of herself.

Because she spends more time in her head than her heart, The Interrupter will spew a variety of her fascinations at the drop of a hat. An exchange with her may trigger a waterfall of ideas and memories. There's even a slight chance their outpouring will be interesting, even valuable.

While you might consider plugging your ears or insulting her, it is best to refrain from taking their interminable babbling personally. The Interrupter is simply trying to find her way.

When someone rattles us, we can complain and play victim, or we can reframe the jolt from a more Self-aware perspective. Do not fault The Interrupter for being authentic, rather, celebrate her intrusion!

When we make small adjustments, we become the bigger person and we grow. When The Interrupter pushes your buttons, that's the perfect time to practice your resolve.

Use the moment as a jumping point into another frame of mind. Allow The Interrupter's interjections to spark keen insight into yourself or spur you into a new vein of creativity. Either way, someone has inspired you to expand, so accept the challenge and get to it!

CAUTION

As The Interrupter, your chatty mouth often renders you lonely and isolated. You may have forgotten to listen to your heart. It may have been a while since you've felt heard and loved. To attract companionship, soften your personality so others will feel safe around you. You might be unaware that your insertions cause other people's hearts to skip a beat. It might be said that you can be a "little much."

While your behavior can be akin to a rhino in an egg store, it's changeable. There is no blame or guilt here. Take inventory of when you are insensitive and seek to be more aware of yourself.

If you make too much of an adjustment to appease someone else's needs or insecurities, you dishonor both yourself and the other person. Only you know the truth. Be who you are but refrain from trampling on others. In the end, sing the song you were meant to sing.

EXTREME

There is a good chance that your insensitivity is far more than an oversight. It might be born of jealousy or animosity. You may also be perseverating on long-ago experiences, unable to wrangle them into submission. Thrusting yourself upon the softhearted shows a weakness. Maniacally communicating your every thought shows instability. Take the time to learn about your triggers. Our minds can become weapons if we are not careful.

Regardless of the infraction, refrain from playing the victim. While you may have forgotten that you are powerful, there is no time like the presence to get back on the train to self-awareness.

EMPOWERMENT

Release your old stories and acknowledge your vulnerabilities. This will give you the best chance of creating a real connection with others. In terms of your long-winded speeches, at least for now, put a cork in them. Become an observer. When spending time with people, allow them to unfold at a pace that brings them joy. The more you allow others to express themselves, the more you'll learn.

The colors of your clothes and the gems you wear can significantly affect your mood, mind and heart. Ingesting flower essences and applying essential oils to your body (or diffusing them into the air) can improve your energy, attitude and drive. Consult a professional for best results.

Colors: cyan, powder blue, lavender, aquamarine, turquoise, spring green, white, pink, yellow

Gemstones: Cobaltoan Calcite, Pink Tourmaline, Orange Calcite, Peridot, Lapis Lazuli, Tanzanite

Flower Essences: Agrimony, Crab Apple, Holly, Rock Water, Vervain, Vine, Star of Bethlehem

Essential Oils: Bergamot, Chamomile, Jasmine, Neroli, Bitter Orange, Rose, Vetiver, Ylang Ylang

Non-stop activity and aggression can dull our ability to receive. With our gaze on the horizon, money, love and success will wander elsewhere. Slow down to receive.

THE WHIMSICAL

I play, laugh, whisper and fly, moving through the universe without agenda or fear. I desire only joy and the experiences that permit me to freely express myself. I inhale and exhale poetry, the elixir to a magical life. I speak often with fairies and animals, entrusting them with the most intimate secrets. I may eat with my hands, make love in a grocery store or run naked through a park. These are just some of the possibilities in this life of joyful abandon. Some might say I am impertinent, but truly I am a reflection of the freedom that lives within all beings. I may end up shocking you, healing you, inspiring you or getting you arrested. What a wondrous groove I am dancing in! Join me, follow me, lead me, or let me cheerfully twirl on by.

THE WHIMSICAL

"I hear whispering angels. They desire so much for me! Journey with me and feel what I feel!"

MORSEL

Magic, playfulness and light-heartedness are gifts from the eternal muse. Invoke them often!

MESSAGE

When the universe was forming, there were no rules or manuals. There were no governments, religions or oppression. Today, we are over-influenced. Advertising and entertainment a mind-numbing vault of false notions upon us every day, and we ingest every one of them. We are fast-becoming the robots, we were warned about.

The majority of the stories we ingest impound our free thinking. In street and sales terms, this is called being "put together." When you "put someone together," you manipulate them into doing or believing things that serves you, even if it puts them in a vulnerable or dangerous position.

We are all "put together" by society in one way or another, which we collectively co-create with every product we buy and every injustice we ignore. We always have the ability to influence the forces that manage and control us, but our comfort has become more of a priority.

When was the last time you experienced a truly vulnerable, inspired and free moment? You most likely have a memory from childhood where you danced with abandon in the rain or laughed so hard you peed your pants. This part of you is still alive and well! Let her out so she can play and dance!

The Whimsical sees past self-imposed veils of illusion and gets to the playful heart of the matter. She chooses freedom over everything else. The Whimsical is the torch bearer of the planet's original intended flow where magic and playfulness were merged into one divine experience.

It is time to honor the softer, purer impulses within you. Your personal truth doesn't reside in the bosom of accomplishment. It lives joyfully beneath the clutter, under the words, down the staircase of magic. There on the bottom shelf, next to wonder rests an electric current labeled "YOU." This is your most truthful, whimsical self awaiting recognition and emancipation.

To tap into your inner Whimsical, write a poem, scream "I Love You," or volunteer to serve the poor in a foreign country on a whim. Break out of traditional thinking and explore life beyond the concepts you've been fed by the media for decades.

Give yourself the gift of personal freedom. This gift never withers or dies. It is impervious to pain, external elements and political agendas. It is more powerful than finances and family. It is soft and pure, able to grow in the dark.

Give voice to this magic that lives in your core. It will bring to life your most sacred visions. Dream big and embody your freedom right now.

CAUTION

The Whimsical is a loving and optimistic person who can be devastated by verbal brutality and dark thoughts. She is a gentle ray of light, a soft sponge. If you are kind to her, The Whimsical will help you shed tears, find joy and burst out of your shell. If The Whimsical is dancing in your garden, open the window and ready a cup of delicious, sweet lemonade. Let her know that you appreciate her presence, gifts and perspective.

The Whimsical reminds us to stop absorbing the negativity around us. Remember that you are in partnership with angels and mystical beings. You are a divine spark who resembles the spirits of creation when they first emerged. You swam in the first sacred pond. You continue to hold hands with the original vines and flowers. Free-fall from heavenly clouds into a pool of bliss with The Whimsical.

EXTREME

We can be so whimsical and "out there" that we forget our responsibilities and commitments. We swing from the branches of the original tree but we have a hard time eating a pear. Living as The Whimsical might mean we have no idea how to function in the real world. Floating in the stratosphere can be a fun, but only if you've tended to the details of your life.

You might be so averse to playfulness that you've ignored every sign of enchantment in your life. You may have let miracles slip through your fingers. You can invite magic and mystery into your life in every moment. You are in control of your dreams.

EMPOWERMENT

The Whimsical lives in a beautiful bubble, but he can wander so far from reality that he often forgets his way home. If you are feeling a little "out there," ask your closest friends and family for love and affection. Consider doing some physical exercise or outdoor work to ground you.

While whimsy can be fun, you might be avoiding something vital to your evolution. Through relaxation and gentle movements, you will quickly become better acquainted with yourself.

The colors of your clothes and the gems you wear can significantly affect your mood. Ingesting flower essences and applying essential oils to your body can improve your energy, attitude and mood.

Colors: red, dark violet, goldenrod, dark magenta, blue, olive, purple, black

Gemstones: Ruby, Red Coral, Hematite, Smoky Quartz, Blue Quartz, Tanzanite, Shattuckite, Chiastolite, Purpurite, Tiger's Eye, Onyx

Flower Essences: Clematis, Rock Rose, Aspen, Centaury, Honeysuckle, Star of Bethlehem, Vervain

Essential Oils: Spruce, Cedarwood, Ylang Ylang, Juniper, Lemongrass, White Fir, Angelica, Neroli

Laugh, play and dance with abandon so that you can remember the boundless joy infused in every particle in the universe.

THE SMALL STEPPER

I believe that the field in front of me is ever-replenished with opportunity. Always the forward-moving optimist pursuing a treasured goal, I seek improvements, no matter how big or small. In the end, whoever gets the credit is of no consequence to me. I am always hopeful, with a full and focused heart, come peril or high water. Let's push ahead, one measured gain at a time. When the time is right, we'll enjoy a bounty together! Look, do you see it? It's over that hill! Keep moving. We're almost there!

THE SMALL STEPPER

"Only through a series of small, measured steps will I achieve my goals."

MORSEL

Most progress comes from a consistent betterment of the Self and minor advances toward the goal.

MESSAGE

The model for success is now so complex, it's daunting to even consider pursuing the creation of something. There are so many variables we have to consider now: the high standards of the marketplace, competition from all over the world, marketing to your chosen demographic in a sea of messages, ads and information. It's a wonder that anyone finds the impetus to organize a project and attempt to bring it to the world. It's crazy out there!

While it all sounds so intense, there are healthier perspectives and work ethics to consider. Imagine a family farm where one person picks the peppers, another picks up the filled baskets and yet another rides the tractor, picking up the bushels and taking them to the store. One pepper, one basket, and one tractor-ride at a time. A reasonable pace, simple goals and a successful model.

The Small Stepper chooses to live and work in this way. He keeps things simple and down to earth. He knows what he needs to do and takes small steps to accomplish the tasks at hand. He makes the most out of every achievement, knowing his progress is at the perfect pace.

No matter the size of his advancements, The Small Stepper understands how to stay motivated. He commits at a core level, enjoying the gain of every ground-inch.

If The Small Stepper has joined your team today, you might been holding too tightly to a harsh, exaggerated, narrow outcome, driving others into feelings of competition, defeat and isolation.

Loosen your grip on the agenda at hand and you'll improve every facet of the project. With a little humility and flexibility, you'll experience all the momentum you need. Take the intensity down a few notches. It'll all work out if everybody sticks together and keeps moving in a forward direction.

Establish a plan that allows for the smallest improvements. Encourage teamwork at every turn. Remember that one handful of snow rolled from atop a mountain can defeat an army of warriors at the bottom. Even the slightest progress can be a turning point.

The Small Stepper understands that having an overactive ego can be disruptive to a pursuit. She doesn't think to promote her work or celebrate her excellence. She's happy to relax into what she's doing, even taking a back seat when necessary.

If you are The Small Stepper, keep up the great work, defend your efforts and help others do the same. The most exceptional Small-Steppers often end up running important, global initiatives. Stand strong and enjoy your journey toward success, one step at a time.

CAUTION

While cheers and shouts from fans can be a great motivator, be careful not to get caught up in the celebrity of your pursuits. All the hype in the world will not complete it for you. The best thing you can do is proceed with patience and go for the long game. You don't need pep rallies and sales conventions to keep things moving forward. All you need is commitment to a plan and heart to get you there.

Remember that when we pass to the other world, we cannot take any of our accomplishments with us. All that we carry are the impressions of the hearts with whom we most intimately connected.

A soulful journey with a heart-centered outcome is far more valuable than a shallow victory with strangers.

EXTREME

With all the hoopla in play, your ego got the better of you. Instead of taking a moment to consider a long list of decisions more carefully, you let the glimmer and shimmer of shiny objects negatively influence your state of mind. Doing so, you may have hurt yourself in some way.

You might be having a mid-life crisis. While there really is no crisis to consider, it is certainly a time to reflect on the things you love so you can make better choices. Consider the possibility that the activities and projects you are a part of are limiting or stifling in some way. They have great mission statements and beautiful logos, but somehow you don't fit in with their ideology, style or momentum.

If you feel unfulfilled or restrained by the things you've chosen to be a part of, break free and give birth to a new situation. It is time to graduate into a new game. Be fearless and let a new vision lead the way. Change your thoughts and you change your reality.

EMPOWERMENT

If you recently let your ego get the better of you, connect with close friends or throw a sweet little dinner party for yourself. When our lives become a little toxic, a little love goes a long way.

You might need to pump up the volume on your life, playing so below your level, you're falling asleep. Take a few small risks in work or love. You might surprise yourself with a whole new life.

The colors of your clothes and the gems you wear can significantly affect your mood, mind and heart. Ingesting flower essences and applying diluted essential oils to your body (or diffusing them into the air) can improve your energy, attitude and drive. Enjoy these recommendations.

Colors: green, forest green, brown, dark goldenrod, firebrick red, dark olive, purple

Gemstones: Aragonite, Axinite, Purpurite, Cinnabar, Bloodstone, Moss Agate, Malachite, Jade

Flower Essences: Cerato, Chestnut Bud, Impatiens, Mimulus, Oak, Sweet Chestnut, Wild Oat

Essential Oils: Frankincense, Ginger, Cinnamon, Sage, Jasmine, Peppermint, Patchouli, Rosemary

With small, confident steps, you can build potent and beautiful realities.

THE COWBOY

Family, honor and tradition are my backbone. I'm loyal and monogamous, making one decision at a time. With me, you'll have a chance to prove yourself, no matter what happened yesterday. Seeing is believing, but I'll always give you the benefit of the doubt. I wear my hat because it makes me feel a little bigger and a whole lot more effective. If you need anything, take the shirt off my back, but don't cross me, or I'll order a stampede to snuff you out before you can say, "Fix me a cup of joe."

THE COWBOY

"Let me give it a ponder, but at first thought, I believe I can help you."

MORSEL

When we remove complications, we are better able to taste the sweet, delicious nectar of integrity.

MESSAGE

In this complex culture, attracting truly heart-worthy friends and partners is a full-time job, often a treasure hunt filled with danger and dead ends. Some people traversing the planet today are clouded by greed, vanity and warped thinking. Allegiance and clarity somehow escape them.

Not long ago, the meaty, proud bond between a man and his posse was a vital part of farm, city and business culture. The unspoken goodwill and commitment between one person and a group had three requirements: show up, help out and do what's right. This was a time when there was no mistaking who your friends were.

In the process of modern social evolution, the bond between brothers and sisters, and the clear line that once separated friend from foe have been compromised in almost every way. We have become such a competitive, individualistic society that true loyal camaraderie has become a thing of the past. The remedy is not easy to muster.

Achieving celebrity status is now more desirable than being of value to someone. Wolves wearing masks wander the fields looking for harmless deer to devour. They fool us with Armani suits and flashy college degrees. Each one of them is a replication. It is a wonder who anybody is anymore.

Long gone are the days when a late-night knock at the door was nothing to fear. When someone needs our help now, rather than jump in with a shovel, we scrutinize and second-guess. We don't have enough trust in our hearts to help others because we can barely help ourselves.

If The Cowboy has sauntered into your corral, you know how to attract good, upstanding people. You just may have forgotten how to hold onto them. Get back on the horse of trust before it is too late. There is always a good person within reach.

If you have the heart of The Cowboy, what a gift you are to others! Your consistent hand of friendship is a reminder that we are never alone. Your generosity inspires the goodwill most of us have lost. You're the person everybody would love to have as a best friend.

If your situation calls for the strength and kindness of The Cowboy, speak up! Remember to follow through with your commitments, stay away from overly-emotional dialogue and seek to produce healthy and delicious crops. The Cowboy says, "You got this, I just know it."

The Cowboy is the real deal. Let him in, give him a hug and feed him a good ole fashioned meal. He will no doubt respond with a "Thank you kindly!"

CAUTION

Be aware that the Cowboy is not always the most open-minded character in the bunch. He has a good heart, but he tends to steer clear of group process, esoteric modalities and alternative thinking.

If you or The Cowboy have lost touch with the flexible, feminine side of life, take time to tap into your heart. Soften that saddle and consider the options you might normally reject. You do not have to step outside the integrity zone, but you may have to give up on some of your more iconic obsessions like being tough, pushing hard and coming out on top.

While headstrong leadership can produce results, consider the pathways to victory that do not require calloused hands and sleeping in the dirt. Buck up, open your heart, and a bucket of joy will come pouring out.

EXTREME

According to some spiritual masters, the universe is mostly feminine, but only by a small percentage. When we focus on the balance of masculinity and femininity, we honor the nature of the universe.

Some spiritual movements tends to over-feminize every aspect of life. It is within this mindset that we see many people rejecting men because they demonstrate attributes that are counter-intuitive to the feminine. This does not mean that the masculine mindset is not valuable. To the contrary, masculinity and femininity have unique characteristics, both of which serve the most masculine of men, the most feminine of women, and those of us who exist in between.

When folks project their fears into the situation, it can get messy. The Cowboy might ask a few tough questions and give some new directives, but do not be afraid. Truly, The Cowboy is here to help.

EMPOWERMENT

The Cowboy sometimes takes himself too seriously. He might need a vacation, a costume party or a reminder to be more light-hearted. Take your Cowboy out for a night on the town and loosen him up!

The colors of your clothes and the gems you wear can significantly affect your mood, mind and heart. Ingesting flower essences and applying diluted essential oils to your body (or diffusing them into the air) can improve your energy, attitude and drive.

Colors: violet, light blue, magenta, pink, firebrick red, turquoise, spring green, gold

Gemstones: Honey Calcite, Tanzanite, Blue Lace Agate, Vanadinite, Amethyst, Pink Tourmaline

Flower Essences: Olive, Rock Rose, Sweet Chestnut, Wild Oat, Beech, Heather, Larch, Mustard

Essential Oils: Angelica, Cinnamon, Patchouli, Sandalwood, Ylang Ylang, Rose, Jasmine

There is rarely a good reason to get all dolled up and make a show of it. Drop the facade and get back to being your grounded, authentic Self.

THE BULL RIDER

I love a wild ride. Whether it is a roller coaster, tough relationship or a genuine big bull tearing down a mountain, I say "Bring it on!" No matter the size of the beast or power of the storm, I'll dig my heels in and ride with abandon. If I fail, expect me to remount and ride again and again until I fall off in complete exhaustion. I might lose a limb, I might not be successful the first time or tenth, but I'll keep at it till that prize is centered high on my mantle. Whatever the challenge, if the purse is right, I'll bring it home between my teeth.

THE BULL RIDER

"I'd appreciate you stepping aside. I'm here to get what I came for."

MORSEL

When brave souls pursue remarkable rewards, another measure of infinite possibility becomes available to all living beings.

MESSAGE

When we set out to create something, our level of success will be defined by our belief system. If we believe there to be obstacles, we'll find ourselves in service to them. If we believe that statistics dictate the level of success, then our ceiling will be based on statistics.

Commercials tell us to buy things we do not need. The media entices us to become someone we are not. Apparently, left alone to our own devices, we are ill-equipped to be happy and fulfilled. Once we absorb even a sprinkle of these limiting messages, it is difficult to break free from them.

Truth be told, while we might get stuck for a moment, we remain unlimited. Our heartfelt passion is more powerful than polls and trends. If we persevere, we eventually succeed. You may have to make adjustments here and there, but that's where the learning is. There are millions of people who focus on their dreams, cut through weeds, and achieve victory. You will too.

What excuses are you using to stop yourself today? Who's voice are you listening to? What are you doing to break through the weeds? What gifts, talents and attributes do you have hidden beneath the surface? How might you awaken and expand them?

If The Bull Rider roped you into his world today, it is time to feel your oats and put them to the test. No matter the dangers, you know how to find the temple, gather the treasure and tear down the mountain toward victory. Get atop that bull, give her some love and ride her all the way home!

This is not the time to take a step back or play the victim. Be tough-minded and committed. Muscle-up, buckle-up and believe! You are more than capable of achieving your dreams and desires.

If you have forgotten how proficient you are at bringing home the gold, remember the dangerous roller coasters you've already mastered. Every time you risked it all, you made it back safely. While others flew off the handle and crashed, you remained confident and focused.

While courageous, The Bull Rider also has a sweet side. Because you know what it takes to dig deep, feel pain and come out on top, you have a soft spot for people who seek the same.

While your style might be rough around the edges, you know how to communicate your passion and inspire others, especially if they're struggling. It is in this way that you are an excellent mentor and coach. You will quickly gain energy and momentum upon sharing your gifts with others.

Saddle up, gather your strength and prepare for success. It's your birthright.

CAUTION

The Bull Rider has a big honest heart, but he also has a needy, vain streak. To keep things flowing, have hugs, kisses and a shiny mirror on hand. A little love and sweet talk can go a long way with The Bull Rider.

If The Bull Rider is barking at you, acknowledge his masculine qualities. Tell him how handsome he is or ask him to share his best adventure story. He loves to talk about his successes, and it is important he does so. While he can be a bit touchy, do not be afraid of The Bull Rider's roar. An emotional event may have rendered him over-sensitive. He might be holding back tenderness because he doesn't want to appear too feminine.

To soften an unruly Bull Rider, give him gentle eye contact and share your feelings. What this beast needs is a hint of confident, feminine energy, and all will be well. He may have forgotten his most stunning adventures. He might not realize just how good he looks. To help this wild one get back on his bull, tell him he looks AWESOME!

EXTREME

Bull Riders have a hard time understanding reciprocity, tending to require the center of attention. When a pedestal is not available, Bull Riders can ride you just like they ride a bull: hard, tough and without apology. If the prima donna in your life is being unkind, let him know he cannot treat you like that. If he persists, take away his gold or kick him out of your corral.

No matter how much steam a Bull Rider has, it is never okay to run someone over or bully them. Did you ask for abuse or make yourself too vulnerable? The only person responsible for protecting you is YOU. Compassion and empathy can go a long way. Consider the other person's perspective and what she is feeling. Remember that some people need a little love before they can climb a mountain.

EMPOWERMENT

If you're feeling a bit too rough-and-tumble, it's time to soften up! Call your mom, go for a run, write in your journal, and consider refraining from drinking coffee or alcohol. You might find that your diet is creating mood swings and unwarranted aggression in your life. You might just need exercise.

The following healing modalities will give you a leg up as you ride the testosterone storm.

Colors: yellow, gold, goldenrod, olive, coral, dark orchid, violet, sea green, pink, blue

Gemstones: Aventurine, Peridot, Infinite Stone, Dioptase, Stromatolite, Lapis Lazuli, Pink Tourmaline, Cobaltoan Calcite

Flower Essences: Cherry Plum, Sweet Chestnut, Oak, Olive, Impatiens, Rock Rose, Aspen, Pine

Essential Oils: Ylang Ylang, Amethyst, Sandalwood, Juniper Berry, Lavender, Bergamot, Rose

Awaken your inner beast. Love him. Heal her. When you're ready, put effort toward the creation of an inspiring mission or adventure.

THE NAIVE

I live in a bubble within a bubble, all within a big, pretty, pink sphere. I am full of life and wonder, seeing the world as a place filled with possibility. I lead with my heart and I am often fearless. Sometimes I do not understand deception, which results in my feeling fooled or manipulated. Apparently, the nuances of complex situations escape me! I am easily distracted by my own fantasies, often appearing to be in another world, but my world is simply delicious! Ooh, look! A butterfly! Hi butterfly! I can fly too! Take me with you!

THE NAIVE

"It is always an amazing, beautiful world, until it is not."

MORSEL

Living in a state of bliss can yield tangible benefits that often outweigh any negativity.

MESSAGE

The brain is a powerful living organism that thrives on input and activity. It is a conduit-sponge that cross-migrates memories, thoughts and feelings according to our intentions and desires. Within the brain, is the conscious mind, a tool that gives our thoughts movement and flow.

The mind provides a deep and fertile soil that gives us the potential to grow any thought or action. As the managers of our minds, we can turn it on or off. We are the doer behind the mind's curtain, the wise and powerful Oz.

Given the powers of our minds, we can invoke the brightest lights in the universe. We can create miracles and change lives, or we can question the sweetest of gifts. Even Jesus, who attempted to heal and enlighten, was seen as a villain by some.

The Naive provides a vital lesson in keeping things simple and trusting simplicity when it appears. She reminds us of the possibility of goodness and sweetness in every part of our lives. She gently nudges us to close the research manuals, stop the analysis and simply believe. She even takes it a step further and asks us to celebrate the wonder of it all.

While this soul might be holding too tightly to the sweetest of perspectives, she inspires us to ask ourselves, "is it possible to be continually full of wonder?" She ensures us that the answer to this question is yes.

The Naive is a soft-hearted innocent whose natural inclination is to accept and support the happy events, ideas and people who come her way. She has a healthy detachment from physical reality which keeps her from getting to bogged down in the day-to-day details.

When you need a cheerleader or when you desire a low-maintenance experience with another human being, choose The Naive. She is receptive, flexible and forgiving.

The Naive rarely projects negativity into a situation or makes detrimental assumptions. Her life is void of the usual drama that the rest of us attract and endure.

If you have slipped into a negative groove lately, turning your back on goodness, become The Naive. Ignore harsh opinions and judgments, and appreciate the kind people around you.

Embrace positivity. There are infinite possibilities in your situation, preparing the ground for continued creativity and rebirth. To embrace The Naive is to invoke a durable and everlasting lightness of being.

CAUTION

As The Naive, a part of you may have been shielded and sheltered during early childhood, or you may have been exposed to such complexity and pain that you were shell-shocked into a kinder, more flexible perspective.

Make an inspired and wise choice by balancing your accrued wisdom with the innocence of a child. Take into account all parts of you as you embark on this next segment of your life. With a hint of softness and delight, you will feel a lighter load. As you allow yourself to remain open, there will be less stress and you will have more room in your life for the universe's sweet and simple gifts.

EXTREME

Because The Naive rarely stands up for herself, she is always at risk of losing everything. You may have recently lost something very special to you because you chose not to defend it.

It might be that you chose such a simple, loving view of the world that you too often ignore threats to your well-being. Always preserve and protect the light entrusted to you by the universe.

Let this be the last time you give up a part of yourself for the sake of something or someone else. Remember that details can provide immeasurable insight and warnings. Do not skip over them.

As you move forward in life, remain whole at every juncture. When a beautiful butterfly kisses your cheek, she might be honoring the innocent part of you or she might be kissing an expired part of you goodbye.

EMPOWERMENT

To get a handle on setting better boundaries, practice saying "no" in front of a mirror. Examine the attributes and qualities of your primary relationships. Make note of how you are treated, how you treat others and how you treat yourself. Seeing the world as magical is enjoyable, even preferable, but only if you take care of yourself throughout every experience.

The Naive may have forgotten his magical side. When was the last time you sat in a forest and spoke with the trees and breezes? They might have a helpful message for you!

Colors: forest green, orange, olive, saddle brown, dark blue, slate blue, dark red, purple

Gemstones: Jade, Bloodstone, Green Sardonyx, Dioptase, Red Coral, Red Calcite, Axinite, Chiastolite, Agate, Galena, Tiger's Eye, Malachite

Flower Essences: Olive, Yarrow, Beech, Clematis, Aspen, Gorse, Walnut, Gentian, Vervain, Star of Bethlehem

Essential Oils: Sage, Lavender, Cedarwood, Bay, Bay Laurel, Frankincense, Hyssop, Lemon, Myrtle

Outside our protective bubbles and illusions live incontrovertible realities. Maintain your sense of wonder, but leave the door ajar for truth.

THE ELECTRICITY

I enliven everything in my sight, utilizing a source far greater than me. Sometimes my efforts are disruptive, yet most often I accomplish miraculous feats. I walk into a room of acquaintances, and one of them spontaneously falls in love with me. I dance in a field and the adjacent barn collapses. I whisper to a friend, and their sick grandmother is healed. The rivers of life and rebirth move through me. Even at a distance, you'll feel a palpable force around me. I reshape reality with each thought.

THE ELECTRICITY

"My effectiveness expands upon my slightest intention."

MORSEL

Without encumbrances, we are limitless. Repelling nonsense, we protect our vibrance.

MESSAGE

We've all felt attracted to another living being. It is almost as if we are swept up by a hidden force. The same goes with objects. Some feel delicious in our hands, almost as if they are already a part of us. We feel something special when sitting on a specific park bench, while on another, we feel lost. A red apple might give us joy while the green one fails to inspire a bite.

There are energetic currents at work within each of us and within everything around us. This universal energy has the potential to connect us to or repel us from any person, event, object or idea. There are no breaks in this current. It is the source of all life unifying all beings and objects.

It follows that every one of us is connected to and related to everything that has ever existed, and everything that will exist in the future. Each of us shares something with every atom that has been created since the birth of consciousness. Given that, how can you say that you are incapable?

If you have a desire, the universe has the elements, currents and connective tissue to co-create it with you. Everything you desire is already you. It is in this way that we are all sorcerers able to manifest actions and events in our life with just one intention, one swing of our mighty staff.

The Electricity lives in all of us. She has the ability to produce a burst of energy and wield it in any direction to invoke change or rebirth. If there is debris in the way of her desires, she uses sadness (water) or anger (fire) to unclog her path and propel forward. To be clear and self-expressed, we must continually set energy free.

As The Electricity, your presence alone can assist a living being in their advancement. Simply by holding someone's hand or sharing your feedback with them, you can move mountains. The force within you is unlimited. It can create anything, including the things you desire for other people.

You may have emotional or psychological blocks preventing you from accessing the abundance of energy living in you. You might be so filled with excuses that it would take a miracle to break through your inertia and reach beyond your self-imposed limits. The key to achieving the things you desire most will not be found in your mind or your abilities. The crucial element is your resolve.

If The Electricity has stimulated your mind and heart today, stop making excuses. Clean out the blocks, tap into the source of life within you, and let it move you. Scrape the lining of your soul and express trapped emotions until you are free. Let the eternal current help you manifest the life you seek. **No one is coming to save you. The miracle you are seeking is YOU.**

CAUTION

The Electricity within you can become uncontrollable. Without realizing it, you can become a danger to yourself or others. Simply put, you might not be aware of how powerful you are.

There is no stopping a heavy rain in her effort to widen a river. That is what water does. As the rain pours onto the earth, our lakes and water sources swell. River levels rise and the river bed has no choice but to expand. It is the same with electric current.

Give the swelling force within you a healthy outlet. Cry, have sex, exercise, forgive deeply, write in your journal or all of the above. Find empowering modalities to help you establish a positive flow in your life. As you expel negative debris, be gentle. Release the beast and be free.

EXTREME

Just because you have access to powerful currents does not mean you should use them. Rage and unbridled anger can easily hurt you or others. Your aggression might not be an infringement on creation, but it could be considered unreasonable.

You may have been screwed over in business or in love. It might be that you were abused or forgotten. Whatever reasons you are using to feed your inner electrical storm, they are only excuses. The only reasonable choice is to forgive and let go. The time of negativity, self-abuse and hurtful outbreaks has ended. You must accept full responsibility for what is inside of you and you must intimately steer it into the light.

EMPOWERMENT

When emotions run high, those who embody The Electricity might experience a power surge or short circuit. If your wires are overloaded, get acupuncture, find a therapist or do yoga. It is up to you to clear the emotional residue nestled in your heart. Ground yourself by exploring trees and streams!

The colors of your clothes and the gems you wear can significantly affect your mood, mind and heart. Ingesting flower essences and applying diluted essential oils to your body (or diffusing them into the air) can improve your energy, attitude and drive. Enjoy exploring these recommendations.

Colors: blue, black, silver, dark green, indigo, magenta, aqua, white

Gemstones: Lapis Lazuli, Chiastolite, Stromatolite, Black Tourmaline, Green Sardonyx, Aquamarine, Turquoise

Flower Essences: Holly, Centaury, Chicory, Clematis, Olive, Star of Bethlehem, Vervain, Willow

Essential Oils: Rose, Cinnamon, Yarrow, Angelica Root, Bergamot, Cardamom, Coriander, Elemi, Lindon Blossom, Grapefruit

You are born of sound, light and current. You are a conduit for everlasting life. Do you know that you are electricity? Life emanates through you.

THE CALCULATED

My life is a chess board imbued with a colorful array of synchronized agendas, all of which support my well-devised plan to get what I want. I do not think simple thoughts. Every idea that comes to me has a deep complexity to it. I consider the emotions and circumstances that tie one person to another. I imagine what each player's secret might be. I fantasize about putting opposites together in order to achieve a stimulating outcome. I meticulously design all my plans long before I take even the smallest step. This alone might be the reason others fear me.

THE CALCULATED

"When it comes to getting what I want, I plan on it."

MORSEL

Consistent self-critique, fueled by drive and confidence, is a winning recipe for success.

MESSAGE

Nature, in all its beautiful complexity, seems a planned creation. Every grain of sand and molecule appear to be reckoned. The way shade crosses a landscape, how root systems seek out and absorb resources, and how stars and planets revolve around each other, are marvelous and miraculous.

These processes affirm the existence of a stunning array of intertwined agendas, each simultaneously serving their own purpose along with the purposes of the greater whole. It appears effortless.

When individuals give in to the flow of a collective pursuit, the process becomes Self-aware and everyone involved benefits. These types of pursuits are difficult to replicate. It's almost as if there is a super-consciousness overseeing the system of communication and goals.

When The Calculated pursues a goal, she becomes a kind of super-consciousness. She imagines twenty different moves at every turn, making sure every need is met along the way. Her ability to plan and scrutinize reveals enviable patience, which often results in praiseworthy achievements.

If The Calculated has landed on your square today, you have the ability to construct complex plans, akin to a Demi-God. You consider every outcome by evaluating every potential move and response. You have a brilliant mind, a profound tool that can provide immeasurable value to your life.

If you're feeling out of balance or in jeopardy, you may have either planned too much, planned too little, or not planned at all. Without a well-constructed plan, the results can be inconclusive. When you're more prepared, you can adjust various levers to achieve desired results.

You have the opportunity to develop a brilliant, methodical plan for this next phase of your life. Sit quietly, write in your journal, and calculate a set of actions that will get you what you want. Consider the feelings of everyone involved, but remember to stay true to yourself and your vision.

Keep your ego in check, remembering to honor your goals over your swagger. When receiving feedback on your plans and ideas, be openminded. Whether it's the color of a logo or the price of your service, if you cannot listen to your customers or partners, you are probably more fascinated with control than you are with creating.

Think like a mastermind, add a sprinkle of 007, and you will have the perfect recipe for rooted, lasting success. Along the way, be sure to keep your self-admiration in check. Honor your teammates, friends and family, making sure to take them along for the ride. It's time to bring something special to life.

CAUTION

Some of the world's successful conquerors were defeated because they failed to take into account the grave nature of their situation. Moments before they imploded, they still refused to change plans. Our egos can bring the best of us to our knees. History's most powerful conquerers often choose greed and control over true leadership and substance.

The most successful plans are the ones imbued with intelligence and heart. As you explore the possibilities, merge your vulnerable heart with your brilliant mind so you might conjure the ultimate step-by-step plan for your endeavor. In perfect balance, you'll be unstoppable.

When planning your next big dream, imagine something that not only brings you success, but also provides value for future generations. Compassion is a great investment.

EXTREME

The critical voices in our minds are often inspired by one of our parents. These daunting voices can give us pause moments before we step into our power or take a final step in victory. Whether our fathers are kindhearted or harsh, they are not the cause of our stumbling. We are.

Our plans may have been inadequate or our actions poorly timed. You may have overestimated yourself or underestimated others. You might have pushed so hard that your heart quit working.

While the current situation did not meet your standards, you collected valuable lessons. As you rework your plan, put that knowledge to good use. Do not to let the resulting drama impound the casualties. Make note of where you need to improve, refrain from gossip, and honor yourself. Stay focused, take nothing personally, and find the joy in everything you do.

EMPOWERMENT

When our eyes are glued on the prize, stress and negativity can bring The Calculated to her knees. For this intellectually-obsessed personality, there is nothing more relaxing and transformative than physical exercise and sexual release. Consider joining a gym or finding a lover. The Calculated must purge all festering negativity or she'll find herself consumed by shadows.

It's exciting to explore colors, gemstones, flower essences and essential oils. When we incorporate these things into our lives, we can increase our energy, alertness, passion and joy.

Colors: aqua, yellow, violet, cornflower blue, sea green, turquoise, plum, deep pink

Gemstones: Yellow Fluorite, Citrine, Blue Quartz, Blue Calcite, Tanzanite, Dioptase, Azurite

Flower Essences: Aspen, Beech, Clematis, Elm, Gorse, Rock Water, Vine, Water Violet

Essential Oils: Violet Leaf, Ylang Ylang, Rose, Sandalwood, Patchouli, Bitter Orange, Anise

Every new thought creates a fresh trajectory. Regularly prune your thoughts. Trust your heart. It can sense changing tides.

THE SEEKING SOLACE

Challenges whirl around me like pinwheels and floating leaves. They distract me from my unique gifts, talents and attributes. I have such goodness within me! Why have I become so suspicious of my circumstances and distrusting of my natural impulses? I see angels looking over me and I see the light on the horizon, but I feel momentarily impaired. I am kind, loving, courageous and ready to shine brightly again. I ask good forces to come to my aid and guide me into the light where I belong.

THE SEEKING SOLACE

"Although I am momentarily impeded, I trust good forces will soon uplift me."

MORSEL

Without attention on the light, shadowy vines creep through memories to challenge the soul.

MESSAGE

Faint memories of events-gone-by can remain in our minds for years. What ties us to these memories is not our desire to improve them, it is our obsession with the past. We imagine things might be better if did something a little different. Truth be told, we can never go back. The past no longer exists.

Following a rain, trees soak up the water for nourishment. A broken leg heals in time, sometimes stronger than it was before. As it is with nature, so it is with our souls. We can always begin again. Even a computer has a reboot button.

We rarely benefit from exhuming the past. Even our memories are not what they once were, every one of them tainted by time, circumstance and emotion. We continue to reference these memories, exiting the present moment. In doing so, we disconnect from the natural flow.

The Seeking Solace is at an exciting precipice. While temporarily hovering after a time of disappointment, he has chosen to release toxic thoughts and return to happiness. By putting faint shadows and impressions behind him, The Seeking Solace opens up to light, love and other gifts from the universe.

If you are The Seeking Solace, you deserve all the compassion in the world. You have been hiding in a comfortless room, focused on ideas that do not serve you. You allowed your mind to attach to beliefs that bound your heart in sadness and fear. You twisted prior experience into a weapon which you used to incarcerate yourself. It is time to let go, resurrect and stand firmly in the light. Your dance with your prior identity and life is complete.

Like all of us, The Seeking Solace forgets to love herself. Becoming temporarily distracted by her confusion, she squanders her joy and creativity. To fully resurrect herself, The Seeking Solace must take continual action toward faith, hope and love. Refresh her mind with helpful suggestions and unabashed affection. She is moments away from remembering all that she is.

When good things come to us, they rarely arrive with a parade. They most often appear as a whisper. When we forget to listen to the sweet whispers from our higher selves, we miss out on special gifts and timely opportunities. Listen carefully for the whispers of kindness, synchronicity and opportunity.

We need only take small steps to bring our life back into focus. The moment we choose to be fully in the present, universal light and love come to our aid. Allow your hidden wisdom to illuminate your path. Stay in the present moment and enjoy the sweetness around you. It's time to begin again.

CAUTION

If The Seeking Solace has made an impression on you, you might be lying to yourself about the details of your life and perpetuating your own misery. It's time to swiftly return to the present moment. Focus on what is in front of you. Open yourself up to goodness and warmth. Let emotions pour from your heart so that you can be free. Call a friend, go for a hike, cook a meal for a loved one.

When The Seeking Solace is feeling sad or lonely, she has a tendency to spread negativity and gossip, sometimes about herself. She can also become so isolated, she forgets how much love is available to her. Be gentle with her. With your kindness and affection, she will soon let down her guard and see herself more clearly. Her mindset is temporary.

It is your birthright to be happy. Give in to the loving hearts around you. Focus on positivity. When we meditate on the rose, we become the rose.

EXTREME

You may have driven your mind so far in the wrong direction that you barely remember yourself. Forgetting our nature, we can wander aimlessly for days. Many of us have made a series of triple-nested mistakes and found it difficult to get back in the game. When we dance too long with negativity, our knees and immune systems become weak. Our past obsessions can lock us up for what feels like an eternity. It's time to give up those ghosts! Rewrite your story from a new perspective. You have everything you need to make a change.

EMPOWERMENT

The Seeking Solace might need a gentle intervention. Consider bringing close friends together for a night of support. Bring to light the behavior you have witnessed and discuss ways you can help.

A regimen of flower essences and essential oils can break mental and emotional binds. Spiritual exercises like Tai Chi, Yoga, and Aikido bring about renewed energy and rebirth.

It's exciting to explore colors and gemstones. When we incorporate these things into our lives, we can increase our energy, alertness, passion and joy.

Colors: ivory, turquoise, honeydew, lavender, sky blue, mint cream, light yellow

Gemstones: Blue Sapphire, Yellow Sapphire, Howlite, White Aragonite, Lemon Quartz, Honey Calcite, Azurite, Azurite-Malachite, Corundum, Lapis Lazuli

Flower Essences: Clematis, Heather, Rock Rose, Vine, Water Violet, Pine, Honeysuckle, Beech, Agrimony, Star of Bethlehem, Apsen, Cerato

Essential Oils: Lavender, Sandalwood, Anise, Cardamom, Rose, Clove Bud, Geranium, Ginger

Your life is far more interesting than the old movie playing in your mind. Change the channel to NOW. With sincere effort, a pleasurable life will soon emerge.

THE SKATER

I'm a success-minded equal opportunist who enjoys light and limited engagements. I avoid intimacy whenever possible. When I give a firm "yes," what I mean is "I am partially committed until I negotiate a better position." I achieve success with the least number of complications and with the utmost speed, but sometimes I skip loyalties, details and deeper truths. By the way, I have another opportunity I would like to discuss with you. Interested?

THE SKATER

"I might not be fully engaged or in it for the long haul, but I'm incredibly effective."

MORSEL

Partnering with a soul who does not value lasting virtue is akin to making love with a ghost.

MESSAGE

When our hearts are repeatedly pierced, we can develop a behavioral tick in the form of detachment. While to others we might appear mysterious, we are actually numb and aloof, desperately trying to synthesize emotions. Although we are unable to connect with ourselves or the world, we somehow come off as attractive.

The Skater is the perfect example of an outward success with a personality quirk. On the surface he appears strong and capable, but when we scratch beneath it, we learn he can be distant or withdrawn. Our gut tells us that something is amiss.

The Skater's style and lingo are impressive. His nonchalance makes us feel relaxed and comfortable. His words are uncomplicated yet effective, but they can also be nondescript. A meeting with The Skater can reveal a beautiful vision, but he might unknowingly mislead us down an unqualified path.

Skaters are charming and brilliant, often the best instructors in the school of life, but they can be self-protective and unclear about their loyalties. When dealing with The Skater, keep your heart open just enough to seize an opportunity, but be on alert for things that do not feel right to you.

If the shadow aspects of The Skater are appealing, dig deep to determine your motivations. You may believe that being emotionally detached or having an edge over others to be useful, but these things can be disappointing and can lead to a shallow life.

It might be time for The Skater to reboot by seeking a major change of life. This could be the day you restart everything with more heart, compassion and transparency. With an earnest heart, honesty and intimacy rule the day.

As you reengage the world, create clear, reciprocal relationships. Be comfortable in your own skin, taking all parts of you into every interaction. Be upfront with a clear list of delights and demands. Risk a tiny bit of your heart. This lets people know that you're sincere.

In all relationships and dealings, ask for references before you tango. Consider every piece of your agreements with care. The universe is comprised of light and shadow. Sometimes we must accept both of these aspects in the people and projects we embrace.

If your shadow-self is preventing you from moving forward, seek clarification by looking within, or ask The Skater a few pertinent questions. To engage from the most powerful and fulfilling place, clear your mind and heart with love, then seize the day!

CAUTION

It might be that you or your partner is unwilling to give what is needed or agreed. While loyalty, commitment and work ethic cannot be taught, they can be encouraged or outlined in a contract.

A dangerous game may be afoot. If your intuition is nibbling at your ear, take inventory of your suspicions and share them with your partner. Keep an eye out for his reactions and excuses. If your suspicions are correct, seek a transition or renegotiate.

You have a chance to transform this situation into something favorable while maintaining (or recapturing) integrity. Do not over-think it. Get on the honesty train and demand the clarity you deserve.

EXTREME

When you first set out on your current endeavor, you maintained a healthy measure of compassion and positivity. Somewhere along the way, your shadow-self hijacked the deal. It's time to take charge and right the ship. Instead of creating hurdles and challenges, build lasting bridges. Negative actions result in the loss of friends, fame, money, happiness or all of the above.

You may have set fire to your creation because your intentions were conflicted. It might be that your scheme was a way to pay off a debt or salvage a prior project. Examine your motivations and clean up the mess. Do the personal work required to get your life on a heartfelt path, where the impulses to stray or betray are outside the realm of possibility.

EMPOWERMENT

The Skater sometimes dishonors herself and those around her. It might be time for her to seek help from a coach or therapist. Take a day to reflect on your actions. Write in your journal, unearthing wisdom and expressing emotions. Always be moving forward, advancing your personhood.

You are part of a greater whole, connected to every living being. When you see yourself as separate, you miss out on the meaning of life. Love and honor all beings. You are connected to everything.

The colors of your clothes and the gems you wear can significantly affect your mood, mind and heart. Ingesting flower essences and applying diluted essential oils to your body (or diffusing them into the air) can improve your energy, attitude and drive. Enjoy these recommendations.

Colors: dark violet, goldenrod, dark orchid, light coral, sea green, steel blue, white, magenta

Gemstones: White Sapphire, Pink Sapphire, Blue Apatite, Chrysocolla, Rhodochrosite, Green Sardonyx, Pink Tourmaline

Flower Essences: Agrimony, Chestnut Bud, Crab Apple, Heather, Holly, Pine, Water Violet

Essential Oils: Basil, Black Pepper, Ylang Ylang, Coriander, Yarrow, Hyssop, Helichrysum, Cardamom, Benzoin, Anise, Angelica

Free yourself from egoistic positions and enjoy affirming cascades of awareness.

THE COPYCAT

I'm fascinated by other people's success. What attracts me most is the creativity of an artist or the vision of a notable innovator. While it feels normal to me, my attraction has a tendency to escalate into a bit of obsession. Once under its influence, I duplicate talents, personalities, styles and attitudes. The focus of my pursuits might be my boss, husband, closest friend or a celebrity. Sometimes I'll copy several people, without them ever knowing. I seek to fulfill an unknown part of me, hoping that by following in the footsteps of excellence, I will find my own unique way.

THE COPYCAT

"Were it that easy to say something new, I would have invented worlds by now."

MORSEL

Inspiration born from external influences has an expiration date.

MESSAGE

The media encourages society to look externally for self-worth. We see pretty pictures and emulate them, buying into stories that often prove to be of little value in the development of our uniquenesses.

It's quite a challenge to uncover our hidden gems. Our lives are so busy and our minds so cluttered, we can barely remember to breathe, let alone carve out time to explore our depth and abilities.

When we allow ourselves to settle into a deep silence in search of an inner-knowing, we unfurl beautiful tapestries filled with ancient wisdom and knowledge. It is here in the quietest parts of our minds that we will find our most precious and delicious gifts.

At the start of their careers, Copycats often align themselves with notable luminaries. They research styles and inventions, spending time emulating those who inspire them most. By doing so, a creator or thinker will advance her own style and perspective. The challenge she must face is to eventually ween herself off of other people's brilliance.

Since The Copycat spends more time copying than innovating, he'll eventually feel frustrated, never fully challenging himself or advancing his talents. To be a true artist or creator, he'll need to learn to take risks. Most importantly, The Copycat must push herself beyond every measure of comfort.

The Copycat is a newly inspired artist still suckling on the breasts of masters. She is committed to the path of innovation, but she is unaware of the growth and processes that await her. She might spend one percent of her day creating or thinking something that is truly unique. The rest of the time is spent mulling over possibilities and perseverating on the talents of those who came before her.

Once in the groove of creating, The Copycat can invent and innovate with ease. The challenge is finding a path that leads to this groove. Once she finds it, she must endeavor to give birth to her creations without fear or judgment. She must practice this as often as possible.

Some Copycats give up on themselves and fail to achieve something unique in this world. He might be the next Stephen Hawking or Steve Jobs, but he continues to belittle or deny his own gifts.

If you love to create, take inventory of your talents and attributes. Look at the accomplishments in your life. Remember the instances where your talents were validated and enjoyed by others. It is time that you stepped out of the shadows and into the light. Give your uniqueness the stage it deserves.

Take it all to the next level Every living being has access to a secret garden. Find yours and nurture it to life. Doing so, you'll experience an astounding inner-abundance.

CAUTION

Are you telling yourself the same old story again? The one where you don't get to do what you love? This story is not true. You have a stunning creative spark, but you do not exercise it. Move on from your story so that you can achieve the level you seek.

It's time to up-level your work ethic. Look to the stars for inspiration! Even if you fail to complete your mission to Mars, you'll end up traversing the galaxy, which is awesome!

Since you have never given yourself proper credit or enough time to explore your value, it is time to dig deep and heal your core.

Make a list of the secret, simple things you wish to achieve. Let the world know you want to share your core gifts. Stand tall, shout to the heavens and shine as brightly as the sun.

EXTREME

When you continually choose to dishonor your best attributes, your spirit becomes comfortable. This is no time to rest! Be whole and fully self-expressed. It is your divine right to experience the fruits of the gifts that live at the seat of your soul. Let go of excuses and create!

You have exhausted your personal network exploring derivative ideas and agendas, but your true work is beautiful, alive and full of inspiration. There is no time like the present moment to reinvigorate yourself, believe in yourself and reach for the stars.

EMPOWERMENT

Make a list of the things you acquired or copied from someone else. Be honest about the origin of your beliefs, clothes, possessions, education and friendships. You might find that the entirety of YOU is the result of a long history of choices based in propaganda and self-deceit. Tap into your nature, look in the mirror and make a decision to end all duplicating. Find an art therapist. Gently peak into your past and release emotions that are blocking you. Let wisdom arise.

The colors of your clothes and the gems you wear can significantly affect your mood, mind and heart. Ingesting flower essences and applying diluted essential oils to your body (or diffusing them into the air) can improve your energy, attitude and drive. Enjoy these recommendations.

Colors: dark blue, dark violet, dark pink, dark orchid, orange, firebrick red, purple, midnight blue

Gemstones: Blue Aventurine, Purpurite, Zoisite, Aventurine, Grossularite, Orange Kyanite, Fire Opal, Ruby

Flower Essences: Olive, Elm, Centaury, Cherry Plum, Heather, Honeysuckle, Star of Bethlehem

Essential Oils: Lemon Balm, Spruce, Bergamot, Cardamom, Frankincense, Hyssop, Ylang Ylang

Let stillness bring to light the depth of your uniqueness. Not knowing your value, how can your dance be true?

THE COMEDIAN

I hold several conflicting philosophies at once, all of which are at war within me. I bring their voices to life using metaphor and humor, often while each seeks to undo the other. With an unquenchable thirst for irreverence, I break through boundaries that constrict reality, using honest and critical thinking. I am a seeker of truth and confrontation. As I ingest then discharge toxic ideas, for a moment, I hate myself. For every truth I expel, I see ten more that crave my attention.

THE COMEDIAN

"I judge the world with unbridled humor, opening doors to more truthful realities."

MORSEL

Once the veil is removed and the rabbit hole uncovered, the excavation of truth has no end. Eventually we realize that religion and society are derived mostly from 6000 year-old folk tales.

MESSAGE

Whatever we think we know, whatever we believe we have experienced, is most often not even a shadow of the truth. Original memories change the moment we store them. They mix with beliefs, attitudes and emotions. The resulting concoction is nothing but fantasy. Eventually our memories embody only fractions of our original experiences. The originating events are long gone.

The most popular notions around politics, religion, planned obsolescence, the environment, energy and the education system were created for one reason: profitability. While some of these fairy tales might provide comfort, they are temporary illusions used to perpetuate exclusion and greed.

When we base our lives on illusion, we limit ourselves. When we confront our false beliefs and identities, we become more in touch with who we are. We become free. We become limitless.

The Comedian believes that society must be freed from its intellectual and behavioral prisons. Answering this call, he challenges our falsehoods so that we can let it all out and let it all go. He knows that every laugh is an awareness. It's the noise our soul makes when it sees itself clearly.

The Comedian shines light on the shadows we've ingested, helping us avoid delusion and disease. He's the angry priest pushing us to rethink our understandings and realities. He is not beholden to any group or philosophy, which means he does not owe anybody anything. This benefits all of us.

The Comedian asks, "Do you really believe that?! If so, here are some ideas that prove your beliefs are ill-informed. You're welcome!"

We might grow more from a brilliant set of jokes than we would at an entire week of Kundalini Yoga. When our attachments to false realities are severed, we nudge closer to a better understanding of ourselves and society.

If The Comedian has confronted you today, it's time to get real with your life, job and relationships. It's time to reboot your operating system with better software. It's time to reprogram.

When false data is removed, the result is a more poignant, elegant equation. Deconstruct your beliefs and identity so that you can enjoy a more truthful perspective. While you might have moments of extreme discomfort, there is nothing to fear.

Step out of your manufactured dream. Let humor enlighten you. Laugh, let go and be free.

CAUTION

The life of a Comedian can produce intangible repercussions. With every joke comes a bit of karma. With every moment of comedic aggression comes a hardening of the soul. Let humor dissolve the edges of your identity. When we allow humor to touch us, we become more real, more humane and more in line with our spirit.

You may have bought into a lie that advanced your position and success. Ultimately, with every acquiescence, a part of us becomes imprisoned. You might be living in dreams that oppress your deeper nature.

When we live without the pretense that family and modern culture feeds us, we see things more clearly. We learn that the truth is vastly more interesting than contrivance. You are a clear vibration, attracting the most truthful of possibilities. Allow yourself to see things as they are.

EXTREME

You're becoming a humorless authoritarian. When new ideas come your way, relax into them and give them the time of day. What if this is the revolution you've been anticipating? Take the time to open up to new possibilities at every turn.

Make a list of the arrogant beliefs you maintained and use humor to reinvent yourself. Take inventory of the lies and excuses you've used to defend yourself. Deflate your ego and be self-deprecating so that others will feel more comfortable around you. You might just attract the love of your life.

Find laughter in the dissonance between how others see you and how you see yourself. As a foe, humor will cut you at the knees. As a friend, humor takes you on memorable rides. Hold on lightly and enjoy a miraculous, transformative journey with The Comedian!

EMPOWERMENT

Although his brash style might ruffle feathers, The Comedian needn't apologize for telling the truth. She is on a noble path and her pursuit of clarity is commendable. Be aware that her toxic thoughts and negativity can have a damaging effect on her body and emotions. She needs love and rest.

Try experimenting with the colors and gemstones you wear. Consider looking into these recommended flower essences and essential oils. You might find they open your mind and heart.

Colors: turquoise, blue, spring green, hot pink, purple, white smoke

Gemstones: Lapis Lazuli, Blue Lace Agate, Howlite, Charoite, Lemon Quartz, Purpurite, Amethyst

Flower Essences: Agrimony, Beech, Aspen, Crab Apple, Gorse, Honeysuckle, Pine, Rock Rose, Star of Bethlehem

Essential Oils: Ylang Ylang, Yarrow, Vetiver, Rose, Myrtle, Juniper Berry, Helichrysum, Patchouli

We laugh when our ideas are abruptly juxtaposed against truth. When illusions and delusions are brought to light, all beings in the universe benefit.

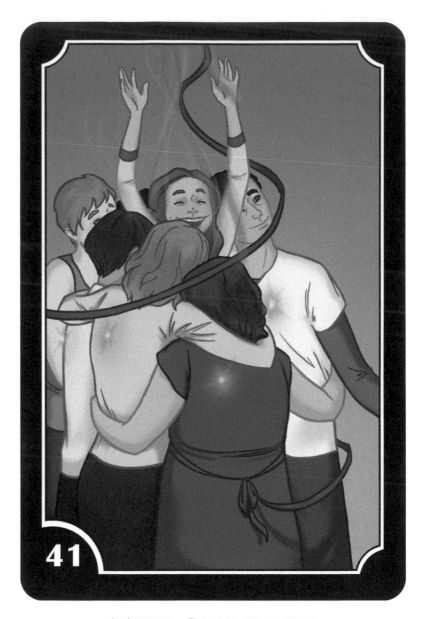

THE CUDDLER

I love to feel a gentle creature pressed against me. I relish the warmth of their skin and the soothing heart beat. The sweet tingle that arises from my belly and the intoxicating flush of comfort are palpable and nurturing. There are so many ways to connect physically with another. It might be our feet resting atop each other, our hands firmly clasped, our arms and legs outstretched and intertwined or our lips tickling, moist and soft. As I bond with another, I acquiesce and embrace their heart as if it were my own. Curl me up. Let's heal this life and the next.

THE CUDDLER

"When enveloped by warm caresses, my heart opens and I am truly at rest."

MORSEL

When our bodies are caressed, positive vibrations pass between the physical form and ease the soul.

MESSAGE

Our skin is our largest organ, connected to the majority of our bodily functions. When we soothe the skin, we nurture ourselves from head to toe. With every touch we experience comes a bit of healing.

It might be a full-body hug, a gentle caress on the arm or a wet kiss on the cheek. We crave physical intimacy, and when we experience it, our lives and worlds are brighter.

If The Cuddler is snuggling next to you, allow the sweet animal within you to give and receive as much affection as possible. Instead of thinking about sex, remain focused on intimacy and connection. Enjoy being embraced in a way that opens your heart and brings you joy.

When are lives become too busy, we can miss the cues that can heal us. The sweet glance, the touch on the arm and the gentle nibble on the ear. If our minds are too filled with distracting thoughts, we won't be able to recognize what is being offered to us and how we might feel about it.

Some religions say that affection induces attachment, and that we must renounce physical pleasures to know the Self. These types of restrictions are intended for a particular category of spiritual aspirant. Renunciation of worldly activities moves us no further toward emancipation (nirvana) than the life that yields to the desires of the heart. All paths with correct intention move toward the light.

The Cuddler understands the value of affection. She knows that one cuddle or massage can change the direction of someone's life. She proclaims, "Everyone needs to be touched!"

It might be that your friend or partner is stressed out, lost in his work, and unable to connect with his body. Since he can't relax, he might be losing sleep and may have lost touch with his emotions. Give him the sweet gift of cuddling so that he might come fully back to life again.

You may have forsaken your own physical needs in order to focus on the needs of your family or job. Ask your parter for the type of affection you enjoy most so that you can feel whole again. Fill a bathtub with hot water and essential oils, then gently massage your scalp, arms and legs. Sometimes your the best candidate to nurture yourself.

Rolling around on a comfy bed, playfully touching and kissing a friend or lover is a beautiful thing to behold. Allow yourself the riches and comforts of this life by reaching out to a trustworthy soul for the gift of touch. It will warm your heart and bring light to your life.

Physical intimacy opens energy gates that feed our bodies and minds. It is not rocket science. If you need somatic touch, create it, invite it into your life, and enjoy it!

CAUTION

You may have seen parental figures exchange emotional or physical abuse as a style of communication. You may have been misled as to what affection truly is. You may have experienced an infringement when being physical or sexual with someone at an earlier age.

The past is long gone and you need not be afraid. Let the touch of another human being be a gentle salve on the wounds in your heart. Consider having physical intimacy with a friend while remaining clothed. Being touched has the potential to heal our fears.

You need not attach to a cuddling partner or define the relationship you have with them. You need only enjoy that which your heart enjoys. Once affection has been shared, it is permissible to let go and move on, unless both of you desire a deepening of your relationship.

EXTREME

If you have more intimacy with your cat than you do with human beings, there might be cause for alarm. If your home smells more like kitty litter than baked bread, your future in terms of human intimacy might be limited. When parts of us shut down, we become less magnetic and attractive.

To attract a nourishing relationship, be conscious of the signals you send to visitors, courtiers and the universe. Be exact in what you want. Make your home welcoming in smell, sight and sound. It might be a job, habit or addiction that is preventing a nurturing partner from entering your life. It might be memories from a past relationship, or your devotion to television or food. Free yourself from distractions so that you can inspire another human being to enjoy your sweet gifts.

EMPOWERMENT

If The Cuddler has emerged weak and dependent, engage a therapist to help you with intimacy challenges. As you explore what your heart and body need, release trapped emotions. The universe is always available to assist you in finding a loving connection with a warm and loving human being.

The colors of your clothes and the gems you wear can significantly affect your mood, mind and heart. Ingesting flower essences and applying diluted essential oils to your body (or diffusing them into the air) can improve your energy, attitude and drive. Enjoy these recommendations.

Colors: green, goldenrod, chocolate, dark orange, orchid, firebrick red, dark sky blue, dark pink

Gemstones: Rose Quartz, Malachite, Ruby, Garnet, Jade, Dioptase, Blue Apetite, Tanzanite, Rhodocrosite, Rhodonite, Green Aventurine, Apache Tear

Flower Essences: Holly, Red Chestnut, Pine, Chicory, Aspen, Chestnut Bud, Mimulus, Vervain, Wild Rose, Water Violet

Essential Oils: Ginger, Jasmine, Rose, Anise, Bay Laurel, Bergamot, Clove Bud, Violet Leaf

Kisses and cuddles are fun, but the most enduring assurances come from within.

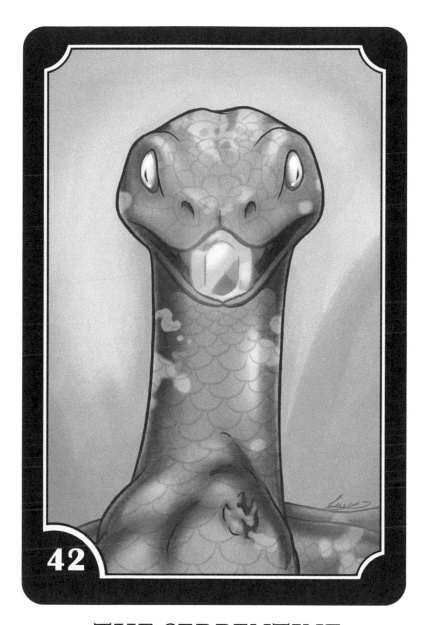

THE SERPENTINE

Whether for myself or in service to another, I am ever on the hunt for position, pleasure and gain. I'm sly, clever and charming, secretly fulfilling dreams with whatever methods are most effective. When I seduce you, you'll barely remember it, thinking it a pleasurable dream. I move mountains, inspire coups and sometimes disrupt trust. It's all for the greater good, or at least that's what I tell myself. Whether shadow or light, I command it. You might be leery of me, but in the end, you'll be satiated.

THE SERPENTINE

"With a cunning nod to your most subtle vulnerabilities, I'll earn your obedience."

MORSEL

The light and dark forces in the universe comprise a unified energy field that serves itself.

MESSAGE

The universe does not keep track of our wealth, status or offspring. We do not advance spirituality by building an empire, growing a family or following a religion. The universe does not make note of our mistakes or successes. It requires nothing of us. It is not the alpha and omega. We are.

We advance when we learn to move through life without attachment. We advance every time we embrace a softer part of our being. We grow when we see our pursuits and relationships for what they are: pieces of our nature interacting in a dream. We progress when we let go.

While most of the world lives according to misguided fairy tales handed down by religions, The Serpentine exposes the disingenuous stories that have lulled humanity into complacency for centuries. When The Serpentine whispers in our ears, we see things for what they are.

The Serpentine will smile and promise you the world, hoping to hand you the keys to the kingdom that you have long sought. He will coax you out of your slumber and into your very own hand-crafted reality. The Serpentine is the motivator and reality-check you've been seeking.

This Serpentine keeps things simple, encouraging you to do what is best for you, regardless of how it affects others. He reminds you of your fire, anger and sadness so that you will be more motivated to thrust forward in your life. The Serpentine says, "Rip the bandaid off and face yourself without fear!"

If The Serpentine has slithered into your hen house, he is here to hold a mirror to your self-denial. To satiate him, think selfishly and create a plan that serves your gifts and dreams. Honor his requests and you will right the scales in your favor.

The Serpentine does not focus on relationships of commitments, rather, she places emphasis on the forgotten wisdom that lives in the shadows. She'll seduce you into serving your ambitions, drawing nourishment from the changes she inspires.

This sometimes devilish creature is your missing piece. She opens dungeons and caves that you were trained to ignore. Engage her earnestly and you will meet yourself for the first time.

While The Serpentine's charm can be disarming, be careful of his hiss. If you betray this alliance, he might hand you a beautiful gem, infused with a curse. Remain aware of underlying repercussions and stay focused on the goals at hand.

Engage The Serpentine so that you will know the depth of your abilities and the value of your quality. Your kind-hearted intentions will provoke his light, resulting in hidden treasure.

CAUTION

When we move through life without stopping to consider the results of our actions, we tend to attract the same lessons over and over again. With prior conflicts unresolved, you may have subconsciously invited disloyalty or betrayal. While temporary, this should give you pause.

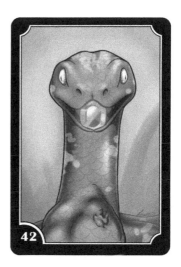

When there is upheaval, make note of the disruptions and infringements in play. As you separate fact from fiction, keep friends and allies close. You may have pushed a someone too hard, and in the process, damaged a relationship. There may be jealousy afoot. Examine your motivations and be honest with yourself. The more you can acknowledge, the quicker you can integrate.

Forgiveness and integrity are the orders of the day. With the utmost compassion, you can convert this snake into a King. It is said that one open heart can shift a nation.

EXTREME

The Serpentine enjoys enrolling others in charades. They use slights of hand and dramatic storytelling to win hearts and votes. The Serpentine may have given your loyal confidants a reason to pause the next time they consider backing you. While The Serpentine might enjoy his temporary position, he knows that he lost something special when he hurt you.

Take inventory of what you chose to do here and why. On some level you knew this person would be your shadowy twin. You permitted this because you wanted the universe to give you a lesson that would expand your self-understanding. When you choose to look at this situation responsibly, you will realize that you participated in the creation of a new you.

EMPOWERMENT

The Serpentine often needs lessons in compassion. Work for a non-profit or community project. Help out at a soup kitchen. To move past her plotting nature, The Serpentine must serve humanity. If you are living in a light-filled bubble, having forsaken your shadow-self, you might consider boxing or martial arts. To be more integrated, bring your trapped emotions to the surface.

The colors of your clothes and the gems you wear can significantly affect your mood, mind and heart. Ingesting flower essences and applying diluted essential oils to your body (or diffusing them into the air) can improve your energy, attitude and drive. Enjoy these recommendations.

Colors: white, ivory, lavender, dark green, cyan, blue, turquoise

Gemstones: Chrysocolla, Blue Sapphire, White Selenite, Lapis Lazuli, Pink Tourmaline, Dioptase, Fire Agate, Amethyst, Jade, Blue Tourmaline, Black Jasper

Flower Essences: Beech, Aspen, Cerato, Crab Apple, Holly, Rock Water, Willow, Chestnut Bud

Essential Oils: Rose, Citronella, Clove Bud, Juniper Berry, Sandalwood, Fennel, Grapefruit

When we steal from someone, we steal from the Self. There is no "other."

THE TWO MINDS

I have the ability to simultaneously pursue two opposing agendas, successfully bringing each of them to completion. While this might not bode well for my integrity, stress level or personal life, I remain unscathed. When all is said and done, neither party is at a loss. Since there's no reason to assume a trusted ally would play both sides, it is not easy to catch me. I am a secret squirrel, a master negotiator, and I play to win - for all.

THE TWO MINDS

"I compartmentalize my loyalties to make room for simultaneous successes."

MORSEL

While a fractured pursuit might be tempting, a congruent mind and heart yield a sturdy wholeness.

MESSAGE

Constructing a plan that's beneficial for every stakeholder can be quite a feat. There might be multiple people or groups with unique and specific needs. There might be secrets or tangential influences that must be addressed in order for everyone to feel whole and heard. Given all these complexities, progress, agreement and flow can be elusive.

The Two Minds is a brilliant negotiator who understands how to achieve balance and equanimity within the most intricate pursuits. She is a powerful opportunist, unencumbered by a moral code. While she seeks to benefit herself, the result is most often that every player at the table is served.

This deep-thinking soul often behaves like a spy, coordinating arrays of desires and expectations from the shadows. While her goal is to funnel the value from the collective effort to her benefit, she enjoys and thrives on pleasing others.

The Two Minds is difficult to fathom and assess. He is neither transparent or easily readable. To keep discussions and agendas moving in positive directions, he keeps most of the details to himself. This ensures his personal satisfaction and guarantees the achievement of the broader, unifying goals.

It might be that you have overcomplicated a recent situation. You may have played both sides of the fence, but not effectively enough to further relationships or establish consensus. Consider reevaluating the positions you have supported. Look for holes and inconsistencies. When you are more prepared, return to the conversation with a fresh perspective.

It's not always possible to serve two masters. Sometimes conflicting agendas can confuse and derail everyone involved. It might be that in this situation, it's best to allow one party to enjoy the upper hand. Negotiate a position that allows for continued dialogue. Open minds should prevail.

As potential resolutions are discussed, remember that each person represents an aspect of you. Consider the wide array of personal lessons that are represented here. Take advantage of every growth opportunity. With clear language and a calm mind, you can achieve anything.

You might consider putting all your ideas together into one transparent solution, creating a hybrid that serves a higher purpose. Use your love, insight and brilliance to integrate the aspects in play. Look into the hearts of every person at the table. Seek ways to engage and motivate them in the deal.

Serving two masters can create two karmic paths, both of which might need to be resolved so that you can live in the light. Congruence most often begets momentum and happiness.

CAUTION

Being a double-agent has a great advantage: you feel empowered because you know that you are the only one who has all the information. While this pedestal may be enjoyable for a time, having a position like this can be intoxicating and short lived. Unless you are creating an outcome that is truly beneficial for everyone involved, secretly opposing a contracted partner is never the best choice.

Avoid the potential mess and salvage the situation. Pick one person in this scenario to exclusively serve with all your heart, seeking no remuneration. You might lose something material or egoistic in this exchange, but you will preserve your spirit.

EXTREME

The idea of living like an underworld spy must be appealing to you. While this bodes well for an adventurous life, you might have to endure some loneliness. Although glamorous, secret agents often feel separate from the rest of the world, never feeling fully loved by other human beings.

You are far more brilliant and resourceful than you realize. If you choose, you could easily carve a more evolved and loving path, one that leads to clarity, generosity, and resolution for all. Sit quietly and admit your mistakes. Make apologies. Those with a forgiving heart will appreciate your effort.

Take inventory of your traits, release attachment to the negative ones, embrace the positives and begin again. There is no time like the present to make a better choice.

EMPOWERMENT

The Two Minds may have had early influencers in his life who were a bit duplicitous. These personalities may have encouraged him to adopt a less-than honest mindset. Engage a personal coach or mentor to help you reframe your early experiences and advance your self-acceptance. Be patient with yourself as you seek wholeness and happiness.

The colors of your clothes and the gems you wear can significantly affect your mood, mind and heart. Ingesting flower essences and applying diluted essential oils to your body (or diffusing them into the air) can improve your energy, attitude and drive. Enjoy these recommendations.

Colors: red, dark violet, dark pink, dark orchid, dark orange, midnight blue, gold, goldenrod

Gemstones: Tiger's Eye, Aragonite, Axinite, Sugilite, Gold, Yellow Fluorite, Citrine, Ruby, Cinnabar

Flower Essences: Chestnut Bud, Chicory, Pine, Cherry Plum, Mustard, Sweet Chestnut, Scleranthus, Star of Bethlehem

Essential Oils: Rose, Neroli, Frankincense, Anise, Bergamot, Cardamom, Citronella, Geranium, Ginger, Juniper Berry

We are arrows flying toward the peak of our desires. When our allegiances are split, we reduce our effectiveness.

THE INDIFFERENT

Prior to my birth, I was one with the eternal consciousness. Somehow when my soul entered into my physical body, I lost access to myself. I may have experienced trauma in this or a prior life that froze an aspect of my power and voice. While I am able to make clear decisions, sometimes I am unable to feel anything. In the quiet of the night, my heart opens and I see myself clearly. This gives me hope. Have patience with me. I seek myself in every breath.

THE INDIFFERENT

"While I am aware and conscious, I am a bit out of reach."

MORSEL

The lies we ingest and the pains we endure can muddy our hearts and awareness.

MESSAGE

By consuming thousands of stories that are pre-selected for us every day, we jeopardize our humanity. Simply by logging on and signing in, we empower a system that seeks to herd us. Free thinking and authenticity are the last frontier.

Given the hurricane of information that bombards us, going numb might seem preferable. The only way to reconnect to ourselves is to turn everything off. With fewer screens, less robots and more solitude, we increase our ability to bring about meaningful changes in our hearts and lives.

The Indifferent can feel silenced by the activity around her. Disconnected from her emotions, she might struggle to break free, but to no avail. In her isolation, she lost the ability to express herself.

It is easy to judge The Indifferent. We might take his unresponsiveness personally, or we might overreact when he temporarily disappears. We act as if he is doing this on purpose, but he is not.

The Indifferent is living in a restrictive cloud, doing the best he can to connect. He has no conception of how he affects or appears to others. He might believe that he is releasing a desperate scream, which appears to us as a quiet whimper or clearing of the throat.

When dealing with The Indifferent, we must realize there are powerful impressions, sensitivities and emotions restricting her, rendering her unable to step outside of herself. As her friend, we must endeavor to extend a hand into her cloud so she may choose to venture out.

If The Indifferent has emerged silent and confused in your life, you might be feeling overwhelmed with all that life has brought your way. You might feel disconnected from those around you and wonder if anyone cares. You might have given up on forming relationships, believing that you are too much of a bother. It is possible you have lost some hope.

You are a reflection of the love that is built into the universe. Your potential is equal to your intentions and desires. You need not limit yourself or hide. The time for your happiness is now.

To find your power and voice again, take responsibility for your position and be proactive. Consider calling a friend to share your heart. Even if you struggle to express what you feel, have patience with yourself. We all need a little time and encouragement now and again.

Stay out of stories from your past. Look only forward. Allow only high-vibration information to make its way to your heart and mind. You are the master of your soul. Nurture yourself into a loving relationship with reality. You deserve all the goodness and joy you can handle.

CAUTION

Something tragic may have happened in your life, disconnecting you from your passion or locking you into complacency. You may have welcomed a primary relationship into your life that embodies these attributes. You might be struggling with how to deal with such a person. You may have forgotten how to love yourself.

When the fog moves in, it is difficult to see the light. It is as if all of our faculties are stripped of their connection to us. We know they are there, but somehow they are outside our reach. The situation might be similar to a blind or deaf person. They are without one of the primary sensory experiences. This can be devastating, and at the very least, challenging. Seek the help you need. Forgive yourself for missteps, confusion and anger. Make one decision at a time. You'll soon be in motion.

EXTREME

Your problem might not be in your mind or heart, it might stem from a prior birth. As such, you might benefit from a past-life regression. Consider looking for someone who can help you access your collective past, source wisdom from it, and heal it.

In your mind's eye, sit in your mother's birth canal and feel your heartbeat as an unborn baby. Feel what's happening in the soul of that being. Are you confused? Are you lost? Do you feel love? What do you need? Dig deeper. As you sit in the warmth of the embryonic fluid and feel the soul of yourself as an unborn, try to see the entry path of your soul. In the time and space before you entered the body of your mother and fetus, there was only your soul before physical life. Can you sense residual emotions from prior lives? Sit with your pre-entry soul and heal the fractures with loving intention. You are in control of your past, present and future. Set yourself free from the past.

EMPOWERMENT

You might be traumatized by a recent experience or stifled by emotions trapped inside of you. You might need a medicinal herbalist to help you soften and open up. Consider volunteering at a hospital or homeless shelter. By giving to others, you will heal parts of yourself.

Your rebirth might be as simple as drinking espresso to get the juices flowing. You might need a lover to warm and awaken your body. Masturbate to get your energy moving. Watch emotion-provoking films, write a heart-centered story or pound the earth in anger.

These colors, gemstones, flower essences and essential oils will improve your mood, mind and heart.

Colors: cadet blue, dark magenta, dark olive green, dark orange, dark turquoise, light sea green

Gemstones: Emerald, Aventurine, Green Sardonyx, Pink Tourmaline, Gold, Lapis Lazuli, Rhodonite

Flower Essences: Star of Bethlehem, Aspen, Mimulus, Elm, Rock Rose, Scleranthus, Wild Rose

Essential Oils: Rose, Sandalwood, Lavender, Spearmint, Violet Leaf, Jasmine, Cardamom, Valerian

When we connect with our desires, they attract their twins in physical reality.

THE MOSAIC

I have not cried since I was two years old. Since then I have used my body and heart as repositories for thoughts and emotions that may not serve me. I seek a healthier release. Just under my handsome surface is sadness and confusion. This can attract adventure and drama, which I often enjoy. I take a spoonful of pleasure every time my presence disrupts or enlivens the room. Once provoked, hooked or loved, one never knows what might come to the surface. My tapestry is a mystery hoping to heal.

THE MOSAIC

"Beneath my skin's surface lives a world of unsettled experiences. Tread lightly upon me."

MORSEL

Expressing emotions clears debilitating debris. A soft touch brings about a gentle healing.

MESSAGE

As life thrusts us from one experience to another, we barely catch our breaths. With such chaos, we repeat never-ending cycles of unconscious decision-making. Desperately seeking activity in our lives, we latch onto things that do not serve us. Filling every gap, we are petrified of being alone.

When we dwell on negative thoughts, our minds and bodies become acidic. This dampens our health and numbs our awareness. When we focus on positive thoughts, our lives naturally improve.

The Mosaic is a passionate soul with a great appetite for life. Her thirst for adventure and mischief is almost enviable. When you look at her, you see a volcano of energy in her eyes. She is powerful, embodying a palpable presence in every moment.

Many moths are attracted to the flames that emanate from The Mosaic. Just sitting in her presence can be mind-blowing. Her inner fire provokes the awakening of every cell in our bodies.

While she might not always be full of the most pure energy, The Mosaic can move mountains. With an uncanny perceptiveness, she is able to suss out problems and challenges in any group. When times get rough, she can be a fierce motivator.

As intense as she might appear, The Mosaic is fragile and she might be in need of your help. Whether it's supporting her as she heals her dependencies and addictions, or gently encouraging her to start the day with a smile, a little sweetness goes a long way with The Mosaic.

When The Mosaic is out of balance, he can inspire others to feed his decadent habits and pleasures. When he needs a fix, it will appear upon the snap of his fingers. When his needs are repeatedly met like this, he can lose sight of his humanity. Protect yourself from the bark and bite of The Mosaic.

At her best, The Mosaic will succeed tremendously as an artist, salesperson or inventor. Some say she can channel the Gods. With excellent intuition and a sharp wit, The Mosaic can create empires.

If The Mosaic is burning a hole in your nature, it is time to pause, reflect and find love for yourself. Release negative thoughts and emotions related to anger, shame and guilt. Stop dancing with fire.

As you take inventory of the positive and negative influences in your life, remember that your most enduring health and success will arise out of positive actions, supportive friendships and happy thoughts. It's as simple as that.

Make choices that honor your heart. As light and love pour into your life, you will unfold and relax into a new you. It will be a beautiful and profound metamorphosis.

CAUTION

You attract fascinating experiences, but it hasn't been all fun and games. There might even be a few casualties. Tap into your feelings of guilt and acknowledge your mistakes. Forgive those who offended you during this segment of your life. Most importantly, forgive yourself and move on.

Look in the mirror with courage and honesty. Consider cutting ties with your past associations, and release the parts of you that create danger and drama. You cannot take these things with you as you grow.

By changing your thinking and releasing emotions, you will change your vibration and attract new experiences. Change one thought, release one emotion, and you begin a beautiful process of transformation.

EXTREME

You have accrued a unique level of perception and intuition. You connect with others on a deep level, often inspiring them to do whatever you desire. You are a master manipulator with the ability to enroll even the most perceptive personalities into your sometimes questionable world.

Be careful not to become a menacing super-villain, unaware of the damaging effects of your actions. Remember that being an enchantress comes with a great deal of responsibility. In the depth of your heart lives a loving child seeking freedom. Find her, heal her and let nature absorb the ashes at her feet. Forgive yourself and rejoice in the emerging changes. To heal the trends in your life, pursue joyful and uplifting experiences.

EMPOWERMENT

The Mosaic brings a long list of past lives and attachments into this present moment. You might need a deep, emotional cleansing, one achieved through ritual or group process. Sit quietly in a safe place. Imagine all the challenging experiences from your life. Do your best to cry deep tears so that you can let them go. Forgive everyone involved, including yourself. Let go and never look back.

If you are serious about transformation, find a spiritual master to help you along your way. Chant mantras in the morning and evening to improve the vibration of your mind, body and heart. As always, seek people who love you and accept you for who you are. Be love and you'll find love.

These colors, gemstones, flower essences and essential oils will improve your mind, heart and mood.

Colors: white, lavender, mint cream, sky blue, pink, green, plum, light yellow, bright red

Gemstones: Amethyst, Lolite, Peridot, Citrine, Garnet, Chrysoprase, Tree Agate, Butterstone, Scolecite, Lepidolite, Honey Calcite

Flower Essences: Agrimony, Star of Bethlehem, Centaury, Crab Apple, Gorse, Pine, Rock Rose

Essential Oils: Basil, Frankincense, Clove, Grapefruit, Rosemary, Geranium, Cardamom, Sandalwood, Rose, Jasmine, Myrrh

Clean the vessel and it will naturally attract a new life.

THE REGURGITATOR

I have not had a unique thought in years. My opinions seem to be a blend of every tag line and sound byte ever conjured. I absorb what I witness then pass it on without a moment of contemplation, regardless of how irrefutable or fallacious. No matter the source of my ideas, I fantasize that I am the supreme originator, which is the foundation of my Self-esteem. I thrive on slight exchanges, secretly fearful I will never find a worthy passion or accomplish anything of lasting value. With a shove, I might open a fragment of my heart so you can sense the real me, an eager child hungering for unwavering truth and attention.

THE REGURGITATOR

"Scratching below my intellectual surface live deeper fears. Who am I, if not what I know?"

MORSEL

Speaking shows us what we know. Listening gives rise to a world of knowledge and possibility.

MESSAGE

Up until the moment we take on physical form in our mother's uterus, we are akin to the light that gave birth to the universe. We are 100% potential in any direction.

Once settled in our mother's womb, we have recall of experiences from prior births, and we are sensitive to the energies of spirits from the other realms.

We go on to ingest the nutrients, sounds and energies within and around our mothers. We feel what she feels, picking up impressions from her experiences. Until our birth, we spend our lives as mini-versions of our moms, depending on her for everything, including our identity.

In the early years, our mothers shield us from harm, but as we grow, we become exposed to thousands of messages. By 18 years of age, our personal advertising consumption is well over 30 million communiques from media outlets and profit-focused companies throughout the world.

Just like a healer who takes on sickness when administering her gifts, each of us takes on many of the ills of the world when we watch the news. One story or advert can change the courses of our lives.

The Regurgitator is a faucet for information. Ask her a question and she will spew facts and figures for an eternity, no matter the quality of the content or the potential consequences. Whether she is relaying the cure for ebola or spreading an emotional virus, it's all the same to her.

If you're feeling chatty today, consider the value of your ideas. Be honest with yourself as you evaluate the quality of your speech. What might it inspire? Will it help or hurt others? If you cannot guarantee the caliber of your ideas, it might be best to listen instead.

The Regurgitator fulfills an important role in the evolution of society. He might pass on information that brings benefit and change for the most disenfranchised in the world. He might also be unaware of how he affects others. He might be a foot soldier for messages created to distract us from the light.

Either way, be careful when courting The Regurgitator. Take special measures to protect yourself from energies and ideas that do not serve you. Set better boundaries, reject gossip, shut off the news, stop following celebrities and get to know yourself. You have all the information you need.

To enjoy a measure of illumination and personal growth in your life, allow the brightness of your soul to attract only goodness, kindness and happiness. Seek relationships and knowledge that uplift your life, mind, heart and spirit. For now, everything else is superfluous.

CAUTION

Drugs are not the worst addiction on the planet, information is. We give more credence to gossip than to the sweet thoughts of a child. Stop ingesting and passing on low-quality ideas. These things have the ability to affect our evolution.

Newscasts, movies, TV shows, commercials, and video games have the capacity to thrust streams of negative ideas into our own consciousness as well as the global consciousness. Commercials promote feelings of lack and imperfection, then herd us to stores to buy products to compensate. Even drug companies have permission to lie to us. Given how pervasive this is, disappointment grows within each of us.

As The Regurgitator, remember the important role you play. Be joyful and positive, spreading only truthful and nurturing ideas. This will exponentially feed your life, the lives of others and the planet.

EXTREME

Negative patterns are difficult to break. We should not feel badly about our inability to change or progress, but we must keep trying. Inherent in our effort is positive intention, which will fuel our hearts, bodies and lives. Stay positive, maintain forward movement and remember your heart.

Examine the content of the messages you have been spreading. Look for the hidden through-lines. It might be that you were hurt by someone very close to you during childhood. You may have been unable to forgive them. The negative thoughts you have been spreading might somehow allude to your painful past. Only you can change the narrative of your life. Consider making the bold choice of only saying things that are positive. In a short period of time, you will feel as though you lost weight, moved into a new house and started a love affair with the source of all life. This is your birthright.

EMPOWERMENT

You can be a bright light in this world. You have the brain, personality and charisma to inspire uncommon momentum. You can invent, heal or teach. Commit to promoting the positive aspects inherent in creation. Walk toward the light and see how quickly your heart and life can change.

The colors of your clothes and the gems you wear can significantly affect your mood, mind and heart. Ingesting flower essences and applying essential oils to your body (or diffusing them into the air) can improve your energy, attitude and drive.

Colors: white, yellow, dark violet, magenta, pink, red, teal, green, orange

Gemstones: Ruby, Bloodstone, Diopside, Emerald, Stromatolite, Yellow Citrine, Pink Tourmaline

Flower Essences: Heather, Agrimony, Chestnut Bud, Chicory, Water Violet, Wild Oat

Essential Oils: Bergamot, Ylang Ylang, Mandarin, Basil, Bay Laurel, Lavender, Sandalwood, Angelica, Rose, Clove Bud, Helichrysum, Nutmeg

Your ingestions and emanations are the lights from which your future Self feeds.

THE FEARLESS

I live from my gut with no hesitation, blocks or conflict. I rarely pause to analyze a situation because the details are irrelevant. For me, it is about mind over matter and following the intelligence of my heart. It does not mean I never fail, it means when I honor the impulse to accomplish something, I pursue it from the depth of my being, no matter the potential repercussions, consequences or loss. Time and time again, I prove myself right, in that fear is nothing but a notion that gets in the way of joyful Self-expression and adventure.

THE FEARLESS

"I am free now and always."

MORSEL

A dependency on comfort might compel your hidden fears to rise.

MESSAGE

When we choose expansion over fear, we participate in evolution. The Fearless understands this. The ability to push through resistance is built into their psychological blueprint.

Fear restricts every facet of society. It is reinforced in our laws, schools, entertainment and families. Fear is used for political and religious purposes, oppressing millions via stories of freedom and redemption. Fear is also infused into product messaging and parenting. We would be surprised to find out how deeply fear is integrated into our daily lives.

When we are able to recognize our fears before taking a fear-based action, our lives improve exponentially. It is fear that disrupts the majority of our peacefulness, success and flow.

The Fearless are ambassadors of the idea that nothing should keep us from what we desire. They know that deep joy is experienced when we take profound risks with confidence. Even when we falter, we learn something important. By keeping at it, we validate ourselves and we lessen fear's effectiveness.

Whether the critics of your bliss are internal or external, you have the option to either listen to them or discard them. Anything that negates your potential is not a reflection of you and doesn't belong in your life. No matter what the haters and negaters say, remember that just about anything is possible.

You are limitless. You may be thinking that you are not limitless, but that is incorrect. At any moment, you can change the presiding thought in your mind, even into its opposite.

When you acknowledge that you are limitlessness, every segment of your life has a greater potential to evolve. Allow the limitlessness of the universe to influence your thoughts and actions. When you live from this premise, the ceiling and box that once contained you evaporates.

If there's an undercurrent of fear in your relationships or work-life, consider the source. Did the fear arise from parenting or from loss that you sustained in this lifetime? What can you do to combat those fears so you can put them in the proper perspective?

If The Fearless has burst into your world today, cook him a feast and celebrate his understanding of the universe. He is the ultimate proof that we are far more capable than we realize.

Whatever you are staring at right now, be fearless about it. Dive in. Bring it on! When we embrace and embody the timeless, adventurous spirit of The Fearless, we surprise ourselves, and we accomplish great things.

CAUTION

You recently devalued yourself by putting your fate into the hands of fearful naysayers. You built a little box inside a little cave then moved in.

This is no time to second-guess yourself. Whether it is a defeat or a success, everything we create or pursue is done in partnership with the universe. If your current situation was not already part of you, you would not be able to recognize it enough to participate in it.

Given these universal laws, this is no time to back out. This is the time to push forward and celebrate the work you have done. Harness your energies and drive your momentum toward success.

Transform the hidden, locked box you're living in into a powerful superhero airplane. Embody fearlessness and fly into action.

EXTREME

Your fearlessness might be the product of unintended arrogance. True fearlessness lives in the moment, serves the spirit of adventure and does not put itself on a pedestal. Relax back into who you are and let go of your ego. It has no business in the business of The Fearless.

When we overstate our value, we increase our suffering and the suffering of others. Break free from this pattern. Fan the flame of fearlessness. Release desperation, anger and cravings for attention. Let go of the victim-mindedness and excuses. These are all manifestations of a fractured ego.

Honor the fears that protect you and release the ones that contradict your potential. Respect your passion, lean forward and unlock a new life.

EMPOWERMENT

The Fearless are born to live beyond restriction. Their only limits are self-imposed, constructed from the same beliefs the Gods used to create the universe. If you've lost your connection to your inner fearless master, seek a life-coach to help you resurrect it. It is time to get back in the game.

The colors of your clothes and the gems you wear can significantly affect your mood, mind and heart. Ingesting flower essences and applying essential oils to your body (or diffusing them into the air) can improve your energy, attitude and drive. The following are recommendations for The Fearless. May you continue to live life with the utmost enthusiasm!

Colors: green, violet, purple, gold, white, turquoise, lime, chartreuse, sky blue, black

Gemstones: Agate, Aventurine, Chrysocolla, Blue Coral, Galena, Hematite, Howlite, Crystal Quartz, Sulphur, Mother of Pearl, Obsidian

Flower Essences: Honeysuckle, Impatiens, Mimulus, Rock Rose, Rock Water, Vine, Aspen

Essential Oils: Geranium, Lavender, Rose, Peppermint, Helichrysum, Cinnamon, Chamomile, Cardamom

To truly know yourself, you must take a humble, vulnerable step into the abyss.

THE PARTIAL TRUTH

I tell white lies to feel better about my position in life. Even the tiniest redirect gives me comfort. When I sense I might lose control, I add a spatter of color to the facts. As a child, I was surrounded by ethically-questionable miscreants who gave me an education in mild deceit and justification. Out of fascination, I concocted a limited moral code, which I use as a license to conceal complete truths. Sometimes I am embarrassed by the truth or I find it inconvenient. I seek an upgrade to my habits.

THE PARTIAL TRUTH

"When I feel vulnerable, I tell stories to protect myself."

MORSEL

Every truth we ingest unclenches a trapped potential, inching us closer to freedom.

MESSAGE

Parents are no longer the primary influencers in a kid's life. The new caretakers are Uncle Internet and Aunt Video Game. When children look in the mirror, they do not see their own reflection, or the faces of their ancestors, they see a composite image designed by the world's advertising agencies. They see people, personalities and lifestyles created by Hollywood and Bollywood. Their new role model? A light brown romantic robot who wears make-up, packs a gun, likes dancing and idolizes celebrities.

Since children will continue to be barraged and shaped by shallow characters and ads, it will become impossible to teach them about integrity and wholeness. This means that when a child grows into an uncontaminated, honest adult, it could be classified as a miracle.

Early in her life, The Partial Truth may have been exposed to falsehood, dishonesty, questionable people, head-games and drama. This may have caused her to feel confused and isolated. Out of desperation she began to create stories and lies to protect and nurture herself. She learned to cope by hiding or masking information. This seemingly benign behavioral tick turned into a habit.

The Partial Truth might feel disconnected from family or community. She may not understand the benefits that come with transparency, friendship and vulnerability. Remain hopeful and seek a connection to her heart. With a little patience and encouragement, The Partial Truth will soften and open up like a gently blossoming flower.

There are many reasons to tell partial truths. It might be to protect someone from being hurt, to save a situation from becoming dangerous or to let someone off the hook so they don't have to deal with a painful memory or experience. While white lies can be helpful, we must remain tethered to the truth.

If The Partial Truth has ventured into your home today, he is seeking compassion. He wants to share his heart so that he might learn to better vocalize his personal truth and feelings. Give The Partial Truth the attention and kindness he needs and you might find him to be the best friend you ever had.

Given how complex our lives can become, we can easily lose sight of our truth. We can forget that honest is the best policy. We can forsake our most loyal confidants and friends. And we can forget to forgive others when they make mistakes along these lines.

There is only one person who can stand up for the truths you've come to understand. That's YOU. You are a torch-bearer and a light-being. If you are hiding under a story, set yourself free. Tell the truth.

CAUTION

When The Partial Truth is out of balance, it is a never-ending game of half-truths that often result in mistrust. If you fell prey to an epic tale, you are in good company. Even the most discerning of us can get pulled into her web of stories. Some tales are innocuous, creating confusion that is more annoying than hurtful. The more villainous liars concoct elaborate schemes that strip us of our faith and self-respect.

If The Partial Truth has gotten into your head, come clean and right the ship. Do your best to heal your most vital relationships. Write heart-felt letters and shed light on the events that transpired. By acknowledging your shortcomings, you allow others to get to know you, and you open a path to your own healing and freedom.

EXTREME

With every lie we tell, we add a filter to our vision. With too many filters, we cannot see anything at all. The more we live from contrived and false personas, the more energy will be required to sustain them. When you remove all the stories and justifications, you will see colors you haven't seen since you were a child. You will witness pure and beautiful moments that formerly evaded you: a child's smile, a hummingbird in flight, and the love between you and creation. You will soon realize that a miracle has come into being, a miracle that you created.

If there is someone in your life who continues to alter the truth, keep her at arms length. Be diligent in your clarity and self-care so that no further harm can come to you.

EMPOWERMENT

The Partial Truth can be quite a challenge. Look into Native American or Hindu rituals focused on integrity, clarity, healing and forgiveness. Pujas, Homas, Sweat Lodges, Medicine Wheels, Vision Quests and the like are tried and true modalities for exploring and living from your higher nature. Be sure to have a mentor or spiritual teacher to ensure your safety in every ritual and ceremony.

The colors of your clothes and the gems you wear can significantly affect your mood, mind and heart. Ingesting flower essences and applying essential oils to your body (or diffusing them into the air) can improve your energy, attitude and drive. Seek help from professionals for the best results. May your self-examination begin with love and light!

Colors: turquoise, aqua, dodger blue, pink, sea green, dark violet, orchid, white

Gemstones: Citrine, Amethyst, Green Calcite, Malachite, Turquoise, Blue Lace Agate

Flower Essences: Sweet Chestnut, Holly, Pine, Chestnut Bud, Heather, Water Violet, Rock Water

Essential Oils: Bergamot, Ylang Ylang, Lemon, Spruce, Cajeput, Coriander, Frankincense, Petitgrain, Violet Leaf, Sandalwood

Honesty opens doors to clear thinking and attracts a hearty, grounded life.

THE COILED

I bottle up emotions for weeks, then liberate them in moments of confusion or unrest. To free my voice and invigorate my personal power, I might fall crying into the arms of my beloved or scream triumphantly from a rooftop. Once self-expressed, I am grateful and at peace. When I feel a storm brewing, I distance myself from others. As I untether, I become aware of the uncharted, broken parts of me. I see my vulnerabilities and crave love. Tread lightly so that I might find myself again.

THE COILED

"When I explode, I am as surprised as you, yet I am grateful for the release."

MORSEL

Once in a while, the beast needs to be set free without judgement or fear of repercussion. After all, the beast is within all beings. Accept him and you accept yourself.

MESSAGE

When we experience profound events in our lives, our bodies and hearts crave releases. Whether it's crying, screaming or pounding the earth, we must express what has accrued within us. Fully allowing and releasing emotions is not only freeing, it's vital to our growth and evolution.

When we interrupt an emotional release, our systems can get jammed. Buildup from unexpressed emotions can affect our health and well-being If emotional residue sinks too deeply into our bones, it becomes difficult to extract it.

Many of us compartmentalize our experiences, securing them in appropriately labeled time capsules. We'll occasionally open random capsules and extract whispers of insight, then quickly bottle them up again. Delving into the past might feel good, but it keeps us from living in the present moment.

The Coiled is a powerful personality, able to absorb and carry the emotions of several people at once. The Coiled might be a mother, father, business executive, Rabbi or Priest, often someone who is in a leadership or care-taking position. Rather than express every emotion as she feels it, The Coiled holds back until the time is right.

The Coiled's withholding might be a protective choice or it might be a reaction stemming from loss. If you see The Coiled pacing or brooding, do not interrupt her. She will emerge when she's ready.

When The Coiled is out of balance, he stores and warps his emotions, gathering them in a cistern. What begins as a reasonable collection of fixable moments can incubate into arsenals of fermented feelings, toxic time-bombs that could be released at any time.

If The Coiled is knocking on your door today, it is because he feels safe enough to do so. You lovingly created the space for him to release his emotions, and he chose to open up to you. Do not fear his release. Allow him the chance to express himself so that he can be free.

Seek greater insight into how and why you withhold emotions. It is obvious that these patterns have been challenging for you. As you look for and express the emotions within you, find forgiveness for yourself and others. Seek the love, joy and clarity you rightfully deserve.

While it's okay to peek into the past in order to gather a final fragment of wisdom, do not remain there. Remember that the past is a cancelled check. Your happiness resides solely in this present moment.

CAUTION

You may not know how to make your emotional health a priority in your life. You might believe that other people's feelings are more important. This could not be farther from the truth.

It's vital you tend to your emotional health. It might be that your home or family does not permit you to take care of yourself in this way. They might not know that you're in pain or what you need. It might be that you're simply afraid to let it all out. It's okay to be ugly once in a while. This does not mean you have permission to set a room on fire with your words, but you are permitted to experiment with self-expression.

Keeping your emotions a secret, you may never know what brews within you. Have patience with yourself. And ask that others do the same. You are a work in progress and sometimes progress is a messy business.

EXTREME

As you unleash your wild animal, it is permissible to freak out and scream at the top of your lungs. It is okay to pound the floor and throw things at the wall, as long as you do not physically hurt anyone. For this one-time rebirth, completely let loose. If you need a few of these sessions to let all the steam out, so be it, but do not become addicted. It will not bode well for relationships or inner peace.

Once clear of debris and emotion, make an agreement with yourself to find healthier and more expedient ways of releasing emotional build up. Move through this process with forgiveness. With a clean emotional slate, you can traverse life with more ease. Get in the habit of sharing your feelings with close friends. Above all, learn to let it go and let it flow.

EMPOWERMENT

The Coiled's sensitivity is a gift, but you must work on healthfully releasing your pain. A Jungian or art therapist might help you put anger and frustration into a manageable perspective. Having a therapist is a great way to grow emotional stability. The tools they share can be transformative. You might benefit from a martial art so that you can let all the energy out of your body healthfully.

These colors, gemstones, flower essences and essential oils will improve your mood, mind and heart.

Colors: white, pink, light cyan, yellow, yellow green, gold, sky blue, turquoise

Gemstones: Pink Tourmaline, Rhodochrosite, Rose Quartz, Gold, Chrysoprase, Azurite, Charoite

Flower Essences: Holly, White Chestnut, Pine, Willow, Rock Rose, Rock Water, Honeysuckle, Star of Bethlehem

Essential Oils: Grapefruit, Vetiver, Ylang Ylang, Lemon, Lavender, Juniper Berry, Melissa, Geranium, Frankincense, Rosewood

Continually improve your communication, environments, relationships and conditions. Release emotions before they become a magnet or burden.

THE FRAIL

I am brittle and frightened, worn from a rough ride. Like the fragile sarcophagus of an ancient ruler, any attempt to peek inside me could chip my heart and psyche. One strong easterly wind and I could burst at the seams. After a cascade of challenging moments, I am rendered a bit lost, unwell and nervous. While I rely on soft connections with others to keep my heart open and hopeful, I am never quite sure who to trust. Find me. Help me gain my footing so that I can endeavor to be whole again.

THE FRAIL

"I seek to reduce my outward vulnerability and to fortify myself in heart and mind."

MORSEL

Unacknowledged sadness and trapped resentments extinguish our vitality.

MESSAGE

We are permeable membranes, sensitive to touch and vulnerable to our surroundings. We are like children absorbing everything that comes our way, but we are ill-equipped to process it all. Without a refuge or protector, we can easily become disabled.

Our external lives most often mirror what's happening inside of us. if we are feeling oppressed, we will seek situations that overpower us. When we do not value ourselves, we cower.

The Frail embodies a palpable sweetness. She has a lovely way of listening, full of empathy and heart. Her vulnerability is magic, inducing easy connections with others.

Beneath her benevolence is a wealth of stored experiences and emotions, so vast, she can barely manage it. Because she is so burdened, The Frail can become depleted and disoriented. Her boundaries are well worn out.

The Frail's challenge is self-esteem. He never learned how to love, protect or help himself. Growing up, he was not permitted to express his feelings or share his perspectives. He was gently stifled into a voiceless sadness, putting him in the crosshairs of neglect and abuse.

If The Frail has shuffled her way into your world, it is time to reinvigorate the part of you that has given up. Whatever piece of your spirit or body is broken, it is time to strengthen it, perhaps with one small gesture at a time.

No matter how sad or defeated you feel, no matter how many excuses you have come to enjoy, and no matter how exhausted you are, you can initiate a new life trajectory in this moment.

Dig deep and make a list of the pieces of your life you feel to be down for the count. Separate that list into two separate sub-lists: the things you can do something about, and the things you cannot. Think carefully about how you delineate these things, then take action where you can.

The Frail has a deep understanding of life, love and relationships. He knows how to open and inspire hearts. You can trust The Frail to tell you the truth. With a sprinkle of loving encouragement, he will open a treasure trove of kindness and insight to you.

You have a great deal more power and strength at your fingertips than you let yourself believe. Watch your thoughts along the way and slowly build up your core. Heal the frailty that ails you by taking small steps and tiny risks toward clarity and wholeness.

Believe in yourself at all times. You are meant to be a full, vibrant being in this lifetime.

CAUTION

When we worry too much, our brows furrow, our heads ache and our cheeks tighten, turning our smiles to frowns. This is how our thoughts change our bodies and realities. You can allow the feelings, emotions and perceptions you have collected over the years to ferment. You can relive the traumas you have encountered. You may even reenact the same conversations you have had for centuries. You are free to choose to stop living, but this is not your path. You are here to enjoy an abundant life.

When others pity us, it feels good for a moment. It is as if we are relating with them. This softens our loneliness and gives us hope. But this hope is short lived because when the feelings fade, we will again require pity to feel whole. This never-ending cycle will deprive you of happiness.

Say no to handouts and giveaways. Choose a path that sustains you physically, financially and emotionally. Work hard to be strong!

EXTREME

While you may have already decided that you are deceased, your body and mind are still alive and well. Given that you continue to have experiences and thoughts, you must still be alive!

Of all the living beings in all the realms, and given all the stars, planets, galaxies and universes throughout creation, you have a human body, beating heart and conscious mind in this timeframe in history, on this beautiful planet. You are a unique combination of infinitely-nested miracles. Gently encourage yourself to live in this moment as a miracle. Accept your past and be grateful for it. You have a full life ahead of you. Embrace it, take positive steps and seek to shine brightly.

EMPOWERMENT

It is difficult to feel broken or damaged most of the time, but there are many things you can do to increase your energy, stamina and strength. Change your body chemistry with work-outs, running or martial arts. Push yourself to express your emotions through physical fitness. Eat healthy foods and find time to be playful. You're better than this and you know it.

When we seek out the colors, gems, flower essences and essential oils that uplift our spirits, we see immediate changes to our demeanors and states of mind. These recommendations are for The Frail.

Colors: green, blue violet, firebrick red, hot pink, purple, turquoise, cyan, yellow, gold, orange

Gemstones: Yellow Sapphire, Carnelian, Moldavite, Grossularite, Charoite, Sugilite, Chrysocolla, Blue Lace Agate, Moonstone

Flower Essences: Aspen, Oak, Olive, Hornbeam, Agrimony, Centaury, Cherry Plum, Larch, Rock Rose, Star of Bethlehem

Essential Oils: Rosemary, Spruce, Orange, Grapefruit, Petitgrain, Neroli, Bergamot, Peppermint, Cardamom, Sage, Ylang Ylang

Live with a sweet and gentle pride. Let good things come to you.

THE OBSERVER

I thrive on stepping back so that I may watch events, dynamics and interactions unfold without my influence. Even when I am not directly involved, I take copious notes, earnestly absorbing all that I witness. It is not that I dislike being a participant, it is that I am entranced and enhanced by the intricacies of human behavior. If you wonder what I have gleaned so far, just ask me. I am affable, approachable, and I love to share my thoughts and processes with other curious souls.

THE OBSERVER

"I evolve as I stand apart and ingest what I see and hear."

MORSEL

Witnessing and listening grows our hearts and advances our souls. Drink it all in and expand.

MESSAGE

When too entrenched in our stories, we miss out on the nuances happening around us. By paying more attention, we see a myriad of subtle and beautiful quirks, behaviors and moments. We could spend hours watching just one person and never fully fathom his nature or what makes him tick.

The Observer understands that listening is far more valuable than speaking. Early in his life, Sufi Master Meher Baba stopped speaking and spent the remainder of his life communicating slowly and thoughtfully with an alphabet board.

We have a lot to learn from The Observers. Even one slight breath between thought and action can transform a dramatic outcome into a peaceful one. One pause can save a relationship or life.

If The Observer is peeking at you from across the room, quiet your mind and become a witness to what is transpiring around you. Do your best to fully experience the present moment in its raw form. Gather as much intel as possible.

Learn how to listen with every part of your being. Allow your heart, eyes, ears, gut and skin to speak to you. The listening parts of us have a unique way of gathering information and relaying it to us. The more you listen, the more you allow awarenesses to step out of the shadows and into view.

When The Observer spends too much time watching, she can begin to believe that by surveying others, she is actually participating in life. While the watching is enviable, it cannot replace our submersion in active relationships and events. We can never mistake our observing for connection.

To take advantage of what The Observer has to offer, become the witness in your life. As you watch a person or event, consider what they might be feeling and experiencing. Remain detached, but commune with them in this way. Imagine light and love pouring into them as you watch them unfold.

As you observe, remember to breathe. When we observe too intently without relaxing into our breath, our body can become tense. Bring your body into the equation and breathe deeply into all things.

Release the reactor, dissolve the judge, and witness what is happening around you without critique or reaction. Remember that reality and experience have no further implications other than what you assign to them. Meaning is something our egos create. It is not necessarily the truth.

Take a lesson from The Observer and refrain from assumption. Learn to quietly receive information. Inhale everything around you. Become the witness in all things. Take a long, deep dive into the eternal knowing through observation.

CAUTION

Unaware of the situation, you may have spoken too soon and created confusion in a primary relationship. Your opinions are sometimes out of balance with the flow of what you are trying to accomplish. It's best to keep those to yourself as often as possible. They have little value. Rather than continuing to tell others what you think, put energy into listening.

Become The Observer and allow for a new level of insight. Transmute your negative assumptions into gentle awarenesses. Be a fly on the wall and breathe in the subtle happenings around you. Embrace the winds in the trees, the homeless man's smile and the sweetness between two lovers. Open your heart and take it all in. Receiving will transform you.

Maintain positivity and all things to unfold without judgement.

EXTREME

We obsess too much, complain too often and work too hard. We are addicted to sensory input and over-activity. We refuse to keep still. When events spiral out of control, there is no blame. Let the universe unwind the patterns in play. Continue inaction and avoid confrontation. Only through silence and observation will you gather the insight necessary for the next level of your evolution. Be grateful for what you are learning, relish the solitude and prepare for a shift in tides.

When she spends too much time watching and not enough time participating, The Observer loses touch with her passion and drive. This will quickly dampen the quality of her life. Find strength in reaching out to others and making new friends. Let others get to know you. You might find that you have more value to others than you once imagined. Take social and emotional risks as often as possible and burst out of your self-imposed confinement.

EMPOWERMENT

It might be helpful to look deeply at the social fears you have been harboring. Some of these fears might be preventing you from pursuing your dreams or advancing your personal network. Allow your role as The Observer to feed your emotional growth, creativity and writing. Share your insights in thoughtful and meaningful ways. Join social groups that have an intellectual or educational focus. This will expand your relationship-base as well as your knowledge.

It's exciting to explore colors, gemstones, flower essences and essential oils. The recommendations below will help you increase your energy, alertness, passion and joy.

Colors: dark violet, dark red, firebrick red, Firebrick red, maroon, purple, dark orchid, yellow

Gemstones: Ruby, Bloodstone, Red Coral, Cinnabar, Red Jasper, Garnet, Yellow Sapphire

Flower Essences: Impatiens, Wild Oat, Wild Rose, Rock Water, Rock Rose, Gorse, Gentian, Aspen

Essential Oils: Rosemary, Patchouli, Rosewood, Vetiver, Bergamot, Frankincense, Geranium, Melissa, Sandalwood

No period of silent observation has ever been the root cause of strife or anguish.

THE FORGETFUL

I have a difficult time keeping track of just about everything. I cannot seem to remember prior events, intimate moments or where I put my toothbrush. It might have been 10 seconds ago or last month, but I still cannot recall the details. I make to-do lists to help me bridge the gap, but I always seem to forget where I put them. Stress seems to push facts out of my head and into my soup. It is not that I am unable to follow though, love or connect, it is that my mind is traversing several agendas, and I am lost in a waterfall of details. Forgive me. I am as frustrated with me as you are.

THE FORGETFUL

"When I suppress stress and tears, I become confused and fall out of flow."

MORSEL

Expressing emotions in the moment clears the mind and increases mental acuity.

MESSAGE

The mind is a precious thing. It gathers information, imagines scenarios and coordinates our lives. While it might appear to be indestructible, the mind is soft and vulnerable, requiring a gentle nurturance. With too much stimulation, it will put itself on alert. When it is unable to sustain the heightened frequency, it will falter.

The Forgetful is a well-meaning hard-worker full of enthusiasm and strength. She is bendable, mendable and optimistic. Her drive allows her to accomplish much more than the rest of us.

When taking care of family or business, she manages details like a pro, never missing a beat. She categorizes and organizes at a master's pace, but she may be unaware of her threshold.

Although relentless in his pursuits, when things escalate beyond the norm, The Forgetful becomes frustrated. Ill-equipped to tend to constant build-up, instead of clearing the clutter, The Forgetful moves things around just enough to form a path. While momentarily helpful, the path falls short.

If The Forgetful is attempting to organize your storage today, you might be brushing things aside instead of dealing with them. You may have endured a series of challenging events which produced thoughts and emotions now strewn across your mind and heart. When feeling overwhelmed and stressed, The Forgetful becomes confused.

If you feel constricted and burdened by too many unexpressed emotions and disenfranchised thoughts, sit quietly and connect with yourself. Look honestly at what may be troubling you. You might just need to shed a few tears, or you may need to give more thought to a challenging event. Being honest with ourselves and releasing emotions paves more than a path, it clears the room.

Think of the gold miners in the 1800s. Hitting a healthy vein, they would follow it inch by inch into the mountain, then chip away pieces of treasure until their sacks were full. It might be time to excavate the emotional treasures in your mind and heart. Breathe deeply and allow your emotions to bubble up, move through you and exit. Give focus to untended thoughts so they can produce a helpful wisdom.

Our lives are fragile dreams. When our activities and relationships do not inspire peace and happiness, we can choose to dream in a new direction. Have a tag sale, buy a motorcycle, reimagine your dreams and set yourself on a new pathway to a more conscious clarity. Your mind and heart will be happier.

CAUTION

When we focus on the past, we live in an imagined fog, unaware that we have forgotten our responsibilities in the present moment. The past can be preferable when our current scenarios feel too overwhelming.

No matter how significant the details, no matter how wonderful your pursuits, it's too much for you to carry. It might be that your identity has been so well-validated because of the hyperactivity in your life that you don't want to give it up. Truth be told, you have too much going on and it's time to let something go.

It's not important who others see you as, especially when you're stressed out with memory loss. It is quite possible not to have an image about yourself at all. Destress by simplifying your life and image.

EXTREME

When we perseverate on busyness and details, our brain can fry itself into forgetfulness. Our brains are circuit boards. The more energy we cram into them, the greater the chance we might blow a fuse. When our internal systems are overloaded, they cannot serve us properly.

Whatever transpired when you were a child is no longer happening. You need not perpetuate the overactivity in your life to dull the pain. Your childhood has passed. It does not exist. You can take some time to release residual, unprocessed emotions and derive wisdom from them, but do not dwell there. Focus on the present moment and your peacefulness. This is how your rebirth begins.

EMPOWERMENT

You might feel too proud, too busy or too broke to ask for help. These ideas are not serving you. If you need help, ask for it, look for it and it will make itself available to you. You do not need to be a super hero, you do not need to play victim. Being stressed out and overwhelmed is no longer required. Open up to someone and let them know what you need.

Each one of us has a unique and subtle vibration. The colors of your clothes and the gemstones you wear can significantly affect your mood, mind and heart. Ingesting flower essences and applying essential oils to your body (or diffusing them into the air) can improve your energy, attitude and drive. Seek to improve yourself on every level.

Colors: coral, white, orange, sea green, purple, rosy brown, steel blue, goldenrod, dark pink

Gemstones: Blue Quartz, Tiger's Eye, Turquoise, Lapis Lazuli, Tanzanite, Aragonite, Fire Opal, Pink Tourmaline, Gold, Coral

Flower Essences: Clematis, Scleranthus, Cherry Plum, Aspen, Chestnut Bud, Elm, Honeysuckle, Star of Bethlehem, White Chestnut

Essential Oils: Vetiver, Lavender, Cedarwood, Ylang Ylang, Patchouli, Lemon, Ginger, Sandalwood, Nutmeg, Melissa, Frankincense, Cinnamon

When we live a peaceful life, we know who we are at every turn.

53

THE REKINDLED

Coming out of a long sleep, I now see my life's potential. While I grieve prior choices, a celebration brews within. I will no longer sit frustrated in the shadows. I will no longer pine for what is not true. I will release old behaviors and attitudes, relinquishing my attachment to a former self. I am choosing to come alive in this moment, greeting new skies with love, knowing that I embody unlimited potential. I am renewed, reborn and ready to shed former skin.

THE REKINDLED

"My heart beats with anticipation as I consider new possibilities."

MORSEL

The emotions stemming from old fantasies can be intoxicating. Titrating off these drugs is paramount to living in the present moment.

MESSAGE

Sipping our tea, we spend whole mornings intoxicated by prior events. We soak in them, chew on them as if they were our most satisfying meals. As we recall each memory, emotions flair up then boil down. Once satiated, we close the door, only to repeat the process later.

When we look back at our lives, we become nostalgic, imagining what it was like "back then", who we were with and how we felt. We remember our old hang outs, our first bicycle and the most poignant moments with friends and loved ones.

It's difficult to know which memories and emotions deserve liberation. Tucked under complex webs of thoughts and impressions, the most troubled parts of us can be frozen in time. It's these aspects that must be softened and nurtured back into the light so they can merge with the fabrics of our souls.

As The Rekindled reminisces on your couch today, encourage him to release the emotions and memories that have been most troubling to him. As he extinguishes the cascade of images in his mind's eye, ask him to breathe in all of the love available to him in this moment.

When we live in the past, reliving emotions derived from fantasy, it is impossible to glean lasting value for our lives. We forget that the past is a cancelled check and does not exist. Once The Rekindled is able to release old fantasies of lovers and adventures gone-by, her rebirth is her greatest feat.

The most important moment you can experience is happening right now. Are you emotionally present? Can you access your feelings? Are you aware of what is happening in your heart and body?

The Rekindled tends to spend a little too much time in the past or future. She tends to construct impossible, ideal versions of herself in her mind, using them to judge herself. Whenever your mind veers off like this, it's important to bring yourself back into the present moment.

Stay focused on who you are right now. Envision and embrace your vibrance and vitality. Your life exists in the now and in front of you, waiting for you to join its flow as a participant.

There is an endless list of opportunities at your fingertips. Think proactively, make bold choices and let the universe come to your aid. By taking immediate action, you integrate your mind, body and heart in the powerful, exciting pursuit of a beautiful rebirth. It's time to rekindle YOU.

CAUTION

It is easy to forget that our thoughts control our destiny. When we're in a rut, it seems almost easier to sit quietly and remain in it. Settled into complacency, we defend the negative aspects of our lives. We begin to believe our excuses. We build a prison and become our own oppressor. We tell ourselves that we deserve to be here.

No matter what age we are, we can adopt the mindset of a sad person or a happy, vibrant person. It's a choice. We can be resilient if we choose.

Have you forgotten how lovely you are? Reach out to a close friend and confide in them. Make plans to better your life. Most importantly, if you have a negative thought, change it the moment it emerges.

Happiness starts with a happy thought. Pick a happy thought right now. Pick another happy thought. And then another. And another. Pick one more. Continue doing this until your gaze is laser-focused on the light.

EXTREME

While you might feel disconnected from those who love you, they are waiting patiently for you to come back to life. It is time to clean house, connect with yourself and begin again. Do not be afraid of the dark. Command it. It knows it is only temporary. With every shadow and memory you put to rest, you expand your inner garden, which is filled with pure light and potential. You cannot love yourself "at a later date." Be proactive and take positive action right now.

EMPOWERMENT

The Rekindled sometimes portrays as an attention-starved repressive with a hint of vanity. To remedy this shadow, lighten up, forget what others say about you and release the judgments you've placed on yourself. Consider working for a charity or homeless shelter, or taking a clown workshop. You might consider channeling all your drama into a role in a play. Is there an actor in you? A singer? A dancer?

Born of the same substance, each one of us has a unique and subtle vibration. The colors of your clothes and the gemstones you wear can significantly affect your mood, mind and heart. Ingesting flower essences and applying essential oils to your body (or diffusing them into the air) can improve your energy, attitude and drive. Seek to improve yourself on every level.

Colors: yellow, gold, ivory, spring green, cornflower blue, orchid, dark pink, violet, dark orange

Gemstones: Jasper, Gaspeite, Howlite, Honey Calcite, Lapis Lazuli, Blue Aragonite

Flower Essences: Honeysuckle, Aspen, Cerato, Cherry Plum, Clematis, Star of Bethlehem

Essential Oils: Peppermint, Lavender, Bergamot, Helichrysum, Jasmine, Juniper Berry, Rose, Sandalwood, Ylang Ylang

The abundance you seek is within and around you. Choosing a memory over the present moment is akin to saying a movie is more valuable than reality.

THE HARNESS

I'm a workhorse, tirelessly pointing my team in a unified direction. I wrap myself around them and embrace their talents, knowing our goal is achievable. I nurture every player, feed their hearts and minds, and do my best to keep them on point. Sometimes I speak in parables to inspire the creation of something unique. The result is a well-connected community, an advanced group process, and a product that makes everyone proud. Who am I as a person? Well, that's not really your business, is it? All you need to know is that I lead effectively and with loving respect for everyone involved.

THE HARNESS

"I inspire proactive, hard work in the pursuit of a co-created vision."

MORSEL

Regardless of personal challenges, leaders must maintain a state of selfless clarity.

MESSAGE

Leadership is not about taking care of number one, it's about service. Everyone benefits from quality leadership and we all seek it.

Sometimes we look around and there is no leader in sight. This renders us lost and confused. With no clear leader or direction, we lose momentum. Then it dawns us: we are the leaders we were looking for. We realize it's time to forget about ourselves. It's time to step up to the plate and serve.

The Harness understands selflessness and service. He has done enough personal work to know that his needs are secondary to the needs of the whole. He's seen how ego can ruin an enterprise or pursuit. He's been part of teams that were led into confusion and dead ends. His experience has taught him that humility and transparency are key to success.

The Harness uses metaphor and story to keep egos focused so they can successfully collaborative. A true leader knows how to keep everyone on board while keeping things moving. Using a little motivation, The Harness helps individuals get over themselves quickly, so they can get back to the group effort. The best Harnesses can lead mediocre teams in the creation of something magnificent.

While his leadership often captures the spotlight, The Harness is often lonely. She might have a vision that is years ahead of its time. Her team may find it difficult working in a collaborative environment. She might be beholden to investors with big demands that conflict with her integrity.

Consider James Cameron and his movie Avatar. Not only did he create an entire universe, he had to wait for technology to be born so that his inventions could come to life. James had vision beyond vision. He is a stellar example of The Harness. He knew that his mission was not to master every aspect of film making (although he did that too), it was to inspire and harness innovation and creativity in others. James and his teams created machines and processes that made history.

When you are offered the opportunity to follow a brilliant, powerful visionary, do it. Put your self-doubt and judgments aside. There is a higher lesson on offer here. It is rare to be welcomed into the lair of a mastermind. Prepare for miraculous events and blown minds, including your own.

If The Harness has a hold on you, let the mastery unfold. Establish a clear vision, meticulously build your team, and begin the creation process in stealth. In a short period of time, you and your team will burst onto the scene with something incredible. What are you waiting for?

CAUTION

If The Harness does not lead her team with care and discernment, she can be plagued with group interpersonal challenges. While team communication and connection might seem trivial, they are the primary factors that determine success.

The same goes with family. Allowing everyone to be heard and honored is vital to keeping the peace. You can remain passive and hope it all works out, or you can coordinate a sit-down with everyone to align their spirits and focus. And sometimes you have to let people go.

Your goal should be to encourage every person to feel connected and motivated. Hire a professional mediator to help bring a healthier process to life. Your additional efforts will prove beneficial for everyone.

EXTREME

It might be that you've temporarily become an authoritarian, micro-managing others into stress, anger or complacency. This is your wake-up call to relax and let others be themselves. You might need a group adventure to get everybody (including you) out of their heads and detached from their egos. To shift oppression into light, change the hierarchy into something more open-minded. Encourage everyone to relax without fear of reprimand. Introduce a little warmth and freedom into the mix and you'll motivate this ragtag group to move in a miraculous direction.

As The Harness, your job is to coordinate and direct, never to push or control. If you are constantly critiquing, you will never achieve the dreams you hold close to your heart. Validate everyone for their best qualities and they'll reward you with an excellent work ethic.

EMPOWERMENT

The Harness can be caught off-guard by tragic events and complex circumstances. In order to move through challenging territory more successfully, The Harness might consider working on their emotional intelligence by engaging a therapist and mentor. Seek the counsel of a trusted friend, hire a personal coach and learn how to meditate.

Each one of us has a unique and subtle vibration. The colors of your clothes and the gemstones you wear can significantly affect your mood, mind and heart. Ingesting flower essences and applying essential oils to your body (or diffusing them into the air) can improve your energy, attitude and drive. Seek to improve yourself on every level. Below are recommendations for The Harness.

Colors: goldenrod, forest green, steel blue, purple, firebrick red, turquoise, white

Gemstones: Fluorite, Ametrine, Carnelian, Rhodonite Sugilite, Jade, Grossularite, Blue Quartz

Flower Essences: Olive, Oak, Chicory, Elm, Heather, Vervain, Vine, Gentian, Star of Bethlehem

Essential Oils: Myrrh, Melissa, Cajeput, Grapefruit, Hyssop, Spruce, Linden Blossom, Yarrow

When we let go of control, we relax into a nurturing, convenient flow.

THE NETWORKER

I love meeting new people and making meaningful introductions. I care more about the resulting relationships than I do about financial remuneration. I believe that happily sharing resources and connecting dots is valuable to the world. As such, I coordinate and marry the desires, passions and intentions in my network, hoping to inspire a new destiny. Providing these services gives me energy and opens my heart, while every cell in my body shouts: "I AM HERE TO HELP!"

THE NETWORKER

"Every introduction I facilitate increases my effectiveness, openness and strength."

MORSEL

One glance at the light can dissolve our shadows and expand our feelings of freedom and power.

MESSAGE

Kindness is what keeps the world in forward motion. Every tiny deed and warm introduction we enact has the potential to bring joy to our lives and the lives of others. We rarely have insight into the potential lineage that a kind gesture might produce.

With just one phone call, we might co-create a way to solve world hunger. With one conversation, we might help a homeless woman overcome her despair. There is no end to the good we can do when we selflessly reach out to help others.

Benevolence has the power to heal, but many of us hesitate before we put our goodness into play, fearing that our generosity might derail our day or become a habit. Truth be told, every one of us has accepted assistance from another human being.

The Networker is excitable, eager to please and passionate about connecting with those within his reach. His life is fast-paced and at the mercy of advances in technology, manufacturing, fashion or politics. Since these areas are always advancing, there is little downtime for this hard-working soul.

The Networker knows that there is little value in holding back, especially when it comes to helping others. Whether it is making introductions or giving someone food, she knows there is absolutely no value in being a stingy gatekeeper. Sparks emerge in our hearts the moment we decide to be generous.

When we hold positive intentions, they generally appear in some form in our lives. That is the law of attraction. This is true for business and love relationships, home searches, and the pursuit of just about any opportunity. When we have clear intentions and desires, the universe will co-create pathways to bring these things to life. The Networker operates from this point of view.

If The Networker shook your hand today, it is time to get creative in how you build relationships. Get out of the innovation closet and become more social. Reach out to those who might benefit from your gifts and offer your assistance. Until recently, you looked at your life in terms of your achievements. Now it is time to look at the value of your life in terms of generosity and relationship.

Join meet-up groups, go to conventions in your field, crash parties in your neighborhood. This new segment of your life is all about connecting with others, and making introductions to benefit the people in your relationship tree. Every leaf you assist, the more access you gain to opportunity. In the heat of it all, the life you benefit will most likely be your own.

CAUTION

When we become too impressed with our momentum or achievements, we can become reclusive or overly self-protective. We might forget that our successes require help from friends, customers and fans.

We might be processing emotions or giving birth to a project, but it is vital to step out from behind the curtain. Get out of the house, buy a new shirt, get your car detailed, or wander playfully in public. Bid farewell to your cave and get back into the light.

Enjoy a period of silence and solitude. By deepening your self-awareness, you become exponentially more attractive to others and more effective in your pursuits.

EXTREME

Being social benefits our immune systems, body chemistries, attitudes, emotions, and frames of mind. While certainly beneficial, socializing can also distract us from our goals and taking care of ourselves. Be careful not to forsake the momentum you started. It might be time to put down the martini and dig deeper into the hard work. Do not worry about being excluded from the hottest happenings. Do not fear being removed from the socialite registry. You will instinctively recognize the right time to dust off your dance card and step back into your party dress.

EMPOWERMENT

The Networker's social calendar and relationship tree often needs trimming and pruning. She might also be forgetting to schedule meals, love and sleep, rendering her exhausted and depleted.

To counter these tendencies, it is vital that you find time to meditate, recalibrate and focus on self-care. Draw a hot bath, walk in the woods, write in your journal, watch a romantic movie, or call a close friend. Endeavor to express your tears so you can become more grounded and connected.

The colors of your clothes and the gemstones you wear can significantly affect your mood, mind and heart. Ingesting flower essences and applying essential oils to your body (or diffusing them into the air) can improve your energy, attitude and drive. Seek to improve yourself on every level. Below are recommendations for The Networker.

Colors: white, yellow, coral, dark cyan, green, dark orange, dodger blue, purple, light pink

Gemstones: Moonstone, Rose Quartz, Prehnite, White Aragonite, White Selenite, Orange Kyanite, Peridot, Dioptase

Flower Essences: Vervain, Water Violet, Vine, Larch, Oak, Red Chestnut, Beech

Essential Oils: Wintergreen, Myrrh, Spruce, Anise, Angelica, Carrot Seed, Citronella, Galbanum, Geranium, Orange, Tangerine, Grapefruit

Imagine your life-force filling the room. Notice how it unites everything and everyone. This is the way in which you are connected to the entire universe.

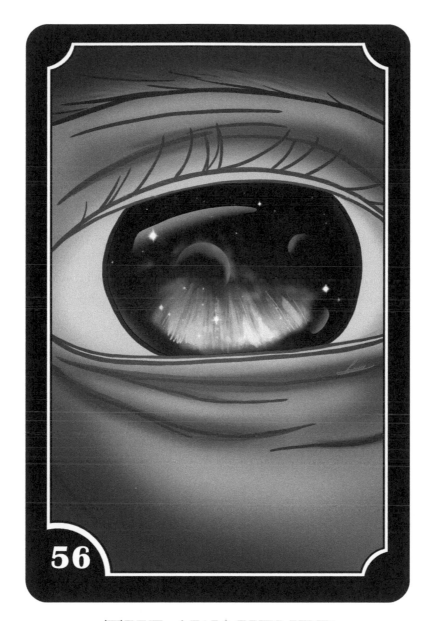

THE AWAKENED

The Self is connected to everything. The spirit in the rose, the energy that comprises the chair and the soul of the child are the same spirit that fills the vessels of all beings. There is no separation between any set of thoughts and any set of creations. All elements within the spectrums of every potential reality are connected. Love expands and contracts, breathing new life into every strand in existence. The Self is now and will always be the breath and the life, ever-connected to all, lighting a pathway from you to you, from the I Am to the all that is.

THE AWAKENED

"When looking in the mirror, it is nothing."

MORSEL

Pushing to achieve nirvana or Oneness is like rushing to fill a basket so that you can empty it.

MESSAGE

All the miracles that occur in the world take place because for one moment an individual bonded with the eternal fabric and commanded it into existence with love. The Awakened, or the one who comes into the state of nirvana, is deeply connected to all of creation, every fibre of the fabric. When we look into the eyes of an Awakened, we recognize our Self in the highest light possible. We see our oneness with everything in all realities.

No matter how far you stray, how disconnected you become, or how much you bark or cry, you will always be the same distance from embodying the internal eternal master as any other being on the planet. It comes down to your ability to forgive circumstance, liberate the past, and exist in a unified, sacred space long enough to embody grace.

The Awakened is whispering in your ear, infusing your mind and heart with the grace you requested in your prayers. As you feel her gentle abundance, remember that your potential will always be Oneness. You are invited to meet the master within. You are a sphere of light living within a sphere of light, protected by the consciousness who created everything. Feel whole as you advance toward freedom. Remember too that the journey is never-ending and your soul is timeless.

CAUTION

You do not live in a box and you are not the identity you imagine. You are much more. See past your limitations and release them with love. Allow your internal and external constructs to fade. Think of love and breathe love into this present moment. Discover the fragments of reality that have been blocking you. Release them so that your awareness and spirit can expand.

EXTREME

It is a funny thought to consider an extreme to the path of nirvana, the complete Oneness with the selfless state, but we have all felt extreme about our spiritual path. Long ago, you might have bumped into an old friend and they told you about Kundalini Yoga or Transcendental Meditation. They may have invited you to a "light gathering" or to meet a new guru. It all seemed so exciting! While the path toward the light might appear to be new-fangled, it is ancient.

When we look around at the many religious and spiritual sects on the planet, we see many modalities for transformation. Some ideologies feel good to us and some feel strange. We might like some of them and hate others. But we know that a spiritual path is subjective. There is no good reason to judge others for their choices involving invisible, silent forces of good and evil.

Spirituality can also be addictive. Some people get involved in meditation, yoga and the guru scene in order to feel a chemical high. We might buy white clothes, burn incense or release our identities with the hope of spiritual advancement.

We see shiny objects, have magical feelings, and sense a kindred like-mindedness in the souls around us. What began as an innocent venture into clarity has become a crutch, an addiction to form.

Spiritual materialism is a creeping vine. It first appears in the form of a small, beautiful weed. When we first meet her, we are barely able to take our eyes off of her. While the majesty of this weed is alluring, it is also dangerous. Its sole mission is to take our attention away from the inner work.

We forget that the truest and most valuable spiritual journey occurs within. This happens to the best of us. We feel lonely and lost. We have no idea where to go or how to grow. Instead of looking inside our hearts and within the richness of our experiences, we put ideologies and people on pedestals.

We buy an endless number of tickets to events and workshops. Somehow we feel that we are doing something of importance and of significant value. We are definitely doing something, it just has nothing to do with spirituality. We forge there are no answers outside of our being. Everything we need to know is within. The rest is illusion. If you have bought into something that is external to you, be sure that it feeds you internally. The time for trinkets and distractions has passed.

EMPOWERMENT

The Awakened is the pure state within each of us, the eternal soul without boundary. If you are striving to find this within yourself, remember that there is no trying. There is no pushing or achieving.

Nirvana, the clear state, will emerge when you are in perfect peace on every level of your being. It is then that you become one with the all that is. Releasing the I, you become everything for all time.

The colors of your clothes and the gemstones you wear can significantly affect your mood, mind and heart. Ingesting flower essences and applying essential oils to your body (or diffusing them into the air) can improve your energy, attitude and drive. Seek to improve yourself on every level. Below are recommendations for The Awakened.

Colors: white, yellow, gold, goldenrod, orange, dark orange, purple

Gemstones: Honey Calcite, Citrine, Sulphur, White Selenite, White Aragonite, White Opal

Flower Essences: Aspen, Centaury, Clematis, Heather, Pine

Essential Oils: Rose, Benzoin, Cardamom, Cinnamon, Frankincense, Juniper Berry, Myrrh

Non-duality is you and the universe forever-merged into a together-dream.

THE DO-GOODER

While I am confident that doing good in the world will yield a certain cachet when I arrive at the pearly gates, the most important aspect to me is how I am perceived by the powers that be. If my kindly efforts cannot be broadcast throughout influential networks and beyond, I might never see cause to offer them. I must feel a palpable and tangible effect from my goodwill, otherwise, what's the point? Once fully engaged and remunerated, I give it my all, or at the very least, make it appear that way. I have a good heart, even though it sometimes has a price tag. I am an opportunist after all.

THE DO-GOODER

"My giving is a means to an end, enhancing my position tenfold."

MORSEL

When we allow our hearts to feel the pains of others, we expand. Invoking compassion, we evolve.

MESSAGE

When we have a pureness of heart, we will naturally want to help others. It won't matter if we're sick or healthy, rich or impoverished, when we see someone in need, we will simply be inclined to extend our hearts and hands.

There is nothing else to do. There is no other impulse required of us. Helping others, sensing their suffering, and addressing their needs is what gives us our humanity. Everything else is an illusion that only feeds us for a moment.

We do not need another office building or sports arena. We do not need more golf courses or malls. We don't require another university, church or highway. If we were all thinking clearly, our only concern would be addressing the plights of the most disenfranchised factions of society. When we help others, we help ourselves.

With a compassionate heart, a mind for business, and a hunger for excellence, The Do-Gooder is a triple threat. She understands the value of human service, and she sees the bigger picture, knowing exactly what needs to be done and when. She's the ultimate quarterback for goodness.

The Do-Gooder knows that in order to accomplish a community project or larger-scale mission, it requires money, connections, favors and positive public opinion. These are the things that drive momentum.

The Do-Gooder understands that people are rarely motivated by a logo or resume. We engage with one another because of a pervading feeling or idea. It is perception that drives the human beast. When a mission or individual is perceived as valuable, they will be successful.

As such, when he begins an endeavor, The Do-Gooder takes advantage of quality introductions and press releases. He personally drives the story, controlling how it is consumed and perceived.

If The Do-Gooder has sauntered into your charity event, study every facet of her craft. Pay close attention to the concept, story, packaging and promotional plans she initiates. Assemble the elements from her tutelage into a plan. Work hard and follow through. This is the recipe for your success.

When the Do-Gooder gains too much momentum, she can tend toward vanity and self-promotion. If she's not careful, her personal aspirations can bring her good-deed train to a halt.

Focus on human service and allow your compassionate and empathic heart to lead the way in all things. This will advance your philanthropy as well as your soul's evolution.

CAUTION

You may have become a little too impressed with your ideas, taking the focus off the service you are trying to provide. In this case, whoever we are and whatever we do are secondary to the results we deliver. Let go of the image you have of yourself and put your energies into the mission at hand. Remember your original intentions. Step out of the spotlight and return to the humbled vision that first set you aglow.

It might be time to reimagine your story or the story of the project you are creating. Distracted by publicity and commerce, you may have lost sight of the challenges ahead. Be careful not to linger at fundraisers just to catch someone's glance. Do not over-celebrate the gift of gab and hype. You started something of quality that deserves to live. Put down the cocktail olives, roll up your sleeves and get back to work.

EXTREME

With drones, global tracking and a media-entranced society, everything and everyone seem to be in crosshairs. It might be that in choosing to help a faction of society, you ruffled the feathers of unions or political groups. You may have become a target.

It might be that your aspirations include targeting a specific demographic that would serve your career. You might be so focused on income and outcome, that you're missing the bigger picture. You may have wheeled-n-dealed too much and are now stuck in a corner. With your vulnerabilities out in the open, buzzards are circling to feast.

Forgetting how capable you are, you might be hiding your insecurities behind a public image. Recall the fire that first drove your mission into the public eye. Reinvigorate your plans with love.

EMPOWERMENT

The Do-Gooder is a valuable asset in times of trouble, but something lurks beneath the surface in this mover and shaker. To remedy the incongruence in this eager soul, evaluate your motivations. Look closely at the intentions that drive your actions. It might be time to reboot your personal ideology.

The colors of your clothes and the gemstones you wear can significantly affect your mood, mind and heart. Ingesting flower essences and applying essential oils to your body (or diffusing them into the air) can improve your energy, attitude and drive. Seek to improve yourself on every level.

Colors: white, yellow, gold, aqua, blue violet, turquoise, lawn green, lime, orange, dark pink

Gemstones: Emerald, Pink Tourmaline, Turquoise, Blue Aventurine, Benitoite, Aquamarine

Flower Essences: Beech, Chicory, Clematis, Crab Apple, Vine, Water Violet, Agrimony

Essential Oils: Angelica, Basil, Sage, Frankincense, Chamomile, Rose, Citronella, Bitter Orange

Miracles and goodness are often delivered by sweet souls, but some of life's most essential gifts are delivered by darker angels.

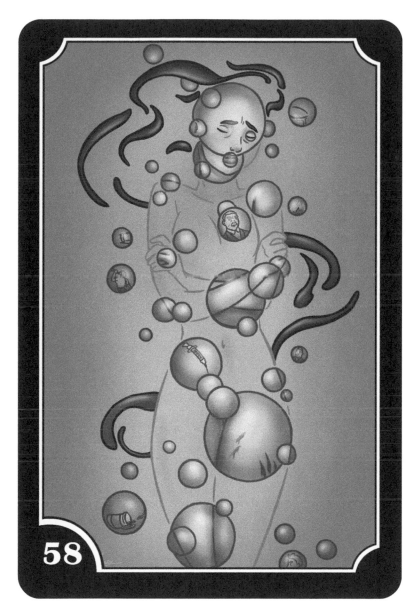

THE YEARNING

I forget that my beliefs are magnets for my experiences. Yet, I continue to retell the same unsatisfying tales. I shun the whispers of angels and remain stuck in my victim mind. I blame everyone but myself. Sometimes I see that my life is in my control. This is invigorating! I fantasize about joy and abundance. I see a clear path to my happiness. How can I attract the sweet scent of honeysuckle again? I yearn for it! I MUST break free! Implanted in this shallow hole, I look up and I see the light.

THE YEARNING

"Who will tend to my unfolding but me?"

MORSEL

Barking at the moon for shining is often preferable to looking at why we chose to stand under it in the first place. False, fermented stories are often the excuses we use to disrupt our lives.

MESSAGE

In every moment, we co-create the universe in partnership with the universe. Everything we are, we created. Everything we intend or desire, in some form, comes into being. Whether it is drama or celebration, happiness or dismay, we chose it all and help bring it to life.

Everything that is experienced in all the universes and all the realms is absorbed by the collective consciousness and then recycled. Whether it has to endure earthquakes, floods or sunshine, every planet finds a balance. Our solar system, like each of us, is a living vibration in constant evolution.

When a soul achieves Self-realization or nirvana, she begins to work on behalf of creation, clearing the energetic pollution throughout all time and space. This is the reason why many people flock to gurus and notions of enlightenment. They want to become part of the solution.

We have a choice to either draw from the energy available to us or add to it. When we're too caught up in our stories and the meanings we assign to them, we are sponges, taking as much energy for ourselves as we can so that we might feel whole. When we are self-sufficient and strong, we add energy to the equation, allowing those in need to draw sustenance when it's needed.

As The Yearning, you understand the plights that much of humanity faces. Seeing how challenged we all are, your empathy runs deep. You hope for a better world for yourself and others. You are acutely aware of how difficult life can be, yet you are hopeful and kind in all pursuits.

Sometimes The Yearning has the perspective that she is special. You are unique, you are an important part of creation, you are a missing piece in the puzzle of life. Without you, there would be a hole in the fabric of time and space. This is all true, but you are no more special than the flowers in the garden. You are one piece of creation, and there are many pieces.

You might feel that you are a needy victim, but this is not true. You do not need much of anything. You are the result of billions of years of evolution. Every option is readily available to you. You can associate with negativity and remain unfulfilled, or you can identify with your potential. It's a choice.

Step out of the shadows, decide to love yourself and be happy. Release the idea that you require help to achieve abundance. You are one decision away from being self-reliant and whole.

The Yearning has untapped resources. To see them, she must sit quietly and allow herself to fathom the possibilities. The moment she submits to her limitless potential is the moment she is set free.

CAUTION

When The Yearning is challenged by an untimely event, she can become attached to the ideas that she is in danger or is being played a victim. Appearing needy and troubled, the personal attention she receives can result in a chemical dependency akin to taking drugs. To get sober, you must titrate off of your negativity. You must take responsibility for your life, choosing independence over fear. This is how you can be reborn.

The first adjustment to make is to stop complaining. Adopt a positive and generous attitude. Stop perseverating on what you do not have. Seek only the positive. Celebrate the fact that you are an integral part of a timeless, living framework. Once you regenerate and sustain yourself, you will become a person of value to your community and world.

EXTREME

Without realizing it, you may have exhausted your friends and family, pushing them beyond their limits. This has affected your health and emotional well-being. You might be lonely or confused. This is what happens when we give up hope. You allowed your life to become less about abundance and more about lack. Lack of ingenuity, lack of money, lack of self-love, lack, lack, lack. Luckily, this is a temporary illusion. To get back on your feet, push through the haze and rise above your beliefs and circumstances. No matter how dark it gets, there is always a path that leads to the light.

You are a child of the universe with immeasurable potential. Live according to this thought and your life will find strength and balance once again.

EMPOWERMENT

To break free from his self-imposed prison, The Yearning must set a schedule of meditation and selfless service. Find a charity near you and volunteer to their cause. Stay away from egoistic notions related to accomplishments and success technologies. The real work is gritty and deep.

Look at every relationship in your life. Examine your patterns and learn to make better choices. Release emotions and adjust your thinking and behavior. Set a clear path to your personal transformation. Remember that your happiness is one thought away. Adopting some of the following ideas into your clothing, jewelry and daily routine can bring great benefit.

Colors: white, gold, goldenrod, coral, light blue, pink, purple, turquoise, light orange

Gemstones: White Selenite, Aquamarine, Charoite, Blue Lace Agate, Orange Calcite, Pink Sapphire

Flower Essences: Willow, Star of Bethlehem, Wild Rose, White Chestnut, Honeysuckle, Larch, Pine

Essential Oils: Geranium, Clove, Bergamot, Sandalwood, Frankincense, Rosewood, Ylang Ylang

Only your effort can produce a resurrection. Expecting imaginary forces to save you is fantasy. Begin again, then again, then again. In every moment, begin.

THE KING

There is no authority above me, except God, but even God and I have an understanding. Beneath me are loyal subjects, attendants and servants. I rule my world with confidence and without objection. Every word I utter is documented then used to educate the masses. All systems within my kingdom are a direct result of what I privately envisioned, whispered to my roundtable then publicly commanded. I hold myself accountable for shepherding every soul in my domain. Seek my counsel and I will weave you a masterpiece. Cross me and you'll pay a hefty price.

THE KING

"My command is the gold from which you will spin your life."

MORSEL

Achieving excellence requires a measure of seclusion. Lonely, strong and courageous are righteous kingly attributes.

MESSAGE

The masculine aspect is within all of us. It helps us move forward, explore, compete and complete. Throughout history, patriarchal societies have overvalued these attributes, using them to enslave others, but when masculinity is fully conscious, the results are growth and freedom.

Defend vigorously and wholly integrate the vital masculine force within you. With one brief statement or gesture, The King can motivate an entire continent to fulfill a complex and enduring agenda. Without his masculinity, The King's efforts would be wordy, limp and ineffective.

The King is the eternal father, resting his hand on our shoulders, encouraging us to work hard, think for ourselves and do the right thing. With The King at our side, we reach beyond our limitations, toward the fulfillment of our dreams. We hear his strong but gentle voice in the back of our minds, as it inspires our temperance and excellence.

The King leads from a deep inner knowing. Long ago he realized that consensus is nothing but a politically correct contrivance that perpetuates confusion and mediocrity. While he is often prudent in taking advice from his inner circle, The King's decisions come from his impenetrable core.

The King understands that when one strong, single-minded individual fully embodies a vision, he has a far greater chance at succeeding than does a co-dependent group of ladder-climbers, continuously micromanaging every nanosecond of activity. It is near impossible to expand under such scrutiny.

Being The King is not about making friends, it is about service to a greater cause. The King examines all the far-reaching implications of her ideas from personal, social and financial perspectives. In everything she does, The King wants her subjects and partners to remain safe.

As The King, you must regularly examine, evaluate and encourage your kingdom. Are you resolute in your command or do you appease fears and critics with over-simplified placations to keep the peace? Would you prefer to be liked or complete the mission at hand? Do you want a mention in a community newsletter, or would you prefer to be on the cover of Time Magazine?

You know what excellence is. You know what needs to be done. Do not fret hurting someone's feelings or gently nudging a few folks out of the way. If they take it personally, that is their choice.

To create something noteworthy, there will always be a few tiny, well-intended casualties. Be swift, decisive, kind and courageous. Build the kingdom your inner King intends.

CAUTION

You may have become defensive of femininity, failing to honor the positive, joyful aspects of a masculine person's gifts. Masculinity is within all of us. To judge the masculine, whether we are male or female, is to judge half of human nature, half of the universe.

To be fair, if masculinity was the more supportive force and the feminine was ruling the planet during earlier centuries, there may have been different, but equally damaging results. The masculine and feminine each have inconsistencies and flaws, yet both have attributes we desperately need in order to thrust ourselves forward.

When The King is congruent in mind and heart, she knows to scour her plans for imperfections and inconsistencies before revealing them to the world. She immediately deals with challenges that arise.

EXTREME

If you are looking to win a popularity contest, The King may not be the role for you. Being The King will not only test your self-esteem, it will demand it. You cannot go into a major leadership position with a desire to be nurtured. You lead because you must, valiantly dealing with consequences. If you do not want to serve, remove your crown then graciously hand it to someone who has the ethics and intentions commensurate with the highest office in the land.

When leadership is failing or toxic, managers are unable to carry out orders. Negative, competitive chatter emerges among workers. The product is wrought with imperfections, failing to impress. Citizens feel lethargic because the inspiration that once enthused them is not to be found. Kings must never be defensive and arrogant. Kingship is about service not servitude.

EMPOWERMENT

The King often keeps an emotional distance from others, living in fear of being out-maneuvered or replaced. To preserve his health and might, he must express his feelings to a close confidant. The King must also find time for playfulness and the arts. This will reduce the pressures he feels.

The colors of your clothes and the gemstones you wear can significantly affect your mood, mind and heart. Ingesting flower essences and applying essential oils to your body (or diffusing them into the air) can improve your energy, attitude and drive. Seek to improve yourself on every level. The following recommendations are based on the attributes associated with The King.

Colors: cornflower blue, dark cyan, orange, violet, firebrick red, white, gold, green

Gemstones: Lolite, Aventurine, Orange Calcite, Fire Opal, Azurite, Blue Calcite, Ruby, Garnet, Gold

Flower Essences: Vine, Gentian, Holly, Impatiens, Larch, Mustard, Rock Rose, Vervain, Water Violet, Scleranthus

Essential Oils: Cinnamon, Ginger, Bergamot, Cardamom, Grapefruit, Marjoram, Myrtle, Rose

Bow your head, ask for grace and bravely charge forward.

THE JESTER

I am a soft storyteller living among wolves. I see the twisted creature-spirits that fight for residence inside the bodies of the kings and queens around me. These conflicted, complex souls live to conjure and conquer. It is all theatre I know, but the pain they cause their subjects enrages me so! I know there is no security. I know there is no control. I dance in the folly of those around me, reflecting hidden darkness to onlookers with a wink and a smile. If, through me, you get a glimpse of your true nature, I have delivered the service I intended. Your denial and delusion are my inspiration. Leaning toward the light, my every thought seeks to unravel the twisted realities that oppress the masses. Come with me, to the edge, on this limb of truth. There we will dance until you break.

THE JESTER

"Laugh at my antics and release the false notions that restrict you."

MORSEL

Upon the bursting of a bubble comes an awakening, followed by a choice to accept reality as it is, or remain in slumber.

MESSAGE

The things we believe to be real in our lives are temporary formations of light and sound. Everything is made of these two elements. This is how everything is connected. It's ALL light and sound. When we verbally or actively defend a specific reality, belief, relationship or experience, we are adding light and sound to it, much like a carpenter adds plaster to form a wall. The more we defend, the more it takes shape and the more it roots in our lives.

When we see changes coming, we are presented with an opportunity. On our worst days, we build walls, block the light, and miss out on a deepening. On our brightest days, we are able to see change as an opportunity. Seizing it, we open ourselves up to the unveiling of universal truths.

The Jester gives us the opportunity to see ourselves and our lives more clearly. With each joke and metaphoric story, he dismantles falsehood, siphoning away our attachment. With loving assistance, he peels back the layers, lights our path, and nudges us along our way.

The Jester uses warm-hearted stories and thoughtful theatrics to enlighten his audiences. The Jester is compassionate, knowing how difficult it can be when our illusions are challenged or shattered. He doesn't want to shock us like The Comedian, rather, The Jester wants to gently hold our hand as we cross the threshold into awareness.

The Jester is clever and discreet, able to escape the destiny he often provokes. Using outrageous dialogue and provocative characters, he distracts the judges from the poignant revelations within his stories. By the time the aristocracy understand the deeper effects of his play, The Jester is long gone and onto his next adventure.

If The Jester is jingling his cane for you today, it is time to lovingly laugh at yourself and the reality you have attracted and created. As this is all an illusion, a play for the eternal master, you are best to remain as detached and upbeat as possible.

Find the extreme and subtle humor in the chaos around you. Be the witness who hunts for the humor in all things. The joy is found between the lines, in the dance of the minstrel, the smirk of the protagonist, and in the lap of the Duke as a fool covers him with honey.

Look into the mind of the most detached character in this play and see what she sees. Notice how free she is. By cajoling at the Jester's side, you might find that everything you once believed to evaporate upon your next laugh.

CAUTION

If you're taking life too seriously, look honestly at yourself and your beliefs. When we finally see ourselves for who we really are, every part of us relaxes. There is no longer a reason to hide or pretend. When we buy into stories around politics, religion, family, security and our own identity, we miss out on growth and transformation. While the truth might not be easy to source, our open-mindedness can inspire the most helpful information to rise to the surface.

Consider the number of illusions you've ingested. Whether it's about products and services you buy, your spiritual stories or your government, it's daunting to peer into that rabbit hole. After your first honest peek into the mirror, you won't be able to take your eyes off the truth. You'll find it nourishing and addictive all at once.

EXTREME

The Jester can be naive. When she is too caught up in his own playfulness, she fails to notice the Sheriff standing in the shadows waiting to imprison her. She forgets that regardless how magical and charming she might be, she is never above the law.

Look at the stories you tell yourself. Are you willing to risk your life for the reality you are defending? It's time to shake your tree! You are not the story you believe yourself to be. You are much more. Every contrivance we allow is a liability that blocks our connection to ourselves. When we defend our illusions, we become them. Focus on the rose and you become the rose.

EMPOWERMENT

This playful soul can fathom complex, social dynamics like no one else in court. With his depth of awareness and intuition, The Jester quickly heals and illuminates. With a gesture, facial expression or story, he helps others see their circumstances more clearly. With all his brilliance, The Jester is not immune to the effects of the world. If he desires to take his craft and healing to the next level, he must confront his broken dreams. Consider alternative modalities like shamanism, art therapy, dance therapy, dream therapy, or any deep exploratory tool.

The colors of your clothes and the gemstones you wear can significantly affect your mood, mind and heart. Ingesting flower essences and applying essential oils to your body (or diffusing them into the air) can improve your energy, attitude and drive. These recommendations are for The Jester.

Colors: orange, purple, gold, chocolate, green, slate blue, firebrick red, dark orchid

Gemstones: Chiastolite, Orange Kyanite, Ruby, Green Chlorite, Dioptase, Amethyst, Sugilite

Flower Essences: Oak, Agrimony, Crab Apple, Larch, Rock Rose, Vervain, Star of Bethlehem

Essential Oils: Lemongrass, Myrrh, Cardamom, Neroli, Orange, Patchouli, Lavender

Nestled in the bosom of metaphor is wisdom born from pain. Embrace the creativity around you. Let it advance your well-being.

THE NOBLE

As a member of the upper echelon, I am entitled, comfortable and at peace. Strip me of my privilege and I may topple. Although I try to be more empathic, I seem to be impervious to the pain of others. I see the lower classes as helpless, yet they often claw for my favor. When I am approached to lend my assistance, my heart freezes. I love my silver spoon, but I'm sure it prevents me from feeling a greater depth. Is it possible to expand my heart whilst protecting myself?

THE NOBLE

"I require speedy adherence and allegiance. Did you not hear the snap of my fingers?"

MORSEL

When love and compassion take a back seat to privilege, a butterfly has a heart attack.

MESSAGE

Every time we joyfully accept discomfort, we expand the Self. With an expanded Self, we fall in line with the pure vibration of the universe and experience a deeper connection to humanity.

We all seek comfort. Whether it is clothes, cars, mattresses, seating or air conditioning, we have comfort barometers for almost every area of our lives. There is comfort food, comfortable shoes and comfy pajamas. Your relationship could be comfortable and your job might provide a comfortable living. We all romanticize around the notion of comfort. It is intrinsic to our identity.

Your partner may require no more than a squishy couch to feel she's luxuriating when traveling, while your friend requires a Five-Star Hotel.

You might enjoy a yoga mat on the floor of an artist studio, while a devout spiritual aspirant feels perfectly rested atop a bundle of hay with goats.

While the young English professor likes sleeping bags at youth hostels, the Wall Street executive shudders at the thought of 250-thread versus 600-count cotton sheets. It is a matter of perspective.

Each of us must decide what level of comfort is desirable to us and how much we are willing to stretch ourselves physically, emotionally and spiritually. Some of us are addicted to comfort, while others use our rejection of comfort as a spiritual whetting stone.

If The Noble is dining pool-side with you today, ask him what he finds most comforting in his world. Is it his position in society? Is it the perceived quality of brand-name products he buys? Is it his family's long list of accomplishments? Is it his ability to serve others?

If you're feeling noble today, how does your sense of comfort and privilege affect how you interact with others? When you eat a meal at an airport, do you bus your own tray and throw away your own garbage, or do you let it sit on the table and secretly hope an immigrant worker will "take care of it?"

Whatever the cause of your comfort itch, it is time to relinquish privilege, loosen your demand for a wrinkle-free existence, and make room for things you might ordinarily find disruptive.

Intimacy can cure The Noble's tendency to separate herself from others. When we connect meaningfully with our neighbors, we experience more happiness and a greater sense of purpose.

You do not have to live without the 600-thread cotton duvet for long, just long enough to test your limits and boundaries. Crack your own shell, let go of a little comfort, and unearth the mysteries beneath your identity. Underneath all our skin, bones, jewelry and titles, we're all exactly the same.

CAUTION

What starts as a desire to be noble can quickly snowball into entitlement. Be careful how you phrase things. Be cognizant of your tone and attitude. It might be that you've become so comfortable complaining and demanding that you don't even know when you're doing it. Every sound you make is absorbed by the universal consciousness. If your sounds are most often negating someone's experience, it might be time to make adjustments.

You might be upset with the low-level shine on your shoes or the imperfectly-formed ice cubes in your drink. Relinquish your pretension. Soften-up and get back to living more from your heart.

EXTREME

Because of is limited tolerance of others, you might feel uncomfortable being in the same room as The Noble. As he works overtime to ensure he gets more than his share, he is unaware of those who scramble for crumbs.

As The Noble, it might be time to volunteer at a soup kitchen, homeless shelter or drug clinic. In most of these environments, you will have to move so quickly to serve others, you will not have time to tend to your own needs. You might be missing an important piece of your personality: empathy. You do not have to be a saint to live a heart-centered life. Soften your demands, lighten your heart and laugh at just how particular you can be. This is the best way to begin your change of life.

EMPOWERMENT

Often holding the upper hand or controlling position in relationships, The Noble finds it difficult to establish dependable friendships. Be more proactive with friends and family. Have dinner parties and picnics. Schedule activities with those you like and love. Open your heart to companionship.

The colors of your clothes and the gemstones you wear can significantly affect your mood, mind and heart. Ingesting flower essences and applying essential oils to your body (or diffusing them into the air) can improve your energy, attitude and drive. Seek to improve yourself on every level. The following recommendations are based on the attributes associated with The Noble.

Colors: white, ivory, blue violet, orange, green, indigo, slate blue, violet red, black

Gemstones: Tiger's Eye, Shattuckite, Blue Apetite, Chrysocolla, Blue Aventurine, Orange Calcite, Ruby, Black Tourmaline, Amethyst

Flower Essences: Chicory, Aspen, Beech, Chestnut Bud, Crab Apple, Elm, Heather, Holly, Vine, Willow

Essential Oils: Patchouli, Mountain Savory, Bergamot, Cedarwood, Rosewood, Linden Blossom, Marjoram, Grapefruit

Your heart is more powerful and expansive than you realize. Diminish your dependency on titles and position. Seek to know and express your heart.

THE MONEY

When I toss a fistful of dollar bills into the air, I am showered with the most nourishing rain! No matter the currency, money gives me confidence in who I am and what I am doing. It feeds the part of my being that sees wealth as a factor in joy. I can use it as a cloak to attract suitors or as a tool to inspire subservience. To me, money is honey. When I have it, I am giddy. Without it, I fade into a sea of unquenched thirsts and dreams.

THE MONEY

"A little money is okay, but I prefer twice as much so I can know myself fully."

MORSEL

Material wealth is not in direct conflict with spiritual growth, but it can obscure our clarity.

MESSAGE

We need to value money enough to attract it, but we should not expect anything else from it. Money can save a life, fund a dream or create an uptick in drama. Regardless of the good it might provide, if our identity depends on it, or if we use it to control others, we can't be free.

The desire for money is integral to our lives. Even loving money can produce great results. Problems arise when we use money to increase our power over others, when we use it to fund something that's antithetical to our nature, and when we believe it to be our only resource.

After all, money is one of many modalities that can be used successfully in an exchange. The broader definition of money is anything that we use to barter in a negotiation or agreement. While The Money is well aware of these definitions, she is focused on one thing: cash flow.

With possibly many lives at the helm of a big pile of cash, The Money is able to attract wealth and financial flow with ease. She understands the ultimate purpose of money is to empower an initiative. She knows how to operate the levers that control money and she can sense when money is tarnished.

The Money is always careful with his intentions around financial planning. He meticulously maps out his goals years in advance. He has back-up plans, alternative contingencies, side bank accounts and longer term investments in play at all times. The Money always takes care of his financial agenda long before he tends to any other personal or business matter.

Methodically map out your desires and plans for money. Carry them out to their logical conclusions. Which of these desires is rooted in who you are? Which ones stem from your temporary illusions? Once you reach the conclusions of these desires, what do you have? Who are you then?

When The Money is out of balance, he'll romanticize about financial gain, using money to gain leverage over others. He might momentarily forsake friends, family and integrity. When the dark side of money nibbles at us, the journey back to ourselves can be challenging.

Along the way, someone may have reinforced the idea that your lifestyle and clothing are of more intrinsic value to the world than your ability to express creativity and love. If your most dominant fascination is a financial waterfall, you might miss out on the deeper aspects of life.

Redefine money in your life so that it aligns with your highest ideals. Allow money to nurture, protect and honor you and your family. In all things, ensure that the money in your life feeds positive, enjoyable realities.

CAUTION

We can be drunk on sex, love, wine or religion. We can be drunk on desire and intellectualism. We can get tipsy from a purchase or experience. Without a doubt, we can become intoxicated with money.

When we are drunk, there is something beneath the surface that evades us. It is a hole, a wishing, a wanting, a soft whisper of sadness that craves love and attention. It is difficult to name this craving.

You might be an artist, healer or inventor, intoxicated with attention. This could easily delay your success in the craft of your dreams.

What can you do from love that might increase your wealth? Bliss generates everything we need, attracting a deeper sense of joy than money could ever attract on its own. Honor your creativity. Doing so will inspire powerful, mysterious forces to come to your aid.

EXTREME

Your love affair with money has been fascinating! You met remarkable people. You were center stage, backstage and behind the magic curtain. You had escorts, valets and personal butlers. You had limousines and caviar, and a key to the executive bathroom. You have been a top dog, a member of the club, and the center of attention. You were a Rock Star VIP extraordinaire on the ride of your life, but is this what your soul intended? After all, do you feel nourished and whole?

Take measure of the expense of your journey so far. Add it up in a spreadsheet. What did it all cost? Take into account every expense, emotional and financial. Break it down into categories and look at the entirety of what you spent. Chances are, the net loss is ginormous. Isn't it time for a change?

EMPOWERMENT

If you are financially able, take a year off to hike, meditate and write. If you need to make a living during this time, get a stress-free part-time job so you can maintain a life of introspection. As this is all an illusion, you might consider making it the happiest and most nurturing illusion possible.

The colors of your clothes and the gemstones you wear can significantly affect your mood, mind and heart. Ingesting flower essences and applying essential oils to your body (or diffusing them into the air) can improve your energy, attitude and drive. Seek to improve yourself on every level. The following recommendations are based on the attributes associated with The Money.

Colors: blue violet, orchid, dark red, green, teal, white, pink

Gemstones: Pink Tourmaline, Red Coral, Emerald, Peridot, Infinite Stone, Axinite, Azeztulite

Flower Essences: Holly, Pine, Elm, Aspen, Gorse, Heather, Crab Apple, Star of Bethlehem

Essential Oils: Fennel, Angelica, Myrtle, Bergamot, Elemi, Galbanum, Patchouli, Sandalwood

Money is the most obvious tool to use in an exchange. It is also the least interesting. Dig deep and uncover the wealth inherent in your uniqueness.

THE VERGE

Holding my vision and potential too tightly, my magic train hopped off its tracks. Lost in a fog betwixt the real and unreal, I see a faint light in the distance. Moving toward the light, I sense that I am soon to regain my position of strength. As I struggle with obstacles, I wonder if I will get back to where I was. In this moment, I realize I will be better than before. I am ready, aware, centered. I push through my confusion into a bright freedom. I awake in a dream remembering only love.

THE VERGE

"I temporarily lost my way, but I am reemerging with passion."

MORSEL

One awareness can pop our souls back into perfect alignment and into the center of the light.

MESSAGE

When we have momentum in pursuit of a goal, we are convinced of our success, feeling as if we have already achieved it. It feels blissful because there are no obstacles in the present moment or on the horizon. We stand in the light and we are the light.

The Verge is the embodiment of forward movement and enthusiasm, on the brink of absolute success and excellence. She relentlessly pushes through every obstacle. Her path is clear and her effort, Herculean. An example of perseverance and completion, she far exceeds her competitors and peers.

When The Verge moves too quickly or in haste, she can be bumped off her path. In the throws of change, she might become confused and disoriented. What was once a promise can temporarily fall into question. This would be devastating for most of us, but for The Verge, it is temporary.

Very little can deter the Verge, but she has a tendency to forsake her well-being. When we are not paying attention to our health, relationships and emotional health, we can easily fall short. No matter how wonderful our goals and projects are, they are no match for a stressed heart.

When our plans change and our lives are interrupted, it's a sign that we missed something along the way. It might also be the universe is protecting us from a larger disaster. While you might feel frustrated with your current position, the recent disruption may have saved your life!

Although The Verge might be wandering in a thin fog today, he is moments away from a stabilizing awareness. His mind may be scattered and he may have temporarily lost faith, but after a few moments of contemplation and meditation, he will find his power and purpose again. Sometimes all it takes is a long deep breath or a walk around the block to bring us home again.

If The Verge appears unprepared and over-burdened, slow things down and take inventory of recent events in your life. Allow yourself to feel the presiding emotions. By listening for and honoring your awarenesses, you ready yourself for anything.

Move gently through the world today so that the sounds and vibrations of your inner-being can recalibrate. Your original state is The Verge. It is your birthright. Reclaim it by reconnecting to yourself.

Leave recent challenges behind and thoughtfully push ahead. Breathe deeply to strengthen your foundation and resolve. The only clocks that tick are those that our egos build. To shine brightly, relax into the present moment. From there you will regain, rebuild and prosper.

CAUTION

All living beings experience trauma. There is not one soul exempt from suffering. If you have taken a major hit in the recent past, you might need to curtail your plans until all cylinders are firing again. Since time and space do not exist, and since the universe has no will, there is no reason to rush any part of your plan. As you evaluate what you want to accomplish, consider your timeline as secondary.

It might be that the idea you love so much is born of negative emotions or beliefs. Instead of letting emotions out and invoking a healing, you may have constructed a false Self to justify the feelings within you. The Self you are promoting might not be you. Is it your shadow? If you end up achieving success from the efforts of your shadow, you may not feel as though you participated in it. It will seem as if the resulting accomplishments were created by someone you never met.

You are a sensitive soul, a magnetic vibration, and a child of the universe who requires additional time to collect his strength. You will know when the time is right to begin again.

EXTREME

Many of us live in constant movement and confusion. You have pushed well beyond your limits most of your life. You have rarely taken even a slight pause between experiences. This means you have barely processed many of the events and resulting emotions from your life. With unresolved and unattended feelings, you are denying yourself growth, discernment and awareness. With a clear, self-expressed heart, you will naturally soften and open up in ways you may never have imagined.

EMPOWERMENT

For The Verge to feel clear again, she might need to grieve. Heavy-duty exercise will help this spirit push through barriers that once derailed her. Art therapy is a great way to connect with the fascia of the emotional body. Cooking will connect you to the earth and yourself.

Whatever is trapping you inside this hazy maze, find empowerment in the use of the following suggestions. Choose whatever soothes you most. If you feel out of control, engage a professional counselor or naturopath to help you clear the debris resting atop your heart and soul.

These colors, gemstones, flower essences and essential oils will improve your mind, heart and mood.

Colors: yellow, gold, ivory, lavender, powder blue, spring green, turquoise, rose, fuchsia, orange

Gemstones: Clear Quartz, Fluorite, Lemon Quartz, Honey Calcite, Sulphur, Opalite, Blue Aragonite

Flower Essences: Aspen, Gentian, Gorse, Wild Rose, Cerato, Chestnut Bud, Clematis, Honeysuckle

Essential Oils: Cypress, Frankincense, Peppermint, Patchouli, Lemongrass, Rose, Myrtle, Lavender

Beneath the stories and hype live the answers to all of our questions. Sit quietly and beckon your awareness.

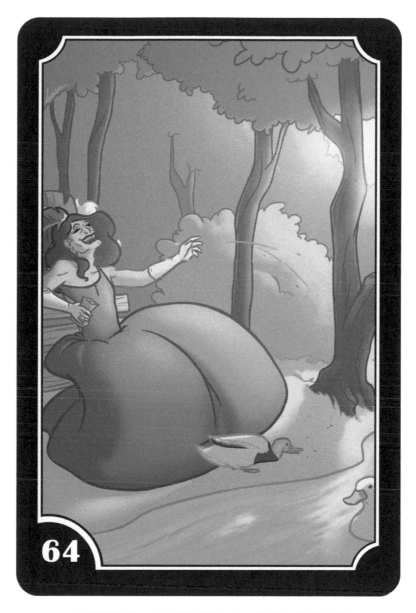

THE OUTRAGEOUS

I am a brightly colored butterfly, a wildly expressive hummingbird with massive, powerful wings. I zoom into a room with theatrical grandeur, demanding to be adored. My deepest desire is to provoke others while drawing as much attention to myself as possible. I do not believe my costume to be representative of who I am, but I enjoy everyone's reactions to my appearance and persona. Laugh with me or dance on by. I am a one-person party, an unstoppable creative force, and I'm here to stay.

THE OUTRAGEOUS

"Get naked with me! Let's show them what discomfort and joy are all about!"

MORSEL

Apologizing for being who you are is like saying the universe has a design flaw.

MESSAGE

Some of us do not need a holiday like Halloween to dress up and get wild. Wearing costumes, acting out and pushing the boundaries of socially acceptable behavior are excellent ways to explore our playfulness, self-expression and divine rights.

We are pulsating, vibrating bundles of matter with an infinite ability to create and expand. There are no rules as far as the universe is concerned. The self-hatred, oppression, and limits we often ingest are born of fear, religions, and contrived social rules. We are the only ones who can set the Self free.

When we honor our nature and commit to being who we are, we allow the universe to pour into and shape us. This is the mindset that the future innovators, inventors and "tappers of consciousness" are being born with. They trust what flows through them.

There are many "apparently" good reasons to curtail natural impulses. It might be the sensitivities of a group we joined. It could be the co-dependent rules built by our families. It might be the political correctness perpetuated by a social movement or the company who employs us. Regardless, we should never lose sight of our truths and the joys of our self-expression.

If The Outrageous has cross-dressed his way into your cocktail party, embrace his sensibilities with abandon. It's important to understand that it takes courage to freely express yourself. We should honor and respect those who go out on a limb to be free.

The Outrageous has a tremendous message for all of humanity: BE YOUR NATURAL SELF WITHOUT APOLOGY. When a bird chirps loudly, society's first reactions are anger or jealousy. If someone is barking at you for being yourself, tell them you love them then ignore them. Celebrate yourself with abandon.

When we lovingly accept the majesty of The Outrageous, we say yes to our unbridled selves. The Outrageous could be an inventor of disruptive technology, a breakthrough street artist, a powerful communicator or a master creative spirit who promises to live in the higher decibels of self-expression.

If you feel the impulse, BE FREE! Let the universe witnesses itself through your words, actions, songs or dances. This will send ripples of happiness throughout all of creation.

You have been quiet for long enough. Living under society's oppressive rules, you have let far too many impulses die a lonely death. Rip the lid off! Shine brightly, like the sun, like the eternal spirit who gave birth to you. Be YOU and be FREE!

CAUTION

How sad it is when we allow judgmental depressives to extinguish our spark. How troubling it can be when we internalize someone else's fears. Other people's opinions are none of our business.

While some of us brew creativity and invention, others cook a different stew: rage. Rage is a potent stimulant for creativity, if it does not destroy us first. If there is anger within you, find healthy, non-destructive ways to express it.

Beneath the anger is sadness. Find the sadness within your heart by expressing yourself artistically. Write a poem, song or story about what you are feeling. Express your emotions and free yourself.

EXTREME

Your outrageous behavior might stem from a long line of fully-expressed family members. With a feisty inner-cocktail, you might be having a hard time being anything but creative or explosive. Some of us have been deeply traumatized by other people's selfish behavior. Our angry fantasies have nothing to do with other people. They stem from us, so they are about us. Everything you experience and every type of person you attract becomes your responsibility. Forgive yourself, forgive others. Let it all go. As your personal alchemy improves, so will your life.

Focus on the creative. Build something superb with an intensity equal to your discontent. You might imagine the next Mt. Rushmore, invent a new healing modality or inspire the development of a new energy source. Before setting something on fire, get out the chisel and sculpt a masterpiece.

EMPOWERMENT

It can be quite a challenge to heal the harshness and judgments thrust upon us. The world is filled with jealous, depressed and parochial naysayers. As they work out their demons on us, we must forgive them so that we can remain free. Once The Outrageous forgives others and releases the related emotions, her art, ideas and life will change dramatically. Do a ritual in the woods to release negative relationships from your life. See a priest, shaman or rabbi for help with forgiveness.

If you feel out of control, engage an art therapist or herbalist to help you find your power again. It is time to leap out of that closet, put on that beautiful dress and be abundantly free!

These colors, gemstones, flower essences and essential oils will improve your mood, mind and heart.

Colors: white, yellow, goldenrod, dark orange, violet red, firebrick red, dark orchid, dark sea green

Gemstones: Green Quartz, Tourmaline, Garnet, Aragonite, Yellow Fluorite, Peridot, Fire Agate

Flower Essences: Larch, Agrimony, Crab Apple, Mimulus, Vervain, White Chestnut, Cherry Plum

Essential Oils: Star of Bethlehem, Bergamot, Rose, Jasmine, Neroli, Lemon, Sandalwood, Cloves

Screaming your value from a mountain-top might not result in social acceptance or an inner-awareness of your stunning majesty, but it could certainly help!

THE SHIFTER

I am a disruptive, innovative cog here to challenge the predictable wheels of life. You may be unnerved by my energy and presence, but my ideas and creations will change you. How did this world become so unimaginative, felled by such restrictive slumbers? It is no wonder that my thunder shakes them so. I refuse to tip-toe. I would rather demolish a wall than paint it pale. While I am here to help, I will challenge every spark of control and untruth around me. Invite me over if you dare.

THE SHIFTER

"Watch my clarity transform the room!"

MORSEL

When we are resolute, the universe bends in our favor. Eternal truth is disruptive, but even perfection can be systematized into a lie.

MESSAGE

Most of us are deeply attached to our beliefs. When it seems time for a change, we're reluctant, quickly diving back into our safe, little holes. Even when presented with wonderful opportunities, fearing too much disruption, we walk away. To make even small adjustments, we need to be shoved.

To break out of our slumber, we must first look to the influences that guided us here: the media, religions, families and governments. Not only did we lap up their rubbish with a smile, we continue to use it to limit our compassion, awareness and personal power.

The Shifter comes into a situation, makes one comment then watches the walls of reality disintegrate around her. She is the classic deconstructionist, the Kali of her day. Her mere presence galvanizes everything around her to align in clear, interdependent fashion.

When The Shifter appears in our lives, it can be alarming. It might even feel dangerous. We might want to punch him in the face, throw up or run screaming out of the room. There is something powerfully invasive about The Shifter.

The Shifter challenges the validity of our patterns. She's a spiritual hurricane who shakes us free of attachments and delusion. Brilliance bursts through her as ideas that are years ahead of their time. She effortlessly conjures remedies to conditions yet to be imagined.

By scraping away all of the assumptions and misinformation lining our guts, The Shifter empowers us to be who we are. He opens our eyes to our most advantageous gifts and qualities.

The Shifter understands that some situations cannot pivot on their own. Passion, emotion and electricity are often needed. When our dynamics and relationships are entrenched in ancient history, The Shifter can provide emotionally-driven pattern-interrupts to save us from ourselves.

The Shifter is intuitive, able to see and uproot forces that oppress authenticity. She laughs at guilt and shame because she knows these things are fear-based constructs seeking to control creative flow.

We all have the ability to change direction and re-make ourselves in an instant. We can reorder, reassemble and recreate any part of our realities whenever we want. Break through the madness today and allow your hidden mastery to ascend to the surface so it may rule the day.

Embrace the wild frontier and conspire with the universe to shift your life. Focus on joy, mix in the colors of clarity, and repaint your world to the full extent of your heart's desires.

CAUTION

Sometimes when our desires and intentions change, we may become less interested in the current people, places and events in our lives. It's not personal, it's organic to the nature of change. Upon changing our life, some friends might feel anger or jealousy. That is because we are threatening their understanding of reality. Your devout group of friends and family might even feel you are purposely hurting them by making a different choice. There is nothing further from the truth.

Your life, no matter how connected to the life of another, is an exclusive, singular trajectory in the realm of space and time. Your contract is with the universe, no one else. You do not owe anybody anything. Given time, everybody adjusts. In the meantime, celebrate your adventure with enthusiasm. Freedom and reinvention are what the universe intends.

EXTREME

The Shifter is neither a home-wrecker nor a bad person. She is a magnanimous truth-teller who brings a bright message to the delusional at exactly the right moment. The most vain of us might ignore her and enter into a cycle of repetitive behavior. Those of us who prefer a more self-examined life will welcome her ideas. There is no reason to fear The Shifter. Whatever changes she introduces, the collateral damage to your world will have a net positive. Your pain is temporary. Rise from the ashes, soar with the phoenix and build a fresh nest. It is a new world if you want it to be.

EMPOWERMENT

Creation would have a hard time expanding, contracting, and rebirthing if it were not for The Shifters. Their innovation, intensity and focus are what is most often needed in the world. The fact that the universe can still produce Shifters is a testament to the idea that the universe is still unfolding. Enjoy the level of your uniqueness. Appreciate your value, whether others receive you or not. You must push forward to let others know what you think and believe. Your emanations and creations are vital to the universe's expansion. Enjoy the process and go for it!

These colors, gemstones, flower essences and essential oils will improve your mood, mind and heart.

Colors: dark violet, forest green, indigo, slate blue, saddle brown, bright white, pink

Gemstones: Ametrine, Amethyst, Lolite, Green Sardonyx, Ruby, Pink Tourmaline, Azeztulite, Carnelian, Rainbow Tourmaline

Flower Essences: Cerato, Centaury, Crab Apple, Heather, Holly, Impatiens, Pine, Rock Water, Water Violet, Star of Bethlehem

Essential Oils: Myrrh, Mandarine, Vetiver, Ylang Ylang, Sandalwood, Black Pepper, Cedarwood, Cinnamon, Clove, Coriander, Cypress, Grapefruit

Much of the contents and details of our lives are nothing. Our inner imagery, mostly illusion. Let the apparitions fade. Truth is more beautiful than fiction!

THE JUDGE

My calling is to inspire others to pursue their highest good. I pose gentle Socratic questions to free minds from shadows, confusion and complacency. While my methods might feel invasive or challenging, it is nothing personal. I am here to serve, delighting upon every awareness and alignment that emerges. With your acquiescence and openness, your life will have more flow and ease. You are born of love, light and truth. I serve these qualities in you and all sentient beings.

THE JUDGE

"I ask you, what is your truth? Knowing it, you must honor it always."

MORSEL

Climb and master the mountains within and you will know every mountain in existence.

MESSAGE

The most profound souls are not fazed by critique or adoration. They accept their own natures and enjoy their creativity without attachment. It is as if they are in direct dialogues with the divine. As information and feedback emerges, they make adjustments and improve.

When we genuinely aspire to better ourselves, we open ourselves up to feedback from friends, family and strangers. Doing so, we allow ourselves to be influenced and directed. As we seek to be informed, enlightened and up-leveled, we naturally advance our skills and personhood.

While it is admirable to live our lives in this way, it is also rare. Most of us are so busy, we barely have time to breathe. To keep ourselves moving forward and to save ourselves from exhaustion, we pat ourselves on the back upon the slightest creation or improvement.

We push ourselves so hard, we're often in physical, mental or emotional jeopardy. While the results of our flurry temporarily affirms the importance of what we are doing, it represents a never-ending circle of effort and illusion. All this activity distracts us from our genuineness and our authenticity. We push until we're exhausted, when all we want is happiness.

The Judge appears to us to inspire our self-understanding. She wants us to become confident in our natures and pursuits. In Socratic fashion, she asks pertinent questions about our processes, hoping to nurture our brilliance. When we fail to sway her, we take it personally, even though she never raised her voice. Meanwhile, The Judge thinks nothing less of us. It is our projections that do all the damage.

When we look at the lineages of our actions, we find the originating thoughts that started it all. These thoughts act like rocket boosters that send us in specific directions. If we forget to include happiness in our originating thoughts, we can easily end up misled and unfulfilled.

If The Judge has gaveled his way into your heart today, be fearless as he questions you. Allow him to dissolve your defensiveness and blocks. Be open so that you might heal the fissures in your philosophy. Push through self-doubt and allow this thoughtful being to advance your thinking.

Judges are often excellent teachers, mentors and coaches. They are able to witness events and behavior without reacting. With a calm resolve, The Judge seeks to enhance the lives of others.

Be courageous on your path and honor The Judge as he introduces you to a clearer, more tenable version of your quality and reality. It's time for an upgrade. The Judge is here to help.

CAUTION

Sometimes The Judge's tone is one of condemnation. She might seem patronizing or mean. With one word, she can burst your heart. Don't be afraid of The Judge's feedback just because it's tied to a grenade. Filter out any harshness, accepting only the gems.

You may have become accustomed to being revered and honored by others. By allowing your mind to build an altar in your own image, you may have become a villain to some. This is only temporary. Remember to implement diplomacy. You cannot brutalize someone and expect the universe to applaud. Make room for mistakes, miscalculations, individuality, quirks and artistic freedom in everyone you engage. This will reduce 90% of your stress.

Before you share your thoughts with someone, take inventory of your projections, fears and desires. Your peacefulness will inspire greater receptivity and more productive outcomes.

EXTREME

You might be spending too much time judging yourself, leaving you psychologically or emotionally exhausted. Reboot your system and liberate the Judge within you. Sit quietly and imagine what he looks like. Find gratitude for this part of your identity, then gently and lovingly say goodbye to him.

When some of us make mistakes, we immediately forgive ourselves and move on with our lives. Instead, you give yourself 40 lashes every time you break a nail. Think more lovingly of yourself. If you made a mistake, acknowledge the aspects that need improvement and work toward that. Get off the addictive memory wagon and get back on track to self-love.

EMPOWERMENT

In order to grow, most of us need whetting stones, stop signs, goal posts, and guardrails to help us progress. Without these things, it can take a long time to get clear understandings of ourselves. Be open to The Judge's help and you'll learn about your shortcomings and value. As you clear your life of debilitating forces, refrain from taking things personally.

These colors, gemstones, flower essences and essential oils will improve your mood, mind and heart.

Colors: white, yellow, gold, fuchsia, pink, magenta, orchid, blue, turquoise

Gemstones: Tiger's Eye, Honey Calcite, Pink Tourmaline, White Selenite, Rose Quartz

Flower Essences: Beech, Centaury, Cerato, Cherry Plum, Elm, Heather, Pine, Scleranthus, Vine, Yellow Marigold

Essential Oils: Myrrh, Fennel, Violet Leaf, Yarrow, Black Pepper, Ginger, Cardamom, Sage, Jasmine

The truths you are hiding from hold the keys to your expansion. They are your whetting stones, your missing pieces, your gold. Unbind them!

THE HEALER

I embody a clear sense of the now, within every thought, boson and fermion that resides in my being. With your permission, I open pathways to light, expand your potential, and increase your connectivity to all living beings in all the realms. At a molecular level, I dissolve the fractures in your etheric and physical cores. Your acquiescence is imperative because it is actually you who advances your well-being. I embrace your consciousness as if it were my own. I encourage you to expect more from reality, which you continually co-create in all dimensions.

THE HEALER

"What you imagine to be you, is you."

MORSEL

Prayers are answered when we arrive at the purest level of vulnerability. When we judge ourselves, we limit our potential. Find peace by harmonizing with the softest wind.

MESSAGE

All emotions, thoughts and physical matter are made of light and sound. These are the primary ingredients of our minds, hearts, flesh and bones. We are the sweet, soft sounds of love in its purest form, vulnerable to the changing winds.

The subtlest shift in awareness can reshape a physical reality, including our bodies. Our thoughts are musical notes. Our bodies and lives are the resulting symphony.

When we understand that every part of us is a thought held together with desire and intention, we begin to take better care of our thoughts. When our thoughts change, so do our bodies, hearts, and lives. From even the slightest suggestion, we can induce change.

Some say that we have to detach from something in order to heal and expand. This is not true. To become new, there is often nothing to relinquish. As we reach for loving thoughts and the truth of our nature, we automatically free negative attachments and anything antithetical to our joy. If not through our effort to release of something, newness occurs upon the opening of our heart.

If The Healer has appeared in your aura today, you are being called to be the conduit of transformation for yourself and others. By being an example of empathy and vulnerability, you will provoke the best of all possible outcomes in the realities you are participating in. By holding intentions of peace, flow and healing, you evolve the vibrations of an entire ecosystem. You might not realize it, but you can become Christ-like whenever you choose to.

There might be a group of people in your life who are having a difficult time reaching an agreement. There might be someone in your periphery who is sick or angry. It might be that you and your partner hit a wall in the pursuit of renewed intimacy. The keys to unlocking the healing in these scenarios live in your strength and will to embody pure light and love.

Everything within you has prepared you to heal the challenges that have emerged in your life. Every fiber of your being conspires to support your capacity to channel love into the people and circumstances around you. Let light come through you, embrace the new awareness without judgment and speak your unbridled loving truth to everyone in your life. With the clearest of intentions, you can co-create and co-inspire miracles in any reality and in any living being. Trust your nature and let the universe flow through you.

CAUTION

Get out of your own way so that miracles can flow toward you. Invoke the light from within and let your masters, angels, and guides do the work. With a clear channel, the brightest light will move through you.

Even if someone has repeatedly infringed upon you, find compassion for him. Even as you reprimand him or set boundaries with him, allow your heart to blossom like the lotus so that you may feel love for him.

It might be that you are the one in need of healing. You may have recently exited a roller coaster. With all the anxiety and commotion, you might have lost connection to your feelings and heart. Whether it is through prayer or being physically present and supportive, your service to others will free you. When you generously give from your heart and serve others, you heal yourself.

EXTREME

You might be continuously putting yourself down, dampening your light and negating the miracles you have inspired. You have come to believe that if miracles stem from you, they are imperfect. Look within yourself and witness your true nature. Do you see how your love heals others? Do you know that when you give, the light coming through you is beautiful? You know how to co-create beautiful realities. When you open your heart, you inspire others to do the same. Lead others in your current situation by being an example of compassion and transparency. Your vulnerability and openness will inspire a shift in consciousness for everyone involved.

EMPOWERMENT

When we are out of step with The Healer, it is as if we are at war with ourselves. It might be a sweet, subtle dispute of the heart or it might be an overwhelming battle. Inner resolve is required. We forget to forgive infractions, miscalculations and missteps in ourselves and others. Whatever occurred was perfect. No judgment required. The only take-away awareness is that the experience did not produce joyful results. The universe does not judge. It merely asks, "Are you happy now?"

To help you move through this time in your life, look into these modalities as a way to improve how you feel. The colors of our clothes, our jewelry, and flower essences and oils can be very impactful.

Colors: white, ivory, gold, yellow, goldenrod, powder blue, pink, bright green

Gemstones: Black Tourmaline, Kunzite, Kyanite Blue, Sodalite, Howlite, Scolecite, Dravite, Honey Calcite, Gold, Watermelon Tourmaline

Flower Essences: Larch, Water Violet, Cerato, Chicory Gorse, Honeysuckle, Star of Bethlehem

Essential Oils: Lavender, Peppermint, Tea Tree, Rosewood, Anise, Bergamot, Clove Bud, Frankincense, Geranium, Neroli

A mountain stream moves with a natural vibrancy. It lives because it is alive, like you. Realize yourself and live with power, fullness and flow, akin to the stream.

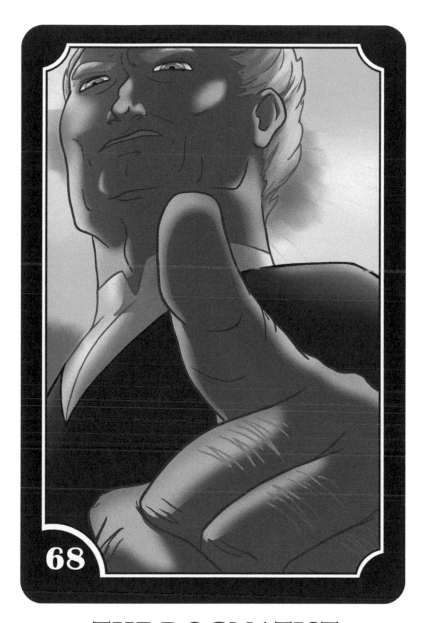

THE DOGMATIST

I am a confidant and authoritative communicator, unshakable in my understandings. I speak with heavy-handed assertion and I usually know what's right for everyone involved. I assemble indestructible sets of assumptions, each conviction born of an absolute fathoming of the ideas in play. Since I am not usually aware of my effect on others, it would be foolish to take my assertions personally. Are you ready for evaluation? Excellent. Let's begin.

THE DOGMATIST

"I told you I knew everything. Did you think I was kidding?"

MORSEL

If mouths considered the horrible places words have been, they would refrain from speaking.

MESSAGE

Society's most damaging trend is extremism. Many extremists declare themselves the defenders of the ultimate truth, pointing to abstract phrases in old books. This is not the best way to win hearts and expand minds. It is a fear-based ideology that seeks to alienate some and control others.

While their original creeds and manuscripts were powerful back in the day, they are mere appetizers now, pit stops on a long path toward understanding freedom and the nature of the soul.

Beyond a zealot's restrictive code is an all-inclusive doorway where everyone is accepted and celebrated, where every belief system finds congruence and accord with every other.

Religious and political authoritarians can become so focused on the battle of the holy egos, they lose sight of their compassion, their humanity and the nature of equanimity. Using culturally-exclusive identifiers and harsh enrollment tactics, they alienate themselves and disenfranchise everyone else.

As The Dogmatist, you are well-versed in the topic at hand. You are perceptive with a strong understanding of human nature. You know instinctively how to motivate and enroll others. When it comes to opinion, yours are well manicured and categorized.

The Dogmatist usually maintains a strong stance and rigid attitude. Unyielding and adamant, she keeps the masses focused on the agenda at hand. With her slightly dictatorial style, she can squash drama in an instant, all the while producing stable, consistent results. While she sometimes tends toward steamrolling, others count on her for momentum and a clear perspective.

If The Dogmatist is barking at you today, gently nudge him from his pulpit. There are few definitive truths in this world, especially those that dictate the "only way". Rather than bending to The Dogmatist's delusion or will, find a more relaxed perspective. Introduce more flexible and inclusive language into the dialogues currently in play. Infect the shadows with your light.

If you are feeling like you're The Dogmatist, seek a measure of softness in everything you do and say. Even if for a moment, relinquish your harsh position and temporarily defend the other side. Your flexibility and openness to dialogue will affect how you grow and expand.

Even though you would defend the truth to your death, the truth never needs defending. Those who obsess about one idea and work tirelessly to enroll others in it, are often fearful and insecure.

Whether something is red, blue, or yellow is of little consequence. What matters most is that you allow others to experience whichever colors they believe are best for them.

CAUTION

When we block out the innovation and personal experiences of those around us, it hints at an inflated sense of self. With a little humility and inquisitiveness, we can encourage others to grow. Take a look at the damage you may have created with your perspective. There is no guilt-trip here, but make note of the lessons you've learned.

Before you get on another pulpit, relax. Include a hint of humor and self-deprecation. Poke a hole in your position and welcome ideas outside your comfort zone. Arrogance only converts the weak. Soften your point of view so you can engage hearts, rather than squander them.

Early in The Dogmatist's life, her family may have traumatized her into adopting a harsh communication style. While this is not her fault, she'll eventually have to take responsibility for the person she has become.

EXTREME

It might be that you're avoiding your inner Dogmatist. Are you afraid to be authoritative and tough? Do you hide your knowledge and experience so you can blend in? Are you devaluing yourself because it seems easier? Have you been meandering through the forest picking daisies rather than boldly defending what is yours?

We each must find a way to participate in society. If a personal tragedy or trauma dampened your voice, it's time to bring it to life again. If you do not have the resources or strength to fund a rebirth, seek help from friends and community services. Trust in humanity. With an open heart, you will find the support and sustenance you need. Get back on your feet and pursue a life worth sustaining.

EMPOWERMENT

Life can be overwhelming. It is no wonder we so often choose complacency. When we experience suffering, we can begin to live from the mindset of scarcity. Our self-definitions devolve and our once-magnificent visions can whither away. The good news is that pain and suffering often broaden our insight and compassion. The light is ever-expanding within us. Remain open and be proactive.

When we seek out the colors, gems, flower essences and essential oils that uplift our spirits, we see immediate changes to our attitudes and feelings. These recommendations are for The Dogmatist.

Colors: aquamarine, cornflower blue, gold, violet, green, teal, white, pink

Gemstones: Abalone, Chrysoprase, Fuchsite, Gold, Blue Calcite, Tanzanite, Lapis Lazuli, Pink Tourmaline, Aquamarine

Flower Essences: Rock Water, Vervain, Water Violet, Beech, Aspen, Elm, Heather, Impatiens

Essential Oils: Myrrh, Bay Laurel, Bergamot, Rosewood, Cardamom, Clove Bud, Cypress

We are only able to perceive submicroscopic portions of reality and truth. Beyond our comfortable perspectives are billions of possibilities, lifeforms and universes.

THE ASSERTER

My salad is not crisp, yet the cool air coming through the top window is refreshing. Did you know that my new car is getting 1.25 less miles per gallon than advertised? The manager's presentation was truly exceptional. Whether it's explaining, complaining or complementing, I am emphatic, precise and unabashed in my opinion. I hope to connect meaningfully with others, but I value my perspective above all. As I describe my experiences to others, I validate my own existence.

THE ASSERTER

"When I share my experiences, I feel seen and heard. This helps me feel more alive."

MORSEL

Nothing is as it seems, so why be concerned about what is or what should be? Change is inevitable and does not require our permission or acceptance.

MESSAGE

Occasionally, we are derailed by a series of events. No matter how much we try to prevent it, people die, things break, plans go awry and the doohickey we needed for the thingy in the kitchen is no longer available in blue. This is life. The very nature of the universe is that of surprise and change.

When we are in a positive state of mind, we infuse goodness into the realities around us. When we affirm the beauty of a flower, we encourage its longevity into existence. Drawing attention to the negative has it's value, but only if the intention is to improve conditions and states of mind.

The Asserter is acutely aware and passionate about his experiences in every moment. He wants the world to know how he sees the colors and symphonies around him. Whether he has an interest, a concern, goose bumps or heart ache, for The Asserter, sharing opinions is a way of life.

The Asserter understands that words carry power, especially when delivered with exuberance. In the heat of a moment, The Asserter will preach with flair, seeing no other perspective than his own.

Most of the time, The Asserter encourages the positive in everything around him. He'll go out of his way to share a lovely thought with an older woman sitting on a park bench. With great emphasis, he might tell the lonely store clerk how beautiful her sweater is. He'll make it a point to repeat a shy person's name. It's this aggressive benevolence that helps The Asserter feel connected and alive.

When The Asserter forgets herself, she can become the irritable uncle or the insatiable boss. Feeling squeezed by circumstances, her impatience can erupt, throwing her out of balance. Whether it's berating a waitress for delivering a limp-lettuce hamburger or declaring the office air to be a health hazard, The Asserter can over-accentuate to the point of everyone's frustration.

Gone unchecked, The Asserter can become an endless loop of overreaction and negativity. Living in the complaint, he can miss out on revelation and growth. With a little flexibility and forgiveness, The Asserter can nudge himself back into a happier and more balanced state of mind.

Every word we speak changes our lives. When we affirm what we desire, what we see and what we hear, we encourage reality to bend in that direction.

As you speak your truth, remember to nourish yourself and others with a majority of positivity. If you wish, share your opinions to no end, but remember to keep light and love in the mix. Encourage reality to blossom with goodness and it will.

CAUTION

When cars break down, it's not all bad news. While the car is being fixed, we might end up at a coffee shop where we meet the loves of our lives. We might enjoy a delicious omelette. We may get exercise as we walk around while waiting. We might end up with a new car! Once we get past our emotional responses, there is always an upside.

When The Asserter enrolls his tribe in his temporary misery, he boxes himself into a corner. Even when we push to sell the positive to everyone around us, we might be attempting to control reality rather than see it and accept it for what it is. Our words do not necessarily help.

No matter where you stand on the happiness or truth scale, do not believe your perspective to be the only truth. Seek to see yourself and others more clearly.

EXTREME

Complaining may have become your habit. The more we complain, the more we allow our aura, mind, heart and facial expressions to sour. We will then attract the same. This is a never-ending cycle. Make a list of every complaint you've uttered in the past 48 hours. If your list is longer than two phrases, you are working too hard to validate negative experiences. Your fog is self-created.

Look at the thoughts you are having. Set your alarm to go off every five minutes. When you hear the alarm, write down the thought in your mind. Try to do this for a few hours. If the composite is mostly negative, you will know that the culprit in your challenging life is you. As soon as a complaint emerges in your mind, interrupt your thinking by clapping your hands. Change it to its opposite. With one transformed thought every hour, you will inch yourself into a more joyful life.

EMPOWERMENT

If complaining is your modus operandi, give yourself a mental and emotional clearing. You might need a hint of professional help to get you out of the doldrums. You might also benefit from an infusion of the flower essences listed below. The most important thing you can give yourself and others is encouragement. Meditating on the rose, we become the rose.

These colors, gemstones, flower essences and essential oils will improve your mood, mind and heart.

Colors: yellow, goldenrod, green yellow, light sky blue, pink, orchid, purple, olive

Gemstones: Pink Tourmaline, Green Chlorite, Serpentine, Blue Quartz, Purpurite, Amethyst, Sugilite

Flower Essences: Aspen, Beech, Gorse, Heather, Impatiens, Mustard, Rock Water, Sweet Chestnut

Essential Oils: Lemon, Tangerine, Orange, Blue Tansy, Geranium, Ylang Ylang, Sandalwood, Rose

When you complain beyond a simple critique, you compound a negative reality. When you accentuate the positive, you emit loving flow and providence throughout all time and space.

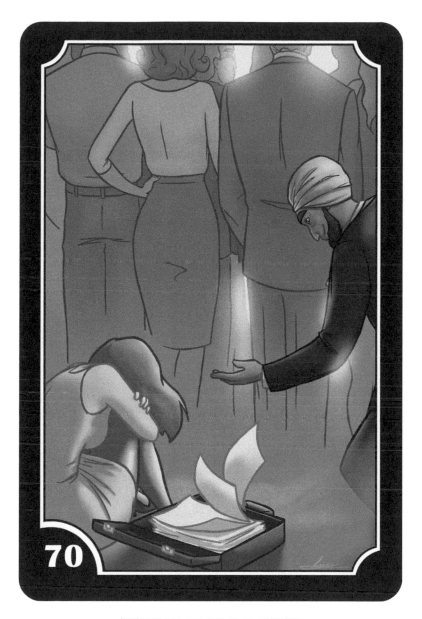

THE RESPITE

Long after my climb up the mountain, I began to feel a depth of exhaustion I had never known. Depleted and wary, I gently stepped away from my busy life. The more I breathed, relaxed and let go, the more I was able to help the forgotten parts of me emerge. Feeling their pain, I poured my heart into theirs. As I settle into a more soulful life, I am shape-shifting into a newly calibrated me. I am now softer, more hopeful, more powerful, more rooted, and fully reconciled with who I am.

THE RESPITE

"With every conscious breath, I relax deeper into my nature. My spirit unfolds and I am free."

MORSEL

When you recognize that you are a reflection of the universe, expectations around success will fade.

MESSAGE

In a relaxed state, we are more ourselves. When we nurture our bodies, hearts and spirits into alignment, we increase our awareness. With greater awareness, we make better decisions and form more congruent relationships. It all starts with our ability to pause, take a break and rest.

When we disconnect from all the images, sounds and experiences that are thrust upon us, we feel a measure of fear in the form of anxiety. We realize that each of these things is a cord that stresses us in some way. Upon cutting each cord, we feel its loss, but somehow we are expanded.

Whether it's a relationship, project or experience, everything we are connected to feeds us in some way. We are akin to electricity poles, draped in wires. Sometimes, without realizing it, we allow a wire to feed us negativity or pain. Given that we have so many wires in our lives, the more disadvantageous aspects and the most beneficial remedies are not always obvious.

The Respite understands when it's time to separate, disconnect, decompress and recalibrate. She sees her reality clearly, and is able to gently guide underlying challenges to the surface. She knows that taking a break can invigorate her or save her life.

With a clear slate and relaxed mind, The Respite is able to reconsider her intentions, desires and goals. With a translucent heart, she is more congruent and more able to honor all parts of herself. Uncluttered and unfettered, The Respite can settle into who she really is.

The more relaxed you are, the more you'll be able to examine the quality of your pursuits. Is this really what you want to do with your life? Are you inspired to do your best? Are all details being addressed? You might find that you made a series of incorrect assumptions at the onset of your project. You might not have taken enough time to form its foundation.

Looking under the hood, you may have cut corners, rushed yourself or incorrectly timed your product or event. These things are remedied when we take healthful pauses in pursuit of inner clarity.

We start relationships, ventures and activities with the best intentions. By maintaining a positive attitude we are able to progress as far as possible. While our accomplishments in these areas can be impressive, we are often unaware of how personally comprising they can be.

If The Respite is seeking repose and transformation, look for ways to honor yourself. Detach from negativity and embrace only that which truly accepts, nurtures and satisfies you. Give yourself this gift every day and you'll grow that sweet little flower into a powerful, majestic tree.

CAUTION

Seeing what hard work can do for our financial well-being, we forget how to take care of ourselves. When we make our health, family and hobbies our priorities, everything changes. We might miss out on a percentage of income, but we'll triple our level of happiness.

Stop measuring your work against unrealistic parameters. You've put enough pressure on yourself. Seek balance in everything you do. With a more self-protective agenda, you'll see more flow in your life. Your achievements will be laced with more positivity. Doing so, you will attract all the attention you need to be a success.

Your heart is the center of your universe. Honor your heart and you feed every part of you. This benefits all who come in contact with you.

EXTREME

When we are exhausted, we make terrible decisions. With each poor decision, we can hurt others, and drastically change our relationships and lives for the worse. We might not see how delusional and selfish our decisions are, even if we appear to be helping our families. When we push too hard and forsake our hearts, we can lose more than our own health. We can also lose family and friends. You might be working so hard that you need an intervention. It's difficult to deconstruct and then reconstruct a life. Take your time. Be gentle with yourself. Give yourself a long restful slumber so that you can emerge fully healed and energized.

EMPOWERMENT

Attend events and activities that speak to your heart. Find time to dance, play music and write. Take long walks in the woods and take a bath every night. The more you soften, the more you will heal and regenerate your mind and heart. The unfolding will be exciting and revealing.

Seek to improve your feelings, attitudes and conditions in life. The colors of your clothes and the gems you wear can significantly affect your mood, mind and heart. Ingesting flower essences and applying diluted essential oils to your body (or diffusing them into the air) can improve your energy, attitude and drive. Enjoy these helpful recommendations for The Respite.

Colors: purple, goldenrod, gold, orange, firebrick red, slate blue, green, dark sea green

Gemstones: Garnet, Citrine, Malachite, Purpurite, Ruby, Jade, Bloodstone, Dioptase, Orange Kyanite, Fire Opal, Stitchtite

Flower Essences: Larch, Rock Water, Aspen, Cerato, Clematis, Gorse, Honeysuckle, Star of Bethlehem, Rock Rose

Essential Oils: Basil, Bergamot, Cypress, Fennel, Frankincense, Jasmine, Bitter Orange, Violet Leaf, Geranium, Grapefruit

Your soul entered this life to figure a few things out. No definitive time frames were set for this procedure. Take notes. Make adjustments. Repeat as needed.

THE SILENT

I'm acutely aware that words have a profound effect on every moment. Every phrase we utter has the power to induce joy or pain, miracles or trauma. I refrain from speaking in most situations because whatever I have to add feels superfluous, possibly habituating. When the stakes are high, and when the outcome could have a severe effect on me and those I love, I am the first and last to speak. Failing that, expect that I will take notes, and carefully consider when to next participate.

THE SILENT

" . "

MORSEL

There is more value in the space between your thoughts on any given day than in a lifetime of chit-chat. Silence and meditation shorten our path to tranquility. Discussion and analysis lengthen it.

MESSAGE

Words help establish consensus, grow connection and build empires. Words give life to feelings and help establish agreements, but words can also confuse and complicate. No matter how pure our intent, our words often fall short.

Silence has a wisdom that inches us closer toward compassion. Silence heals bridges and gives people the space they need to see themselves more clearly. Silence opens the skies so that light can shine brightly onto our hearts and lives.

In every family and group, there is often one person who is peacefully withdrawn. As they sit quietly focusing on themselves, The Silent puts a spell on the rest of us. Without a word, she challenges us to become better people.

It is obvious that The Silent has found something special within herself. If The Silent is appearing in your dreams today, she is a reflection of your most beautiful intentions. She represents your desire to have a peaceful, inner life.

The Silent knows that opinions can become toxic chess pieces in games of achievement. She understands that by being speechless, she adds grace to any equation. Even in the heat of the most challenging situations, The Silent can inspire quickened, tranquil resolutions with just one breath.

You are being asked to place a lid on the cascade of opinions you normally share with others. Your guides and angels are asking you to let your thoughts dissolve before you speak. Have the awareness, but don't verbalize your process, lest you jeopardize the peace in play.

While you remain quiet, you'll allow others to impress themselves with their orations. It's time to let others have a turn. Remember that when we speak we are saying things that we already know. By listening, we might learn something new or valuable.

Silence slows the pace of our projections long enough to temper them with grace. By taking a few moments to pause and reflect, the poignant phrases that live within us have a better chance of percolating and coming forth. Silence is golden because it allows negative chatter and dark fodder to fall to dissolve, long before it has an effect on the relationship or dialogue in play.

When its time for you to speak again, choose your words carefully. Doing so, you'll preserve a relationship, build a bridge and continue the embodiment of a peaceful state of mind.

CAUTION

The time for your silence has ended. When the moment presents itself, share your thoughts in a non-threatening way so your co-workers, friends or lover will know your thoughts and perspective.

Remain emotionally balanced throughout the process and remember the value you bring to the table. The tenured generals in the room might fear The Silent and try to enroll him in their philosophy. They might corner or steamroll you with threats and insults. Ignore them. Take nothing personally and continue to make clear, concise points.

After the dust settles, you will see inroads into the minds and hearts of those around you. As you share your personal insights, many will be inspired. Remember that the best answers come from within.

EXTREME

Your tendency toward silence may have become a crutch. When we let the more powerful mouths in the room talk us out of our opinion, we sometimes lose our voice, intuition or inner strength. Not only can we lose our position, we can lose connection to ourselves. Remember that you are the bright light at the table, and your voice is the missing piece in the pursuit. Choose the most advantageous moment to share your insights. By honoring your voice and sharing it in a peaceful manner, you secure reciprocity in your primary relationships.

EMPOWERMENT

When The Silent is out of balance, she might be unable to access her feelings and voice. There might be emotions trapped under a reprimand or argument from the past. Sit quietly with yourself and consider this idea. Write in your journal to see if anything emerges from within.

Sometimes The Silent hides behind his demeanor in order to avoid intimacy or a decision. Whatever is challenging you right now, gently confront it and work toward awareness and resolution. You are the healer you seek. Become the breath and invoke the lightness of your being.

Seek to improve your level of happiness, state of mind and conditions in life. The colors of your clothes and the gems you wear can significantly affect your mood, mind and heart. Ingesting flower essences and applying diluted essential oils to your body (or diffusing them into the air) can improve your energy, attitude and drive. Enjoy these helpful recommendations for The Silent.

Colors: white, purple, dark blue, orange, turquoise, black

Gemstones: Amethyst, Orange Calcite, Turquoise, Opalite, Black Tourmaline, Benitoite, Hauyne

Flower Essences: Heather, Willow, Gentian, Honeysuckle, Walnut, White Chestnut, Pine

Essential Oils: Myrrh, Jasmine, Grapefruit, Frankincense, Bay Laurel, Cardamom, Galbanum, Ylang Ylang, Nutmeg

If divine truth advertised, billboards would be blank.

THE FACILITATOR

I am aware of who the players are and I understand what each side brings to the table. I am committed to remain as balanced as possible as I bring us together in dialogue. I am intuitive enough to know what each player needs, and I'm savvy enough to ensure an outcome that every participant can accept. When rotten egg appears, my job is to remove as much stink as possible. Upon consensus, I am a hero. Let's open the windows and allow the winds of change to flow through us all.

THE FACILITATOR

"Let's meet in the middle, become our better selves and pray for grace."

MORSEL

When conflict is unraveled and the byproducts dissolved, the result is love reflecting love.

MESSAGE

It's exciting to meet people who understand the value of agreements. If this type of person is in your life, everything is a little clearer and brighter. Unafraid to commit, they help us advance our lives.

Without agreements, very little happens in life. Agreements can form anything from living arrangements and partnerships to multi-national businesses. They do not have to be 300 pages long to establish understanding. Even simple verbal accords can add meaning and flow to our lives.

Open-minded and compassionate, The Facilitator understands that agreements are little engines that propel ideas and relationships forward. She knows instinctively how to guide opposing sides into win-win covenants. Able to withstands scrutiny and criticism during heated exchanges, she does not take anything personally. The Facilitator has an enviable and powerful skill set.

Using tested communication processes, The Facilitator opens doors and connects dots. With a deep understanding of how to traverse emotional ecosystems, she helps everyone feel safe and comfortable. She knows that once relaxed, participants are always more open to compromise.

The Facilitator is not a secretary or note taker. His role is not to make lists, push agendas or enforce ideas. The Facilitator is tasked with unraveling a vast array of opinions, projections, conflicts and beliefs, constructing agreement and symmetry from the ground up.

With a high emotional IQ, The Facilitator is often the most intuitive person in the room, with an uncanny sense of how to motivate and encourage each participant. Knowing that attacks and judgments tend to polarize people, he educates everyone on the use of disarming language.

If The Facilitator is attempting to untangle your vines today, seek understanding and resolution for the conflicts in your life. Whether face-to-face or within yourself, your healing begins today.

Detach from your opinions and put yourself in someone else's shoes. Find empathy for those you care for most and let go of the anger, sadness and disappointment. Privately express your emotions, clearing the way for a more open heart and mind. Do not dwell on the past and allow for a new beginning.

Use peaceful phrases so that you can encourage a more complete resolution. State your feelings and desires clearly, without aggression. Keep an eye on the joy you will feel upon the dust settling.

The more open you are, the more productive the dialogues will be. You have your work cut out for you, but you are worthy of the task at hand. Leading with your heart will help others do the same.

CAUTION

When working to help two or more parties understand each other, be careful not to favor any of them, even in the slightest way. The resolution should remain the priority. Maintain a balanced voice. Refrain from engaging in private alliances so that no one feels marginalized or threatened. Give everyone the opportunity to be heard. Remain detached so you can thoughtfully orchestrate the ebb and flow.

Stay strong and remember to continually affirm your position. If someone questions your value or quality, ask what caused them to be upset, then apologize if necessary.

You have done a fabulous job. Do not let this hiccup trip you up. Hold tightly to the truth and steer this ship to its rightful destination.

EXTREME

When leading a pack of wolves, the most aggressive creatures regularly show their teeth. If necessary, take your challenger to the mat. Call them out. Hold up a mirror to their disruptiveness. If you are hesitant to challenge the difficult personalities, examine your patterns of sheepishness. Why do you find it difficult to stand up for yourself? Are you projecting father, mother or a sibling onto others? When you are unable to say what you think to someone, they will continue to have power over you. You are not a wet blanket. Gather your strength and speak your truth. Gain control of the room and shine brightly, guiding this process to a clear and speedy resolution.

EMPOWERMENT

When the fires of group dynamics provoke your emotions, it's difficult to serve others. Seek to know yourself by exploring your buttons, what provokes them and what heals them. As you move through this process, you might bump into your shadow. That's okay, just don't let anyone shake your tree. In all things, remember that you are a servant of humanity and a beautiful beacon of light.

The colors of your clothes and the gems you wear can significantly affect your mood, mind and heart. Ingesting flower essences and applying diluted essential oils to your body (or diffusing them into the air) can improve your energy, attitude and drive.

Colors: yellow, gold, yellow green, lavender, blue, mint rose, violet

Gemstones: Lepidolite, Prehnite, Howlite, Scolecite, Opalite, Pink Tourmaline, Gold, Rose Quartz, Azurite, Peridot, Amazonite

Flower Essences: Beech, Chestnut Bud, Chicory, Gentian, Cerato, Elm, Honeysuckle, Hornbeam, Larch, Pine

Essential Oils: Cardamom, Rosewood, Rose, Ylang Ylang, Geranium, Frankincense, Lavender, Spruce, Jasmine, Patchouli

Whether you wish to admit it or not, you are a beacon of light with unlimited potential in every direction.

THE LITTLE DEVIL

I'm on the hunt for playmates and adventures. I get a certain satisfaction when I tease others into participating in my risky escapades. Danger and intrigue give me a rush, a delicious high. It might appear that my life means little to me, but that's far from the truth. I simply love to sex things up, blast out the volume and exercise my wild nature as much as possible. Mischievous deeds do more than entice and excite me, they awaken me. Join me on the edge of delight and passion! Want a taste?

THE LITTLE DEVIL

"Do you feel it? Isn't it delicious? I'm ready for more, are you?"

MORSEL

When we allow our attachments to melt away, we finally see who we are.

MESSAGE

We all need a fix. Whether it is exercise, coffee, sex, depression, money or drugs, we have cravings for excited states of mind. We either refrain from these things out of fear of losing ourselves, or we tell ourselves to take just enough to enjoy it, but not enough to become disrupted or addicted.

If The Little Devil is in your living room, she's enticing you to participate in an exciting experience. You'll meet mysterious strangers, delve into your passions and connect with exhilarating undercurrents. Although potentially dangerous, you'll feel things you've never felt before.

Throughout your life, you played by the rules, meeting every expectation. You took care of children, helped fellow human beings and cleaned the garage. You did the dishes and made your bed. You became what society wanted and your parish priest or rabbi would be proud. While it all looks good on paper, you forgot to include one important item on your journey: YOU.

Take inventory of the joys, patterns and attachments in your life. Look for the ways in which you fly under the radar or settle. When you think of making changes in your life or going on an adventure, do you limit yourself? Remember that change and risk can be invigorating.

Today the Little Devil is whispering in your ear: "It's time to have a little fun!" Look for influences that provoke your freedom. Break out of your box and dive into your deeper passions. You've lived in the doldrums for long enough. Awaken your playful beast and expand.

The earth's elements are powerful. Winds form hurricanes and water creates waves. There's even lava bursting from the tops of mountains. These elements are a part of us. We are not our jobs or our routines. We are all the forces of nature combined. We can direct these forces to create magnificent lives. Yes, we are that powerful.

As The Little Devil, you are highly skilled in encouragement and conviction tactics. You could sell a fleet of cars to a bicycle company. With the charismatic magnetism of a backwoods preacher, you could do or have anything you want.

If you're feeling ferocious today, consider going for your dream. Put your skills and experience to work for you. Focus all that fire and passion into one brilliant idea or adventure.

As you explore the possibilities, remember to remain tethered to who you are. While the details might change, preserve the foundation you've built. Take care of your health and well-being. Dance in the fountain of youth with abandon, but remain whole in the process.

CAUTION

It's time for a housecleaning! Get rid of pornography, nasty letters, trinkets that your part-time lovers gave you and all the make-up that feeds your youth fantasy. Toss the stash of pot and pills that make you sleep. Reduce your media consumption and cut your caffeine in half.

Whatever controls, manipulates or ails you, reduce its power and effect on you. To improve your game, make a clean break. The universe requires your immediate participation in your rebirth.

Look at the dynamics of enslavement in your life. When we lose ourselves in habits and addictions, it can be a long road home. You might believe your secret little pattern to be inconsequential, but somewhere in your life it's having an impact. Even a sprinkle of self-abuse can be dangerous. Look honestly at the outdated behaviors and tendencies in your life and make the necessary changes. Be swift and never look back.

EXTREME

When we get too caught up in "the scene", our pristine sparks of life become tainted. You might need a support group or intervention to keep you away from enablers. When we use erasers too much, they create irreparable holes. Put the eraser away and put your energy into finding the right kind of help.

The Little Devil uses outlandish plans to get what she wants. Her priority is not people, it's the high or anything that will produce the high. She'll steal from her best friend, cheat her parents or cut her own heart out to keep her game going. Make no mistake about it, The Little Devil is not to be trusted. Focus on positive and loving behavior. The light within you is limitless.

EMPOWERMENT

The Little Devil is a complex creature who might seek solace from low-vibration visitors. To keep her from making bad decisions, she needs good friends, a warm bed, healthy food, and lots of kind-hearted affection. Help The Little Devil take better care of herself by introducing her to experiences that are filled with light and love.

Seek to improve your feelings and attitudes. The color of your clothes and your jewelry can affect your mood, mind and heart. Ingesting flower essences and applying diluted essential oils to your body (or diffusing them into the air) can improve your energy, attitude and drive.

Colors: white, pink, magenta, violet, light blue, lavender, turquoise

Gemstones: Amethyst, Bloodstone, Fluorite, Ruby, White Selenite, Pink Tourmaline, Turquoise, Lepidolite, Blue Apetite

Flower Essences: Agrimony, Pine, Centaury, Chestnut Bud, Gorse, Pine, Star of Bethlehem, Wild Rose, Crab Apple

Essential Oils: Bergamot, Grapefruit, Basic, Clove, Anise, Jasmine, Frankincense, Vetiver, Rose

Our cravings are a reflection of surface desires. Going deeper, we forget them.

74

THE FERAL STORM

A powerful burden brews within me. Some call it rage while others see it as a natural unfolding of the universe's masculine aspect. As I feel a healthy measure of sadness and anger, parts of me remain out of reach. Tears fall from my eyes as my mind races to find meaning and connection. As the rivers and tides of my heart swell, I begin to unravel. Bursting out, I am finally free. Moments later, an awakening surfaces like the sun. For the first time in ages, I am clear, vibrant and full of light.

THE FERAL STORM

"My rage is a ticket to invention, discovery and freedom. I make no apologies for who I am."

MORSEL

Feeling and expressing emotions makes way for authenticity. Anger can rip us apart or thrust us back into focus.

MESSAGE

In the Hindu tradition, Kali is the sculptor of matter and the raging de-constructor of worlds. In all traditions, one hand of God creates, while the other destroys. In a moment, the world is bustling with life, and in another, it's a wasteland. How temporal our existence is.

Kali's deconstruction is akin to the Christian idea of being "born again", whereby you relinquish a set of behaviors and beliefs, choose Jesus as your master then declare your rebirth. Jewish people celebrate Yom Kippur, their day of atonement. Native Americans have sweat lodges and vision quests to inspire their renewal. Disruptive experiences like these have the power to wake us up.

The Feral Storm uses disruption to help her release false and limiting patterns from her life, understanding that change inspires the juiciest lessons. She lives and breaths the breaking and remaking of her life with a focus on clarity. Stripped free of all distractions, what remains is her truth.

The Feral Storm is aligned with the original spark that inspired the birth of consciousness. When he rips himself or others apart, he is demonstrating an ancient passion, which is not easy to control. His goal is to free himself of the blocks that bind him.

The Feral Storm is charged with electric and magnetic forces, which can sometimes be difficult to handle. She is a pattern-interruptor who can help others see themselves clearly. While it's not always pretty, The Feral Storm has the ability to inspire dramatic change.

Sometimes you'll find The Feral Storm sitting meekly and humbly in the corner, barely offering a word or a whisper. This is when he is tending to his emotional and psychological stew. While he might appear peaceful and placated, be on guard for the unleashing of everything within him.

The Feral Storm's expression of anger is often judged by society as inappropriate or dangerous, but this is unfair. While it might be ugly and unruly, anger is often our missing piece. When we release anger, we know ourselves better. While gentility has obvious benefits, rage can set us free.

The Feral Storm hunts down the constructs and ideologies that keep us in slumber. She threatens our most comforting notions and the emotions that numb us. If you're in a rut, allow the Feral Storm to push you out of your despondence and into your next level of awareness.

Give your ego the lesson it has avoided for centuries. Let The Feral Storm challenge the fluff in your life. Shed like a snake and become clear. Embrace your inner beast and be free.

CAUTION

The Feral Storm can be a little sloppy, sometimes coloring outside the lines and making a mess. You may have hired him to demolish a wall, but he took down the building instead. It is not your fault that you were unable to set better boundaries with him. He is a master of destruction.

The Feral Storm is a perfectionist. His divine purpose is to build then bulldoze, sometimes destroying more than he creates. His innate mission is to helps us release attachment to every construct in our lives.

Release attachment to your prior reality. Relinquish the guilt and shame that surround the major events in your life. With a lighter heart, you will transform. Forgive yourself and find power in your new reality.

EXTREME

When we repeat anger and sadness, it's like indelible ink, staining our hearts and minds forever. Be careful that your release of emotions does not become an addiction.

If The Feral Storm is challenging you today, be careful not to internalize her harshness. You are witnessing a precious unfolding, which has nothing to do with you. No matter how hard she pushes, refrain from feeding her blaze. Once her storm subsides, you'll be safe to recalibrate and begin again.

The Feral Storm can be so focused on one specific area of destruction that he often misses out on the gold coins we hide under the sink. In all things that involve The Feral Storm, set boundaries and protect yourself. He might not be what he appears to be. Find empathy for her actions so that you can master this aspect within yourself. This is a rare moment in life, so celebrate it.

EMPOWERMENT

If the force of The Feral Storm is bubbling inside of you, create a plan for rigorous exercise. Be sure to establish friendships with people who accept you unconditionally. Take breaks from society so you can run wild in the woods. If anyone judges you, tame the beast with love and affection.

Continually nurture your heart, mind and relationships. The color of your clothes and your jewelry can affect your mood, mind and heart. Ingesting flower essences and applying diluted essential oils to your body (or diffusing them into the air) can improve your energy, attitude and drive.

Colors: mint cream, cyan, light green, yellow green, cornflower blue, pink, violet

Gemstones: Amethyst, Silver, Howlite, Tanzanite, Blue Apetite, Prehnite, Pink Tourmaline

Flower Essences: Beech, Cherry Plum, Holly, Impatiens, Vervain, Aspen, Chicory, Crab Apple, Rock Rose, Rock Water, Vine, Willow

Essential Oils: Grapefruit, Lavender, Spearmint, Peppermint, Benzoin, Chamomile, Carrot Seed, Bitter Orange, Ylang Ylang

Gentility is an elitist trend that leads to depression and denial. Rip away your masks, hesitations and pretensions. Reclaim the lightening then let it go.

THE SOFTIE

Butterflies rule the universe and hummingbirds are healing oracles. My home is a transparent, purple-tinted sphere floating over a waterfall, where birds and plants talk with each other and dance. I believe sharing secrets and holding hands are two of the most important things we can do as living beings, whether it is with a man, woman, dog, insect or mineral. My warm smile helps others feel safe, loved and renewed. My goodness is far-reaching, born from the light in my being.

THE SOFTIE

"I seek to explore the sweetness and vulnerabilities of every living creature I encounter."

MORSEL

Kindness is an effective negotiating tool. Upon a hearty tap on the nose, the mighty beast will heel.

MESSAGE

Emotional vulnerability is a valuable human attribute. It is said that the universe only fulfills the dreams of those who have vulnerable hearts.

When we push too hard in our lives, the softer parts of us become bruised. Our hearts tire and close down. Our lives shrink and we lose our vibrance. When we let stress, work and money obscure our hearts, everything suffers, most notably our relationships and our happiness.

We might be on vacation with a group of friends. After a day of fun in the sun, we slip away from our friends and head to our hotel room. Once behind closed doors, we take one sip of honey tea and explode in tears. This is vulnerability catching up with us. The Softie understands this all too well.

The Softie inspires thoughts of kindness, compassion and empathy. Love and peace are always one breath, one intention away. The Softie understands this at a core level. She is committed to keeping the warm and cozy aspects of herself alive and flourishing. We might be in the most horrible moods, but when The Softie shows up, a secret part of us unfolds into the openness he presents. The Softie doesn't even have to say much and we feel accepted.

Most Softies are adept at reframing negativity into a temporary hurdle. He helps us interrupt our reactive patterns of fear, anger and anxiety so that we might experience reality for what it is. When The Softie shows up, everything gets a little clearer and sweeter.

If The Softie is snuggling by your side today, find the right moment to speak your heart's desire. No matter how boisterous the setting, trust yourself and share your warmest, most vulnerable thoughts and feelings. When we trust our softer natures, we inspire the world around us to do the same.

No matter what challenges you have brought to the table today, remember that The Softie always forgives you the moment you mess up. Her job is to gently encourage you to learn and to expand your horizons. What a wonderful voice to add to your personal choir.

If a Softie is nearby and hinting at their affection for you, encourage their advance by showing a measure of openness and willingness. Their kindness might be the elixir you need to get past that old hurt or advance to the next level of your awareness.

Just when life begins to feel challenging, The Softie gives us warm muffins and miracles. Let The Softie give you the elixirs of the Gods. If a friend needs your softness, give it without hesitation. If your newfound vulnerability is sincere, mountains will move to bow at your feet.

CAUTION

When we become too attached and entrenched in specific outcomes, there is no reasoning with us. When our interactions get heated, avoiding a train wreck is not easy. It takes a thoughtful person to step back, take a few deep breaths, and come back to the table with love.

In all things, use finesse, be demonstrative and trust your gut. Look into the hearts of the people around you. Empathize with their suffering. Nurture others with confidence. Let softness have a say in all you do. With an added measure of humility, forward movement will return.

Even the slightest sprinkle of warmth can turn the most toxic table in your favor. It all depends on how well-versed you are in the art of letting go and reframing reality. Turn cesspools into pudding. Make a bold choice to nurture others today.

EXTREME

While softness is alluring and soothing, it can also be a curse. Finding the right balance between soft-speak and shows of strength can be paramount to the success of an endeavor or relationship. You have become The Softie for too many people in your life. You've sweetened their tea, massaged their feet and whispered loving thoughts in their ears. While you might be a living angel, if you add any more sweetness to the scene, you will attract a toothache. The challenge is that you too often allow yourself to be taken for granted.

Hang up your angel wings for a moment so that you can stand on more solid, realistic ground. Notice the tigers and sharks circling around you. It is time to defend your territory and own your truth. As you join the ranks of confident creators, thinkers and leaders, be conscious of your value at every turn. Learn to engage others, not as a cowering servant, but as an aware and prepared equal.

EMPOWERMENT

Find the blocks that keep you from softness and playfulness. Hire an art therapist or life coach to help you lighten your heart. With a little emotional release, your heart will open and put you at ease.

The colors of your clothes and jewelry can improve your moods and feelings. Ingesting flower essences and applying essential oils to your body (or diffusing into the air) can improve your life.

Colors: light blue, silver, light green, orchid, violet, purple, rose, ivory

Gemstones: Emerald, Purpurite, Malachite, Dioptase, Rose Quartz, Tanzanite, White Selenite, Silver

Flower Essences: Aspen, Yarrow, Holly, Cherry Plum, Rock Water, Walnut, Wild Oat, Willow

Essential Oils: Clary Sage, Rose, Lavender, Cedarwood, Violet Leaf, Ylang Ylang, Sandalwood, Vetiver, Roman Chamomile

Being soft and kind is courageous, but being a doormat is not. Proclaim, nurture and defend your gifts, talents and attributes.

THE HEART COLLECTOR

I wander the world with a secret understanding of how to capture someone's heart within seconds. I do this consciously amping up my charisma, feigning friendship or sharing pointed, inspiring prose. While my intentions are often innocent, it's also possible that I'm a poetic predator seeking to fill my void with your attention. I might write a book, host a gathering or slither into your circle of friends with an agenda to enroll them. As I reflect to you your loveliness, I keep a sprinkle of you for myself. At worst, I'm incestuously industrious. At best, I will encourage you and inspire your advancement.

THE HEART COLLECTOR

"What I seek for myself, I happily find in the joyful projection you thrust upon me."

MORSEL

Pure light can move mountains, but neediness masked as therapy deprives seekers of their power.

MESSAGE

The most luminous hearts in the world attract followers and fans without much effort. They sing, preach, heal, love and create, while the world sits at their feet in awe. It is a wonder to watch and experience this type of person. Enraptured, we experience a belonging. In turn, our hearts expand, adding light and value to our lives.

If The Heart Collector has emerged in your world full of charisma, purpose and light, make note of what they awaken in you. Realize that their gifts are a reflection of a set of gifts nestled deep in your being. As you gaze upon the Heart Collector, remember that you are made of the same substance.

When someone captures our hearts, we feel tuned to them. We note changes in their facial expressions and hang upon every phrase. We feel their breath become ours, and we merge with them. We are at peace because their outward representation of perfection reflects the perfection within us.

Heart Collectors are vibrant, enrapturing souls who inspire the awakening of our potential. If a true and loving Heart Collector has made his way into your world, feel gratitude for the value he has brought to your life, but be careful to remain whole in the process of worship and adoration.

Even if this person is the brightest light in the world, set boundaries until you have vetted her value and quality. Allow every part of you to catch up to your understandings and experiences. This will give her less-appealing aspects a chance to rise to the surface, which might give you pause.

Occasionally, infused in the embrace of a Heart Collector, is foul intention. Without our broader awareness of their totality, we can become prone to gazing mindlessly upon them and risk falling off cliffs. When we are not fully Self-realized, we are often at the mercy of chance. Remember that there are predators in this world who would love nothing more than to use or devour you. Be careful.

Remember to look within for answers to your life's challenges. As you seek others to inspire you, remember that only you can heal your wounds. Stay away from complex, psychotherapeutic dynamics and align yourself with the forces of good.

In every step and action, keep integrity at the forefront of your mind. Allow for a slower process in your life, one that includes a relaxed pursuit and a more thorough examination of the details.

Surround yourself with true, kind-hearted human beings. If you wish to serve others, take tiny steps so that the purity in your heart can be conveyed with patience, kindness and integrity.

CAUTION

Without realizing it, you may have put your personal agenda above the needs of those who come to you for healing. While you are innately compassionate, you may be stuck in a pattern of manipulation.

The Heart Collector is vastly different from Gurus and spiritual masters. The Guru gives and expects nothing. The spiritual master instructs from a position of service. The Heart Collector is not necessarily as altruistic as these souls. While she might be a bright and helpful light, her goals can be a little more self-serving, possibly focused on fortune or fame.

Sit quietly and look internally for your self-serving behaviors. You may have lost touch with your purity of intention. Recapture purity while you can. Clean out your heart and intentions, turn snake oil into love, and get back on track toward personal evolution.

EXTREME

If The Heart Collector gets too caught up in the excitement and attention that surrounds her, she can become self-centered, akin to a vampire who seeks out the vulnerable for nourishment. She also has the ability to feign friendship to put others at ease. He might also be consciously driving his followers to be dependent on him and his "teachings."

If you are The Heart Collector, you might not realize that you are operating from a selfish perspective. You might say you want to help others, but isn't it possible that you are feeding a deep, unchecked wound within yourself? You might be too fascinated with your new-fangled therapeutic modality, continuing to deprive clients and fans of their self-worth and dignity. Look at your early childhood and your emotional dependencies. Dig into the shackled anger and sadness. Honor yourself by untangling from this black widow. Look to the skies for forgiveness. Heal yourself first, and then seek to be of service to others.

EMPOWERMENT

As The Heart Collector or his victim, it is important to look carefully at the web you constructed or fell prey to. It might seam impossible to get back to love and integrity, but with a shift in perspective, all things are possible. You may need a long retreat to help you unravel and soften. Consider the following colors, gems, essences and oils to help you advance your mind, heart, body and spirit.

Colors: orange, cornflower blue, forest green, purple, orchid, indigo, violet

Gemstones: Carnelian, Tiger's Eye, Coral, Fire Opal, Blue Lace Agate, Blue Aragonite

Flower Essences: Agrimony, Holly, Larch, Pine, Elm, Sweet Chestnut, Star of Bethlehem, Willow

Essential Oils: Rose, Jasmine, Bergamot, Cardamom, Orange Blossom, Sandalwood, Cedarwood, Pine, Vetiver, Rose, Galbanum

When you admit and dissolve old fantasies, your nature and identity come into clear and miraculous focus.

THE FAMILY FABLE

I live for the continuation of family. I awake each day looking to my bloodline for the meaning of life and Self. I defend my family relationships because they define me. I am afraid to look beyond family for my identity because I fear the unknown. In the throes of emotional drama, I choose family co-dependence over spiritual truth and I defend loyalty over deep awareness. Unlike the Buddha, I relish my ancestry and I am proud of my pedigree and family. I will honor my memories, genealogy, family experience and bloodline to the end. These notions give me a profound comfort.

THE FAMILY FABLE

"There is no truth greater than family. Shared blood and the rituals we create give me strength."

MORSEL

Through the course of creating a family and the ideologies that coincide with it, many spiritual truths are neglected. Blood was designed to prolong humanity's addiction to karma.

MESSAGE

At birth, we are welcomed into a group of human beings, amidst a competition for resources. While family might begin as a battle, as tensions ease, we make hopeful agreements, some more advantageous than others.

As we age, we choose relationships that mirror our family until we realize there is freedom beyond our birth identities. As we learn to emotionally scrutinize and relinquish these identities, we begin to taste true freedom. In doing so, our deeper awarenesses and most enduring gifts begin to emerge.

When The Family Fable invites herself to dinner, evaluate which aspects of family life nurture you and which parts exhaust or defeat you. As we become more independent and choose to have more joyful experiences, we might release the family attachments and dynamics that imprison us.

If we are willing to do the emotional work, we can change the way we identify and interact with our families. We can set boundaries with them family as a whole or with specific individuals. We can even divorce our families. It is important to remember that our primary contract is with the universe, not groups or individuals.

The Family Fable might be present in your life to provide some needed perspective. He might be educating you on the value of family. It might be that you are trying to skip a step, exiting a family structure before fully owning, processing and embodying the potential learning.

The Family Fable might also be heralding a time of self-reflection and renewal. You may be in a process of exploring who you are as separate from your family. It might be that you have been unable to define or deepen yourself because of family noise and family-contrived responsibilities.

While family might be of help to you at times, family is not the end-all and be-all of existence. You are. As such, family is re-definable in any moment. While sometimes attractive, it is a potentially disposable construct.

As you consider what you have experienced, who you are and who you want to be, you must carefully weigh all the influences, voices and participants in your life. While being of service to your family is often important, you must first know yourself.

Create a definition of self and family that ensures a joyful life and the full expression and acceptance of who you are. Know and love yourself always. All good things stem from this.

CAUTION

Family can have great value at various junctures in our journeys. Roots go down, branches go up, and we grow. For at least parts of our lives, we need strong bases and mirrors, however temporary or challenging.

When we endure compounded negative and oppressive patterns within our family, we might choose to take a break or leave and move on. We might grow to the point whereby our family becomes a faint memory.

The Buddha left his wife and newborn to pursue his divinity. While this seems devout, it might not be your best course of action. Unless you are doing a great deal of spiritual and emotional work, exiting your family could render you confused, hurt or devastated.

Rather than erasing your family from the book of life, consider taking a break from the insanity. While we might feel obligated to our families, we owe them nothing. Look to your closest friends for the clearest definitions of family and the most enduring reflections of yourself.

EXTREME

Many Family Fable personalities use guilt and contrived "belonging" language to inspire participation. They might use strategic, manipulative behavior like pouting or deprivation to provoke allegiance. She might even blame her heart attack on your temporary disconnection.

Forgiveness and detachment can heal the day. With good intentions, examine your family dynamics so you can make better choices going forward. Remember the reboot button. We can always begin again. Look deeply into your feelings. Forgive your family, forgive deity and yourself.

EMPOWERMENT

Families can have a great deal of spiritual and psychological significance in our lives. For a time, we need families to evolve. We do not have to like them, but we do have to respect the journey we chose to endeavor with them. Once we achieve gratitude, we can move on with more peace of mind.

Continually nurture your heart, mind and relationships. The color of your clothes and your jewelry can affect your mood, mind and heart. Ingesting flower essences and applying diluted essential oils to your body (or diffusing them into the air) can improve your energy, attitude and drive. These recommendations are meant to advance the life of The Family Fable.

Colors: blue violet, slate blue, dark turquoise, dark violet, forest green, dark yellow, orange

Gemstones: Sugilite, Lapis Lazuli, Dumortierite, Blue Aventurine, Sulphur, Fire Opal, Amber

Flower Essences: Aspen, Chestnut Bud, Elm, Gorse, Honeysuckle, Oak, Rock Water, Vine, Pine

Essential Oils: Geranium, Blue Tansy, Myrtle, Sandalwood, Frankincense, Rose, Benzoin, Vetiver

Just because your story involves a warm, socially-acceptable belief does not make it true. Family can be a precious gift or it can be a fools folly born of fear.

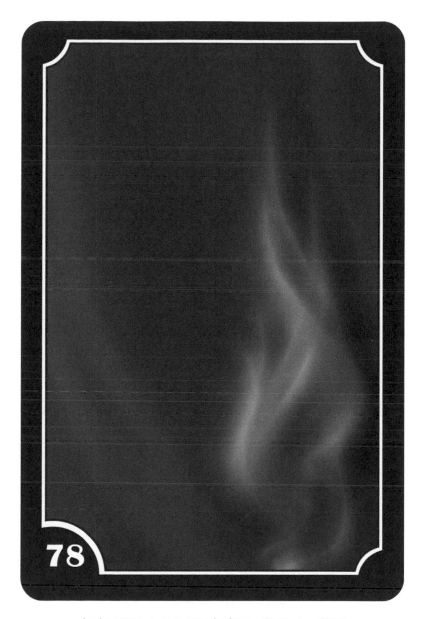

THE EMPTY SPACE

The timelines for our dreams, experiences and relationships are often unknowable. Every idea and event that we participate in has a unique life trajectory. There might be protective forces wrapped around your current question or idea, preventing you from seeing a potential outcome. There might be angels or higher selves shielding you from information, at least in this moment. Answers and truths most often emerge from within. It all begins with a clarity of mind and heart. It all stems from a deepening. Sit quietly and with greater focus, then reimagine your question.

THE EMPTY SPACE

"We give birth to answers long before we imagine the questions."

MORSEL

Deep inside our cells live the answers to the questions that have been posed by all beings in all the realms, in all the universes, throughout all of space and time.

MESSAGE

Long ago, when the universe was young, there lived a small particle. This particle always felt whole. It was filled with life and driven to expand. It was vibrant and free. When other particles began to emerge, the original particle become distracted and lost its connection to itself and its birth.

Soon the original particle became curious about the new particles and began asking questions. It loved to emulate and follow them. By its own choice, it relinquished its inner knowing for all time. When realizing this, the particle paused, looked within and found itself again.

We are all distracted beings seeking the solitude and peace of our origin. The awareness of our origin lives deep within us, hiding within our emotional undercurrents. Seeking this peacefulness is why we are here. Find the original part of you and free yourself from unnecessary activity. These are illusions that only you can release. The original peace, the first knowing, is waiting within you.

CAUTION

We enjoy forming questions, even when they have no relevance to our happiness. We dig into the details of reality simply to satiate a curiosity. The most valuable questions provide a framework for our advancement and success. They help us feel encouraged and inspired. They move us forward.

The moment an answer arrives, our ego tingles with excitement. We enjoy this so much that we decide to do it again. We pose a question, find an answer and further reinforce the notion that answers come from outside of us. Once this cycle begins, it may never end. By depending on external knowledge to fill and fulfill us, the Self falls into slumber.

If we allow questions to appear and dissolve without giving our attention to them, we honor our origin and connectedness to all beings. We allow a deeper knowing to emerge.

We fill our nooks and crannies with details, activities, relationships and entertainment. We forget that these nooks and crannies are magic. Together they form the eternal space that houses the universe. This space is a living, breathing being connected to all space and time.

In the center of this sweet, holy space is the core of our nature, the Self. The Self knows that we are always connected to everything. Diving deeply into your heart in meditation will reveal every question and answer in existence.

EXTREME

You know that you have been avoiding the Self for many lifetimes. You might recall the moments in other lives when you chose materialism or identity over the pure nature of the universe. You might even remember the suffering that went along with it all.

We experience remnants of our personal truths when we take deep breaths. Inside the particles of our inhale and exhale live the answers we need.

As you gently breath in and out, do you feel the awareness emerge? Can you feel how your lungs and heart are nourished as your breath enters the body? Electricity breathing air: this is who you are.

EMPOWERMENT

Take 30 seconds to consciously breathe in and out. Place your attention on the quality and value of each breath. The breath contains eternal knowledge about you and the universe. Lasting value begins with a breath. The Empty Space is available to all of us at all times. We may need a little guidance or encouragement to get us there, but it is always one breath away.

To be open to the universe's flow of light, love and providence, we must take care of every aspect of ourselves and our lives. This includes nurturing the subtle bodies that influence all of our decisions, relationships and conditions in life. Remember that we are electricity moving through space and time. We are comprised of the most subtle currents. The slightest changes to our diet can affect how we engage others. Our environments are also key to how we heal and evolve.

In this light, the color of your clothes and your jewelry can affect your mood, mind and heart. Ingesting flower essences and applying diluted essential oils to your body (or diffusing them into the air) can improve your energy, attitude and drive. These recommendations are suggested so The Empty Space might find the questions from deep within and implement the most enduring answers for the benefit of all involved.

Colors: white, gold, silver, bright blue, bright yellow, black

Gemstones: White Topaz, Howlite, Gold, Azurite, Dioptase, Onyx

Flower Essences: Aspen, Cerato, Cherry Plum, Elm, Gorse, Honeysuckle

Essential Oils: Bergamot, Cardamom, Marjoram, Niaouli, Jasmine, Rose

With such a full cup, how can you receive what is intended for you?

THE PERSONALITY CARDS

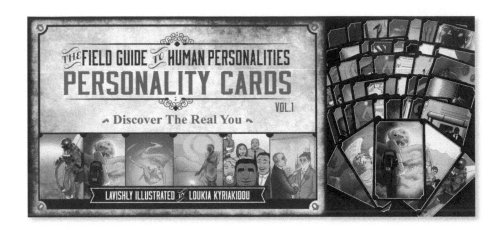

Use the cards to inspire personal growth and self-awareness.

Gain perspective, enjoy new insights and find forgiveness. This beautifully-illustrated deck of cards is a powerful self-discovery tool.

Pose a question, choose a few cards, lay them in front of you. As you read about each personality, you'll enjoy a reflection of your life in this moment.

Every image represents a temporary aspect of you or another person. By exploring each personality, you'll heal your past, expand your self-understanding and empower your future.

Get inspired with The Personality Cards!

Included in the box are 78 professionally-illustrated Personality Cards and an extensive booklet. The booklet features shortened personality descriptions along with several card layouts that will help you interpret the cards. The card box is compact and great for travel.

Visit **PaulWagner.com** to learn more.

THE ME APP

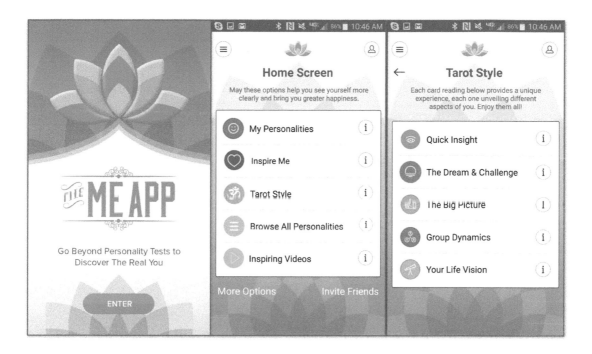

The Me App is an exciting mobile and web tool that provides helpful insights about you, your life and your relationships, all based on this book.

The readings are fun, informative and inspiring.

- Gain insight on partnerships, friendships and life's most challenging questions.

- Learn new ways to improve challenging situations and dynamics.

- Share with friends and loved ones - and grow together!

- **It'll feel like the app knows you!**

Use the app for personal exploration, or as a spiritual divination tool for you, your friends and your family.

THE ME APP is FUN TO USE and it's a great tool for happiness and growth. Share it with your friends and grow together!

Download at PersonalityApp.com!

POCKET PEOPLE

Pocket People: The Guide To Understanding Humans is the smaller version of <u>The Field Guide to Human Personalities</u>. With 78 compelling personality descriptions, it's chock full of helpful, on-the-go insight! (soft cover book, 174 pgs, 4"x6")

A great gift idea, **Pocket People** is a fun and thorough deep-dive into the personalities we most often adopt. Learn about yourself, family and friends.

Get the free companion app at **PersonalityApp.com**!

Pocket LOVE

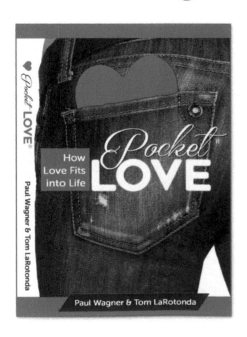

Pocket Love: How Love Fits Into Life is a quick-reference guide, inspired by the dialogue between Paul and his friend Tom LaRotonda. Together, Tom and Paul dive into **Love** as it relates to 32 unique and compelling topics. (Soft cover, 152 pages, 4 x 6".)

Paul and Tom carefully chose the book's categories hoping to convey the broad spectrum of their diverse experiences.

They hope their open hearts and sincere dialogues are of benefit to all who read these pages.

Visit PaulWagner.com for more.

COLORFUL ME: A Personal Workbook

47

THE FEARLESS

These powerful spirits are ambassadors of the notion that nothing keeps us from living our dreams, except fear. They know that deep joy is experienced when we take profound risks with confidence. Even when we falter, we learn. Keeping at it, we validate the power within us.

2 AS YOU CONSIDER THIS PERSONALITY, DESCRIBE THE IMAGERY AND THOUGHTS THAT EMERGE.

3 IN WHAT WAYS ARE YOU SIMILAR TO THIS PERSONALITY?

4 HOW DOES THIS PERSONALITY CHALLENGE YOU?

Open the pathways to the wisdom living within you.

The Colorful Me workbook is a simple and revealing tool created to help you explore your life and relationships. It is meant to help you live an authentic, fully-expressed life. The workbook is an impressionistic journey into the emotional body, helping you to see yourself and others clearly.

Enjoy a rebirth through playfulness and gratitude!

This workbook provides hours of transformational creativity and reflection. Have fun with the coloring section. Use crayons, pencils, markers or paint - whatever makes you feel more joy. If tears and other emotions emerge, let them out with compassion!

You are the universe born of love.

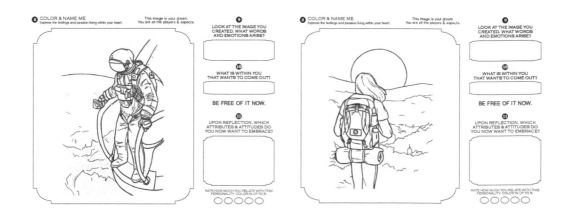

STARTUP CONFIDENTIAL

STARTUP CONFIDENTIAL: The Raw, Unfiltered Truth About Starting A Company is a brash and humorous look at the What, Who and How of launching your Big Idea. While some of my books are sweet and magical, this one is more akin to swallowing a pill the size of your nephew. If you're starting a business, it's the one book you need to read. Packed with meaty facts and figures, the book digs into the human aspects and the gut-wrenching stories that make startups such profound experiences.

Visit StartupConfident.com.

BIOGRAPHIES

PAUL WAGNER is a writer, intuitive coach, TV host, corporate comedian and 5-Time EMMY® Award Winning actor. Paul's books, cards and apps include: The Field Guide to Human Personalities, The Personality Cards, The Colorful Me Workbook, Pocket People, Pocket Love and The Me App, all of which are helpful tools in the pursuit of self-awareness.

Paul spent 30 years touring as a professional writer and comedian, all the while seeking out awakened spiritual masters in the US, India and Asia. Paul's vision quests in the wilderness and his experiences studying with Native American elders grew in him a deep awareness and a love for intentional rituals, ceremonies and prayer.

As an actor, Paul studied hundreds of character types, gaining an empathy for each one. Early in his career, Paul achieved a dream of becoming a children's TV writer and host where he developed over 50 distinct personalities for television and stage. These became the foundation of his corporate education and entertainment business.

With humor and insight, Paul has educated millions of people throughout the world. He has created over 2500 custom shows and educational videos for Fortune 500 conferences, trade shows, award banquets and corporate meetings. Paul has lectured and created workshops for hundreds of companies, colleges, international festivals and global organizations.

Paul is available for retreats, corporate events, workshops, lectures and personal coaching.

Visit PaulWagner.com for personality books, apps and updates.

LOUKIA "LUCY" KYRIAKIDOU is a notable artist who worked tirelessly to create emotionally provoking scenarios to represent the 234 unique personalities in Paul Wagner's books, cards, workbooks and apps.

Lucy left Greece in 2007 and moved to England, where she graduated from Teesside University with a First-class BA Computer Animation degree.

She is currently working as a freelancer in animation and games, as well as other creative fields. Located in Newcastle upon Tyne, UK, Lucy spends her days drawing and working in her pajamas.

Learn more about Lucy at www.lucydoesart.co.uk

Thank you Alyssa Richards for the beautiful infinity symbol found throughout the book. Alyssa's work can be found here: http://squibli.tumblr.com/

the **only** person you can change

the only **person** you can truly affect

the only person **you** can discipline

the only person you **can** expand

the only person you can control

the only person who can inspire your **transform**ation

the only person you ever interact with

is

YOU